ENGLISH RELIGIOUS
TRADITION
AND THE
GENIUS
OF
ANGLICANISM

THE
ENGLISH RELIGIOUS TRADITION
AND THE
GENIUS
OF
ANGLICANISM

Edited by

GEOFFREY ROWELL

Chaplain of Keble College, Oxford

With a Foreword by

THE ARCHBISHOP OF CANTERBURY

Copyright © Keble College, Oxford 1992

First published in Great Britain by
IKON Productions Ltd
Manor Farm House
Manor Road
WANTAGE OX12 8NE

Reprinted 1993

British Library Cataloguing-in-Publication Data

A catalogue record for this book is available
from the British Library

ISBN: 1 871805 01 5 hardback
ISBN: 1 871805 02 3 paperback

Typeset by Oxuniprint, Oxford University Press
Printed and bound in Great Britain by
Butler & Tanner Ltd, Frome and London

CONTENTS

ACKNOWLEDGEMENTS

The quotations from T. S. Eliot, *For Lancelot Andrewes: Essays on Style and Order* (London, 1928) are reproduced in this volume with kind permission of the publishers, Faber and Faber Ltd.

Foreword

by

THE ARCHBISHOP OF CANTERBURY

IN THE SPRING of 1992, a series of lectures was held in the Chapel of Keble College, Oxford, to celebrate the bi-centenary of the birth of John Keble, poet, priest and pastor.

This book is a record of those lectures. Twelve distinguished scholars present the English religious tradition as it has come down to us through the centuries from pre-Reformation times, and the genius of Anglicanism as reflected in the lives of those writers and teachers who served and helped to shape it. In its character and wisdom, the English religious tradition displays an underlying consistency. As an expression of the continuity inherent in English spiritual life, it is an appropriate tribute to John Keble, since his ministry was distinctively Anglican in its loyalty to the English Church and its traditions.

This set of lectures directs us to the foundations of that loyalty. As the Visitor of Keble College, I am glad that they were first presented in the College dedicated to his memory, and I am delighted that, through this publication, they are now available to a wider audience.

+ George Cantuar

GEOFFREY ROWELL

Introduction

ON 27 SEPTEMBER 1836, John Keble preached a notable sermon in Winchester Cathedral on 'Primitive Tradition'. Less well known than his Assize Sermon of 14 July 1833 on 'National Apostasy', it is an exposition of one of the major theological themes of the Oxford Movement. The constitutional changes of the late 1820s and early 1830s raised important questions of identity for the Church of England. When Newman asked in the first of the *Tracts for the Times*, 'On what ground do you stand, O presbyter of the Church of England?', he answered with reference to the sacramental continuity of the historic ministry of the Church expressed by the doctrine of apostolic succession. No less a concern was the living continuity of faith and practice represented by the theme of apostolic tradition. Against rationalist re-interpretation, and the private judgement of an individualist Evangelicalism, Keble, Newman, Pusey and the other leaders of the Oxford Movement re-asserted the corporate nature of Christian faith, the normative character of the creeds which embodied the faith of the early Church, and the devotional and sacramental pattern which was an essential element in creating and maintaining Christian identity and continuity. They emphasized that the Christian faith was at one and the same time a revelation and a mystery — a revelation to be received and a mystery to be lived out. The notes of awe, wonder, reverence and reserve, were essential characteristics of Christian believing. As Newman put it, 'Christians receive the gospel literally on their knees, and in a temper altogether different from that critical and argumentative spirit which sitting and listening engender'.[1] For Keble 'in the substance of faith there is no such thing as improvement, discovery, evolution of new truths; none of those processes, which are the pride of human reason and knowledge'. Theology, he believed, was not 'like any human science', a subject in which every succeeding age might be expected to advance on the former'.[2] He protested against 'the *nominalism*' of the day, 'the habit of resolving the high mysteries of faith into mere circumstances of languages, methods of speaking adapted to our weak understanding, but with no real counterpart in the nature of things'.[3]

The words and doctrines of the Christian tradition were, as Coleridge might have put it, 'the living educts of the Christian imagination'. As such they were to be received reverently. They were matter for prayer before they were matter for investigation.

Part of the concerns of Newman and Keble were framed by their knowledge of the Fathers, and their endeavour to guard and express the apostolic faith that had been handed on to them. For Keble in particular this patristic inheritance came through the more immediate tradition of Richard Hooker and the seventeenth-century Anglican divines, men such as Lancelot Andrewes, Henry Hammond, and Herbert Thorndike. It was his family tradition, and one which he believed embodied the genius of Anglicanism, though the phrase would have been alien to him. It was characteristic of the Oxford Movement that it was a 'revolution by tradition'. When Newman dedicated the *Lectures on the Prophetical Office of the Church* to the venerable President of Magdalen, Martin Routh, it was with the epigraph that he had 'been reserved to report to a forgetful generation what was the theology of their fathers'. Anglican identity was to be discovered by a return to roots.

It was such characteristic emphases in the thought of John Keble and the other leaders of the Oxford Movement which made it appropriate to plan a series of lectures on 'The English Religious Tradition and the Genius of Anglicanism' to mark the bi-centenary of the birth of John Keble. Eleven scholars were invited to speak on significant figures in the history of the Church in England; a twelfth, Stephen Sykes, the Bishop of Ely, who has written much on the identity of Anglicanism and on some of the contemporary issues facing the Anglican Communion, was invited to reflect on the 'genius of Anglicanism' in the final lecture. The lecture series drew a large audience to Keble College Chapel over a term and a half, and it is good that lectures of such high quality now have a permanent form.

The first four lectures were devoted to the pre-Reformation church and one of the interesting features of these lectures is that it has been possible to identify in these early figures characteristics of the Anglican ethos. With only twelve lectures the choice of significant figures across the centuries was not always easy, but since a selection had to be made the choice was, it is hoped, both judicious, and appropriate to the one whose bi-centenary of birth it was. Keble himself was a poet, and it is notable that so many of those studied in these lectures were significant not only for their religious insight but also for their stature as writers.

In addition to the twelve lectures this collection includes two sermons preached at Fairford and at Keble College Chapel during the anniversary weekend. In their different ways they try to draw out something of Keble's continuing importance for Christians. He himself wrote the lines inscribed on the memorial tablet in Fairford Church — 'so glorious let thy pastors shine, that by their speaking lives the world may learn'. His was indeed a speaking life. Like Teresa of Avila, Keble knew that humility is endless. The 'condition of complete simplicity' costs 'not less than everything'. 'Purity of heart' is indeed, as Kierkegaard reminded us, 'to will one thing'.

> Bless'd are the pure in heart,
> For they shall see our God,
> The secret of the Lord is theirs,
> Their soul is Christ's abode.

NOTES

[1] T. Gornall, ed., *The Letters and Diaries of John Henry Newman* V, (Oxford, 1981), p. 46. (Newman to Sir James Stephen, 16 March 1835.

[2] J. Keble, 'Primitive Tradition' in E. R. Fairweather, ed., *The Oxford Movement* (Oxford and New York, 1964), p. 86.

[3] ibid.

PATRICK WORMALD

The Venerable Bede and the 'Church of the English'

IT IS APPROPRIATE that Bede should have a place in a book on 'The English Religious Tradition and the Genius of Anglicanism'.[1] But I do not intend to argue that Bede was a prototype of Anglican churchmanship. I shall begin by trying to show that the part he has undeniably played in the historical image of insular protest against Rome is ironic and by him entirely unintended. I will go on to argue that, in founding the history of the *Church of the English*, indeed of the English themselves, he did make a central (if again unintended) contribution to the eventual emergence of a *Church of England*. Those who created the Church of England were very far from unaware of the inspiration they could draw from Bede.

The Church of England was not the only one to seek its charter in the earlier history of its nation's Christianity. From the days of George Buchanan, supplying initial historical propaganda for the makers of the Scottish kirk, until a startlingly recent date, there was warrant for an anti-Roman, anti-episcopal and, in the nineteenth century, anti-Establishment stance in the Columban or 'Celtic' Church. Here is the peroration of a respectably learned book reprinted in 1957: 'When the Columban Church itself passed away, [independence] was the legacy that the Church of Columba bequeathed to the Church which was to be built at the Reformation upon the ruins of the Church of Rome, and which has been completed in the Church of Scotland — the most independent national Church in Christendom'.[2] The idea that there *was* a 'Celtic Church' in something of a post-Reformation sense is still maddeningly in-eradicable from the minds of students.

One of the misconceptions involved is that there was a 'Roman Church' to which the 'Celtic' was notionally opposed. The pre-Gregorian Latin Church exhibits a rich variety of liturgies, and even organizational principles, as well as Easters. And the Irish variety, as we shall see, was marked as much by devotion to the Petrine cult as by peculiarities absorbed from its exceptionally re-silient secular traditions.[3] But what I wish to highlight is the extent to which the whole fallacy was affected by what Bede wrote. I begin with a model of judicious and unemotional scholarship by the greatest (for historians at least) of Keble alumni. Sir Frank Stenton saw in the work of Aidan and his followers, 'all the characteristics of a Celtic missionary enterprise':

> The original community at Lindisfarne lived in gaunt auster-ity. . . . Aidan himself was an ascetic evangelist . . . influencing men of all ranks by his humility and devotion. . . . He and his companions were monks, and the monastic note runs all through their work. . . . In their general conception of the religious call-ing, and especially in their tendency towards asceticism, the monastic communities founded by Aidan differed widely from those of the Roman pattern. But his own moderation was re-membered. . . . On many points of ecclesiastical order, the Irish Church . . . differed from the prevailing custom of the West. . . . In organization, it was monastic rather than territorial . . . author-ity rested with the abbot of the chief monastery in each tribe. . . . Above all, in its method of calculating Easter, the Irish Church was governed by principles which differed fundamentally from those accepted at Rome or in the English churches founded under Roman influence.

I quote this passage at length, because it encapsulates almost all the features that historians have thought characteristic of the 'Celtic Church'; and even if this careful scholar tends to speak of 'Irish' rather than 'Celtic', he went on to make St Cuthberht the repre-sentative of the 'Celtic strains in the English Church'.[4]

Relatively few of the features attributed to Celtic Christianity by Stenton would come through the searching (not to say excoriat-ing) tests of Irish historical scholarship today. But for present pur-poses it is more instructive to consider the views on the Irish and the *Frankish* Church proposed by a continental scholar who was fully Stenton's peer. Wilhelm Levison did not find Easter a critical issue, and he was among the first to show that the Irish were prominent in the spread of the cult of St Peter on the Continent.[5] He was not much impressed by the idea of the Irish as missionaries: evangelical efforts receive some attention, but are not seen as a primary motive of Irish activities. Above all, there is no suggestion that early Irish Christians were *moderates*. Levison's word for St Columbanus, the Irish founder of Luxeuil and Bobbio, and the inspiration behind a 'new wave' of Frankish monasticism, is '*kampfesroh*'. Levison took the lineaments of his picture from the rich hagiographical literature of the Columbanian monastic circle in seventh-century Gaul and Italy, especially the superb biography of the saint by Jonas. Jonas says nothing about Easter, comparatively little about evangelization, and a great deal about his hero's spectacular confrontations with the Frankish Establishment. Not everyone could expect to march out of the royal court after announcing that a Merovingian of illegitimate birth was debarred from the throne, nor to be accompanied as he did so by a clap of thunder.[6]

It is possible that Columba and Columbanus were men of different mettle. Jonas may simply be a less reliable witness than Stenton's main source, who is of course Bede. Yet, as James Campbell has observed, we can find more than a hint of a Columbanian approach between the lines of Bede's account of the Lindisfarne Church, as well as in the masterly *Life of Columba* by Adomnan that is the insular counterpart to Jonas.[7] Aidan, like Columbanus, repudiated a handsome royal gift, even if he is not said to have remarked that 'the Most High is displeased with the offerings of the wicked'.[8] Cedd, Aidan's disciple, consigned a king to the vengeance of the incestuous kindred with whom he was consorting, in a gesture reminiscent of both Columba and Columbanus. (Plummer noted that 'the frequency with which Irish saints distribute curses . . . is indeed remarkable in persons with a reputation for holiness'.)[9] Like Jonas, Adomnan says nothing about Easter; and if one suspects that recent embarrassments played a part in both silences, one can add that Columbanian devotion to St Peter has a close equivalent in Adomnan's use, among hagiographical models quoted to shed lustre on his hero, of the *Actus Sylvestri*, forerunner and, in part, source of the notorious papalist forgery, *The Donation of Constantine*.[10] So it may be that it *is* Bede and historians in these islands who follow him that are the odd ones out.

We return, then, to the features extracted by Stenton from Bede. It is Bede whose description of the 'unusual' constitution of Iona and its *parochia* led almost all historians until recently to see abbatial rule rather than episcopacy as characteristic of the 'Celtic

Church'. 'Unusual' would in fact have been the *mot juste* for Iona when compared to other early Irish Churches, and those of Wales too.[11] It is Bede, *not* Adomnan, who makes Columba 'convert the Picts to Christ by his words and example'. Even if there was an element of wishful Pictish thinking here, as my ex-colleague Professor Duncan forcibly argues, Bede's words are very characteristically his own.[12] That the Lindisfarne Church was responsible for a prolonged and fruitful English mission under royal auspices is not open to doubt. But we may begin to wonder whether such activity was as *typical* of the Irish Church as Bede certainly implies, when we turn to the use he made of an extant Merovingian *Life* of St Fursa. All the *Life* says of evangelization in East Anglia is that Fursa 'softened the king's barbarous heart'. But for Bede, he 'followed his usual task of preaching the Gospel, and converted many unbelievers by the example of his virtue and the encouragement of his preaching'.[13] Above all, it is surely Bede's four immortal portraits of the lifestyle of 'Celtic' churchmen, Aidan himself, the Lindisfarne community on the eve of its departure, Chad, and Cuthberht, which underlie our impression of a 'gaunt austerity' that would not perhaps have been the first impression of a seventh-century visitor to Armagh; which sound the 'monastic note' so strongly; and which leave a lasting aftertaste of 'humility' and (most precious of virtues) 'moderation'.[14] In short, Bede has done more than anyone, more even than Adomnan and picturesque scenes of beehive huts, to make these 'Celtic' saints lovable.

Now, as Alan Thacker has convincingly shown, there is very little doubt about the palette on which Bede's unforgettable colours were mixed. At the very end of his life, he told Bishop Ecgberht that he should be reading Pope Gregory's *Book of Pastoral Rule*. In setting up the Lindisfarne community as a contrast to the 'sloth of our time', it very much looks as though he had Gregorian virtues in mind.[15] He gives as his explicit reason for commending the monastic way of life on Lindisfarne that it corresponded to what Gregory enjoined on Augustine at Canterbury (as, on the whole, it did not).[16] Not just the necessity of preaching but the technique of conversion *by example* are absolutely central Gregorian themes, as was the humility that a bishop must cultivate — though never to excess — in his dire need to avoid the danger of pride. And if there was a primer of moderation in the vast range of patristic literature, it was the *Pastoral Rule*; though Gregory's and Bede's preferred term was 'discretion'. It may be that Aidan did, in a well-known Bedan tableau, rebuke a failed predecessor for 'unreasonable harshness', and recommend a 'little-by-little' approach. If so, he contrived to use remarkably Gregorian words when scarcely likely to have read the book.[17] Mr Campbell has taught us that Bede wrote history to preach the examples of the past to his contemporaries.[18] The lessons he sought to teach were those of orthodox churchmanship. It was in so far as they encapsulated these lessons, or seemed to, that he praised the Irish in Northumbria. So it is that, by not the least of the ironies of historiography, prototypes of Protestantism have been found in a model whose main lines were drawn by a pope.

If that seems too much to believe, there is one aspect of 'Celtic Church' history for which Bede's responsibility is undeniable. The Scottish Divinity Faculty where, till not long ago, the Church History course ran from Acts to 664 before resuming in 1560, may have been an isolated case. But that the Synod of Whitby had a nigh-cosmic significance in the relations of the Church of Rome with those of the British Isles and beyond is a conviction that still seems unshakable. Most scholars today accept that the decision related to Easter and the tonsure only, not to allegedly more fundamental underlying issues of organization and discipline. Many are aware that it concerned only the part of the English Church answerable to Lindisfarne. Most of these know that this was just one chapter in the long-running saga of paschal disputes within the Irish Churches, themselves merely one set of episodes among several that were more or less comparable in the Latin Churches at large.[19] None of these provisos seems sufficient to persuade scholars to give Whitby rather less prominence than Archbishop Theodore's Synod of Hertford in 672, which *did* discuss Easter, but which *also* covered a series of crucial disciplinary matters, and involved the *whole* English Church (of which it might well be seen as the founding charter). The reason is clear. Bede's unrivalled artistry made Whitby a central dramatic episode, perhaps *the* climactic episode, in his story; whereas, though in no doubt of Hertford's importance, he reported simply its decisions rather than the whole course of an impassioned debate.[20] A world grown used to confrontations with St Peter, and their not infrequently tragic outcomes, will never forget that of Columba, nor how the power of the keys swung the decision against him.

But we should not forget that Bede's account of the Easter controversy has no counterpart in scale or drama throughout the literature of Christianity: not even in Eusebius, who was in so many respects Bede's model; not in Gregory of Tours, otherwise his nearest equivalent; not in Eddius' *Life of Wilfrid*, a Whitby protagonist, where it takes up one not especially lengthy chapter; not in Adomnan or Jonas, if perhaps, as I say, for rather special reasons; not in the

Irish Church as a whole, where Cummian's polemic devoted solely to this issue is not much longer than the account of the Synod of Whitby that is far from Bede's only discussion of the matter in a book concerned with the Church in general.[21] There are perhaps three reasons why Bede was so preoccupied with Easter as to leave the impression of a Church fighting for its 'independence'. First, Easter was Bede's obsession. He was after all the author of the all-time definitive treatment of the subject, and was not the last scholar to let his speciality dominate his perspective. Second, he wrote from a distinctly Canterbury angle. To judge from one preface to the *Historia Ecclesiastica*, he owed Canterbury's Abbot Albinus not only much of his information but also the very idea of writing the book.[22] The unity of the English Church was a matter of the most passionate concern to him, and it was in this one respect that the Irish example was *bad*. Third, this was only one aspect of Bede's commitment to unity in the whole Church. Paul Meyvaert has strikingly observed that Gregory the Great might well *not* have shared Bede's paschal obsession, certainly not his belief in a uniform tonsure: 'A Gregory the Great must never be confused with a Gregory VII, and on the issues at stake Bede's mind was probably closer to the latter than to the former'.[23] Bede in some ways anticipates that sense of the need for uniformity which is already a Carolingian principle two and a half centuries before Hildebrand. So another irony is that someone who said so much of disunity precisely because he so detested it should unwittingly have immortalized the image of a Church in defiance of Rome.

Bede cannot then be the apostle of a Church for whom it still remains axiomatic that the truest wisdom resides (to quote words that Bede ascribes to Wilfrid) 'in the two remotest islands of the Ocean'.[24] But that is far from all there is to say on the matter. To have agreed to speak for Bede in this series would hardly do, had I not thought that he did indeed play an indispensable part in the ultimate emergence of a 'Church of England'. I shall now go on to argue that he, more than anyone else, inspired the idea of the English as one people, called into existence by the special favour of God.

This argument is best begun at the end. One can make a good case — in view of the improbabilities involved, an astonishingly good case — that words like 'England' and 'English' were used by 1066 in very much the way they are still used. The vernacular is already English as a matter of course. In the last and in many ways definitive pre-Conquest law-code, Cnut legislates as 'king of all *Engla lond*', according to '*Engla* law'.[25] The terminology is not confined to formal texts. It is absolutely normal in any phase and all versions of the *Anglo-Saxon Chronicle*. 'Some thought that it would be great folly to join battle because in the two armies were most of what was noblest in *Ængla landa*; 'it was hateful to almost all to fight against men of their own *cynnes*, because there was little else that was worth anything apart from *Englisce* on either side'.[26] If the Chroniclers be suspected of having axes to grind, as they not infrequently had, there is also the homilist Ælfric on the Romano-British martyr St Alban: 'the murderous persecution of the wicked emperor came to *engla lande*' — an authentic early instance of the Englishman's tendency to confuse the identities of 'England' and 'Britain'.[27] And if the Winchester-educated Ælfric could also be thought *parti pris*, we have a fragment in an eleventh-century manuscript with Worcester connections of what may be the sole surviving private letter from one relatively 'ordinary' Anglo-Saxon to his 'brother Edward'. The letter's first complaint relates to his brother's hairstyle: 'You do wrong in abandoning the English practices which your fathers followed, and in loving the practices of heathen men, and in so doing show by such evil habits that you despise your race and ancestors, since in insult to them you dress in Danish style with bared necks and blinded eyes'.[28] The point here is not that an Englishman is imitating foreign fashions, for far from the last time. It is that he is being told that it is 'un-English' to do so.

Three points need to be made about this sense of England and the English. First, it was unparalleled in the Europe of the time. The '*regnum Francorum*' extended in both Merovingian and Carolingian eras over all of what is now France and much more besides. The Franks were taught to think of themselves as a holy '*gens*' ruling an '*imperium Christianum*'. But for a while yet, very far from all the king's subjects thought themselves Franks. To the civilized *gentes* south of the Loire, the term seemed suitable only for the barbarians living to its north. There has been much debate in the last generation about whether a single reference to the '*regnum Teutonicorum*' is genuinely tenth-century or a later interpolation. The significant point is that so much hangs on one disputed text. The concept of *Deutschland* made notoriously little headway against other German allegiances for centuries to come.[29] Given the political realities, there was a surprisingly strong sense of the 'Men of Ireland'. But the learned classes who did most to burnish this image were so committed by their *raison d'être* to traditional patterns, that they continued to write of Ireland's 'Fifths' (Ulster, Leinster, etc.), regardless of the fact that this immemorial structure had been rendered obsolescent in the immediately prehistoric period by the Uí Néill dynasts with the most realistic prospect of turning myth into political fact.[30]

Second, such a sense of 'Englishness' was not even new in the eleventh century. A Mercian royal charter of 855 grants freedom from 'lodging all riders of English race (*Angelcynnes*) and foreigners'. A Kentish nobleman's will of much the same date is to be valid 'so long as baptism exists in the *Angelcynnes* island'.[31] When King Alfred wrote, in a famous passage from his translation (into '*englisc*') of Gregory's *Pastoral Rule*, about the decline of Church, learning and happiness 'among all *Angelcynn*', he reflected a contemporary trend.[32] Third and last, however, there was very little basis for the growth of so strong an ethnic sense in Britain's post-Roman history. One of the signs that no sub-Roman aristocracy survived in Britain, as it did in Italy, Spain or Gaul, to mould the political imagination of incoming Germanic warbands, is that there is so *little* evidence of an idea that *Britannia* should be subject to unitary rule. Many of us grew up with Stenton's notion of a '*bretwalda*' (he was too good a Keble scholar to tolerate the neologism, '*Bretwalda-ship*').[33] Ten years ago, I expressed doubts that so thin an evidential base could possibly bear the historical weight resting on it. I am now thought conservative.[34] In that overlordship was contested by various kingdoms, like the not dissimilar 'Kingship of Tara' in Ireland, it gave rise to resentments that did nothing to foster feelings of 'togetherness'.

My argument in 1983 was, and is still, that the clue to this conundrum lies in the use of the word 'English'. Bede identifies the invaders as Saxon and Jute as well as Angle. The special virtue of Angles was not so much that they supplied nearly all the newcomers' most powerful rulers for two centuries after 616. This would hardly have commended the term to the West Saxon Alfred. It was chiefly that it was in their name that Christianity was restored to what had once been *Britannia*. So far as we know, the first person to *assume* that the Germanic-speaking inhabitants of Britain were all called Angles was Gregory the Great. Whatever the truth of the notorious story of his encounter with 'angelic' slave-boys, it is a fact that the copious correspondence with which he launched his mission to the pagans of Britain never calls them anything but 'Angles'. On the Latin-speaking Continent in the sixth century, and for some time afterwards, normal usage was 'Saxon'. Everyone in *Britannia* whose language was Germanic seemed, whatever their real ancestry, to be descended from its pagan invaders. It followed that all were 'Angles', owing their Christian faith to Gregory's mission, and to the 'church of the Angles' that it had founded at Canterbury. The outcome is neatly illustrated by Ælfric's homily for Gregory's feast-day. The slave-boys are still said to be '*Angle*', but they come from '*Engla lond*', and are being sold in Rome by '*Englisce* merchants'.[35]

The nostrum that the English were unified ecclesiastically well before they were united politically thus acquires extra significance. The Church brought more than a new communal persona. It gave it a name. English identity was not, like Frankish or (Continental) Saxon, the badge of the most successful of the peoples contesting supremacy in a given sphere. It was what each Anglo-Saxon was called in heaven. The idea of '*Angelcynn*' was conceived not, like that of 'the Men of Ireland' in the mists of legendary antiquity, but in the mind of God. Yet not even Canterbury possessed the ideological clout to impose a new ethnicity unaided. It was Bede who gave 'Englishness' a manifesto of unique grace and power. When contemplating the divergent destinies of early medieval hegemonies, nothing is so suggestive as the contrast between their programmatic historians. 'The History of the Franks' was not Gregory of Tours' own title, nor in fact is it what he wrote. He and his successors gave the Franks an image of their special status, but the imagery was wasted on those of the Carolingians' subjects who did not consider themselves Franks. Widukind of Korvey, trumpeting the rise of a German monarchy, called his book '*Res Gestae Saxonicae*'. It was indeed a specifically Saxon, not a German, history. Its heroes are almost as much the Saxon nobility, even in rebellion, as Otto the Great himself. This was anything but a warrant for Saxon acceptance of non-Saxon rule.

The very first words of Bede's preface, on the other hand, are '*Historiam ecclesiasticam gentis Anglorum*'. Professor Walter Goffart and others have recently wondered whether Bede's 'Angles' were not in fact his fellow Northumbrians, *technically* Angles, rather than 'Englishmen' in general, i.e. Anglo-Saxons. Facing this challenge will regrettably take us into the dusty, if not entirely infertile, fields of semantic analysis.[36] In the *Ecclesiastical History*, the word 'Angle' occurs 179 times (discounting specifically 'East' and 'Middle' varieties). On no less than seventy-eight occasions, it *must* mean 'English', in the sense of 'Angles, Saxons, Jutes and the rest', those of ostensibly Germanic origin in contradistinction to Britons, Irish and Picts. Fifty-seven such cases denote the 'English' as a religious entity, but twenty-one more give the term an emphatically secular connotation. Cadwallon's determination to extirpate 'the whole *genus Anglorum* from the bounds of Britain' clearly does not refer merely to the Northumbrians. King Earconberht of Kent, '*primus rex Anglorum*' to order the destruction of idols and the observance of Lent, was neither Northumbrian nor technically Anglian; nor, when his daughters sought convents '*in regione Francorum*' because there were yet few '*in regione Anglorum*', was it a shortage of houses north of the Humber they had in mind. Especially instructive are the headings for the famous chapter on the arrival of Angles, Saxons and Jutes, '*ut invitata Britanniam gens Anglorum*'; and for the concluding survey of the current state of all Anglo-Saxon kingdoms and bishoprics, '*qui sit in praesenti status gentis Anglorum vel Britanniae totius*'.[37] We can add to such surely unambiguous instances, twenty-seven uses of the word to denote Germanic as opposed to Celtic or Latin speech. Seventeen places or items thus designated are Northumbrian or otherwise Anglian, but ten are not.[38] So on a minimalist reckoning (ten plus seventy-eight), Bede's 'Angles' were what we mean by 'Englishmen' nearly as often as they were not.

We are left with seventy-four further instances of the word. On just seven occasions (four in the 'arrivals' chapter), Bede means Angle as opposed to Saxon.[39] On another forty-four, he can reasonably be taken to mean 'Northumbrian', in that the individual or collective thus indicated was in fact Northumbrian. Yet there is scarcely one case where the more general meaning 'English', would not do as well. If we are to read 'Northumbrian' into the word as applied to achievements of Kings Æthelfrith, Edwin, Oswald, Oswiu or Aldfrith, we should note that it had previously been applied in very similar contexts to Æthelberht of Kent.[40] If it means 'Northumbrian' when used of actual Northumbrians like Benedict Biscop, it can hardly do so when used of the luckless Kentish cleric who died in Rome before he could be consecrated archbishop.[41] Those who subjected Whithorn to the '*gens Anglorum*', or whose power waned with the loss of lands north of the Forth, were indeed Northumbrian, but also 'English' in so far as their rivals in each sphere were Celts.[42] Besides these forty-four cases, where a wider meaning is at least possible, twenty-one are more truly ambiguous. The Anglo-Saxons who founded Mayo, six times described as 'Angles', were probably mostly Northumbrian, but it is unlikely that Bede thought all of them were. The same goes for 'Anglian' visitors to Ireland at large (three references), or the four 'Anglian' kingdoms whose relations with Celtic neighbours are assessed in the summarizing chapter. And while it is impossible to say whether the '*alii in gente Anglorum*', whose poetry Bede thought inferior to Caedmon's, were Northumbrians specifically or Anglo-Saxons in general, the latter is as good a guess as the former.[43] In short, eighty-two cases where it makes sense to read 'Northumbrian', but rarely makes nonsense to read 'English', contrast with eighty-eight where 'English' is really the only feasible meaning. Scholars preferring the narrow interpretation face a burden of proof such as to render Atlas enviable.

To turn from terminology to content, it is of course true that a high proportion of the *Ecclesiastical History* is about Northumbria. Given the geographical bias of Bede's information (Canterbury apart), and his understandable pride in the rulers and saints of his own kingdom, it would be surprising if it were not. The heavily northern orientation of Book V thus arises from Bede's predictable interest in the miracles of the bishop who ordained him, in the life of Wilfrid, predecessor and mentor of Acca, his current diocesan and dedicatee of most of his other books, and in what his own Abbot Ceolfrith wrote to the king of the Picts about Easter — not to forget his own re-write of Adomnan's book on the Holy Places. Naturally too, he could describe a Northumbrian's vision of the afterlife in the man's own words, but knew less of a Mercian's comparable experience.[44] Yet Bede would hardly have sought out informants from other kingdoms had he not intended to tell the story of the English as a whole. His abiding interest in the wider picture emerges from his two final chapters: that on 'current affairs' referred to already, and a chronological summary with as many entries (including the last) about Anglo-Saxons overall as about Northumbrians.[45] It therefore seems safe to view the *Ecclesiastical History* as later generations of Anglo-Saxons from all parts of the island certainly did. It was indeed a spiritual history of a single '*gens*', albeit one divided into several '*gentes*'.[46] That Bede was himself an Angle affected its matter but not its message. His view of the 'Angles' was that of Canterbury and of Gregory beyond.

This is not to say that Bede's objective was English political unity. At the same time, his book had an underlying message that drew on decades of study of the history of Israel as deployed in the Bible. Bede had Gregory's exegesis to teach him that the 'literal' or 'moral' methods of interpreting Scripture were particularly suitable for the instruction of 'the little ones'.[47] In two biblical commentaries at least, he dwelt systematically on 'literal' or 'moral' meanings, and emerged with interpretations that have a startling relevance to what he would later write in the *Ecclesiastical History*. So David's dance before the Ark as it came up to Jerusalem showed the need for humility in kings (like Oswald); the instant death of the priest who reached out to steady it as it wobbled on its cart signified the 'presumptuous Jewish people', who aimed to keep salvation for themselves (like the Britons).[48] Bede's mind was already attuned to the moral lessons of one people's past. In turning to instruct his own 'little ones', the '*nostrae . . . Anglorum gentis inertiae*', through their own history, he naturally understood it in similar terms.[49] The *Ecclesiastical History* opens with a detailed account of Britain as a land of plenty. Next, its inhabitants, the Britons, are introduced by Rome to civilization, and eventually the Faith. But Rome withdraws, and the Britons fall into sin. They ignore the warnings of Gildas, 'their *historicus*'. They are scourged by invasion, but fail to learn its lessons. After defeating the invaders, they relapse into their old ways. They do not trouble to pass Christianity on to their new Germanic neighbours. As Bede knew and Gildas did not, the scourge comes again, and there is this time no recovery. God abandons the Britons. They lose their lovely land to those they have left in ignorance of Him. Yet 'God in his goodness did not reject the people whom he foreknew'. Rome comes again to Kent, in the person of Augustine, not Julius Caesar. The English are the heirs not only to the island but also to the religion that its original inhabitants have abused, and (as regards the date of Easter) are still abusing. Bede's story ends on a note of apparent euphoria. But it has a stern moral; one which we know was in Bede's mind, because the letter that he wrote three years later to his pupil, Bishop Ecgberht of York, was anything but euphoric. If the English sin as the Britons had, they face the same fate. The *Gens Anglorum* is a people with a Covenant, like Israel. Its future depends on keeping its side of a bargain with a God who is in every sense its maker.[50]

The attitude of their historians was in the first instance an effect, but ultimately also a cause, of the contrasting histories of England, France and Germany. For, whether intentionally or no, Bede's biblical model had immense political potential. Successful hegemonies in the early medieval West tended to exploit a common fear of a common enemy: an enemy who was preferably infidel, so threatening not only the interests but also the cherished assumptions of an otherwise fissiparous society. Power was established by effective leadership against a yet greater evil than a busily interventionist government. The Alfredian dynasty's campaigns against the Vikings were cast in the same ideological mould as the Carolingian claim to be rescuing the Christians of Gaul from advancing Islam, or the Lechfeld triumph of the Ottonians over the mortal danger that the Magyars posed to all Germans. But Alfred and his heirs had the additional advantage that their role made sense of the pattern of Anglo-Saxon history, as Bede had unforgettably laid it out.

A single people may not need a single ruler. But a people of the Covenant does. Israel, after all, was the archetype of the 'Kingdom divided against itself', and of its lamentable results. By directly tracing English destinies to God's plan, Bede lent the campaign for a united 'English' kingdom an urgency that soi-disant kings of Tara might well envy. Alfred's sketch in his *Pastoral Rule* preface of 'happy times', when 'kings were obedient to God and his messengers, and upheld peace and morals and authority at home, and also extended their territory abroad, and prospered both in warfare and in wisdom', was clearly drawn from Bede's picture of the seventh-century 'Golden Age' of the English Church. In stressing 'what temporal punishments [i.e. Vikings] came upon us when we possessed only the name of Christians, and few possessed the virtues', he implicitly invoked the English Covenant.[51] His lawbook opens with another remarkable preface: a translation of nearly three chapters of Mosaic law from the Book of Exodus, followed up by the story of how the Church had modified and transmitted this law 'throughout the whole world, and also to the *Angelcynn*'. This had the effect of showing Anglo-Saxons how similar were their laws to those of Ancient Israel. It also invited them to remodel themselves as a new Chosen People. Such was the foundation of a vigorous law-and-order campaign, designed to *make* the English into deserving recipients of God's favour, and sharing (I would argue) many of the features and all the brutality of the criminal law whose introduction is conventionally ascribed to Henry II.[52]

> There was a historian in the times of the Britons, called Gildas, who wrote about their misdeeds, how with their sins they angered God so excessively that finally He allowed the army of the English to conquer their land. . . . Let us take . . . warning. . . . we know worse deeds among the English than we have heard of . . . among the Britons. . . . Let us love God and follow God's laws. . . . Let us carefully keep oath and pledge, and have some loyalty between us without deceit.

This is Archbishop Wulfstan's great 'Sermon of the Wolf' from the grim year of 1014, when the English kingdom faced the first of its two eleventh-century conquests. Wulfstan is quoting a letter of Alcuin, written in shock at the Viking sack of the holy island of Lindisfarne in 793. Alcuin, who knew men who had known Bede, can be trusted to have grasped the message of the *Ecclesiastical History*. Wulfstan was himself the draftsman of many later Anglo-Saxon law-codes. His laws trouble the tidy minds of legal historians, because they are so very like his sermons. His confusion of these media in the urgent pursuit of his message epitomizes the linkage between Bede's vision of English history and the attempt to make society holy by law.[53]

The widespread dissemination of 'English' identity, and the nowadays generally acknowledged power of Old English govern-

ment, each imply that the message was getting through. It is understandable that it should. Any early medieval *gens* could see its mirror
image in the Old Testament. Some did. But English identification
with Israel arose from direct experience. This was, for West Saxon,
Kentishman, Mercian and Northumbrian alike, that Bede's warning had all but been realized in the ninth century. Their hard-won
promised land had almost been lost, along with the Faith introduced
by Rome itself, to another wave of pagan invaders from across the
North Sea. The tenth century, by contrast, brought triumphs unprecedented since the sixth, under kings who made it their business
to see that society 'possessed the virtues' as well as the 'name of
Christians'. But one more lapse could mean final disaster: the English would suffer from the Vikings what the Britons once suffered
from them. Compliance with unification was not only symbolically
proper; it was also a condition of survival. The high costs of allegiance to Alfred's house were paid, because the Anglo-Saxons had
already been taught by *their* historian to accept the terms of their
special relationship with the Almighty.

My argument, then, is that Bede's *Ecclesiastical History* had
some of the role in defining English national identity and English
national destiny that the narrative books of the Old Testament had
for Israel itself, or Homer for the Greeks, or Virgil (rather than Livy)
for the Romans. There is a natural tendency to wonder whether a
work so suffused with an intellectual's piety could possibly have had
such an impact. It should be resisted. Manuscripts of the *Ecclesiastical History* from pre-Conquest England number nine in Latin, and
six in Old English translation. If this does not seem a lot, it is more
than those of any other non-biblical book, except Ælfric's *Homilies*
(25), and Boethius' *Consolation of Philosophy* (18). It outstrips even
the *Pastoral Rule* and the *Rule of St Benedict*.[54] And if the number of
pre-1066 manuscripts is more impressive than it looks at first, it is far
outstripped by the number from the century that followed. Bede's
popularity in the twelfth century has been attributed recently to the
appeal that his portraits of pristine Irish ascetics had for the new
monastic orders. Yet only three copies are from Cistercian libraries,
and more than half the twenty-six that are placeable come from the
great Benedictine houses that were always the most closely associated with medieval ruling-class mentalities.[55] One of the most interesting is from Battle Abbey itself, the Abbey that Henry II's
justiciar (the abbot's brother) saw as the charter of the new regime.[56]
The main appeal of the *Ecclesiastical History* may therefore have been
that it continued to make sense of English experience. When the
Vikings did come again in 1066, with all the ruinous effects feared

by the makers of *Angelcynn*, the model proved its versatility. Two half-Englishmen in the early twelfth century wrote histories which adapted it to the new conditions. The *Gesta Regum Anglorum* (kings from Hengest to Henry I) was written by William of Malmesbury in self-conscious succession to Bede. He was among the first to make the equation between the Norman Conquest and an unreformed English Church that haunts our textbooks still. Orderic Vitalis personally penned a copy of Bede, as well as composing an *Ecclesiastical History* of his own that was modelled on Bede's in more respects than its title.[57] An account 'of deeds of Normans for Normans', it can also be seen as a *Historia Ecclesiastica Gentis Normannorum*, and is very much a story of conquerors operating as the instrument of God's punishment for sin. In short, the English were not forgotten by God, only scourged. By learning their lesson, they could flourish again.

So we come at last to the 'genius of Anglicanism'. God's Englishmen had a long future. It has been argued that Wyclif's sense of an '*ecclesia Anglicana*' was based in part on knowledge of Bede's 'Golden Age', and indeed of his angry denunciation of growing abuses in his *Letter to Ecgberht*.[58] As we enter the sixteenth century, there is no question at all about the importance that Matthew Parker attached to Bede, Alfred and Ælfric; this was his main motive in building up the manuscript collection at his old college of Corpus Christi, Cambridge, which is still one of the chief foundations of Anglo-Saxon studies. The idea of England as 'an elect nation enjoying God's special favour' was not a Tudor coinage. To say that the sixteenth century saw many conditions of the tenth recreated is not to give artificial respiration to the myth of a primitive Church of England which Maitland smothered with such brio. But if Hooker had written, as he very nearly did write, 'there is not any man of the *ecclesia Anglorum* but the same man is also a member of the *regnum Anglorum*', Wulfstan would have understood him perfectly.[59] The same exclusive allegiance was in each era melded by the same sense of a special Church, and the same fear of a godless enemy. In the next century, a much greater Englishman than Hooker or Wulfstan (though no Anglican) had an exceptionally creative sense of England as 'an elect nation'. The works of Milton include a *History of Britain* which, as it stands, is in effect a history of Anglo-Saxon England. It is also the last serious attempt to understand historical process in terms of the relationship between God and a Chosen People.[60] But that was not of course the end of the idea. English imperialism was to have a notably Messianic flavour, and its nineteenth-century apogee was another age when the first

English received special attention. And who is to say, in the light of current controversies, that we have yet heard the last of this self-consciously Chosen Race, or of its sense of a unique political and spiritual destiny?

NOTES

[1] My thanks are due to Geoffrey Rowell, Eric Stone and the Warden and Fellows of Keble College for inviting me to take part in this series; and to Simon Keynes, Veronica Ortenberg, Eric Stanley and, as ever, Jenny Wormald for constructive comments on my lecture. The notes that follow are largely restricted to references given in the text, together with English translations where available. The following abbreviations are used: *HE* = Bede's *Historia Ecclesiastica Gentis Anglorum*, ed. C. Plummer in *Baedae Opera Historica* (2 vols, Oxford, 1896) — I have preferred to use this edition, because it also contains *Ep. Ecgb* = Bede's *Epistola ad Ecgbertum*, but an acceptable translation is offered in *Bede's Ecclesiastical History of the English People*, ed. & tr. B. Colgrave & R.A.B. Mynors (Oxford Medieval Texts, 1969); *CCSL* = *Corpus Christianorum Series Latina* (Turnholt); *EHD I, II* = *English Historical Documents, Vol. I, c. 550 - 1042*, ed. D. Whitelock, 2nd edn. (London, 1979), *Vol. II, 1042 - 1189*, ed. D.C. Douglas, 2nd edn. (London, 1980); MGH, SRM = Monumenta Germaniae Historica, Scriptores Rerum Merovingicarum; *PL* = *Patrologia Latina*.

[2] G. Buchanan, *History of Scotland*, tr. J. Aikman, 4 vols, (Glasgow, 1827), I, pp. 249-50, 275, 308 etc.; J.A. Duke, *The Columban Church* (Edinburgh, 1932, repr. 1957), p. 138 (cf. p. 110: King Nechtan's attack on Iona was 'the First Disruption'). Cf. M. Lynch, *Scotland: A New History* (Edinburgh, 1991), pp. 26, 31 and n. 11 (p. 452).

[3] The late Kathleen Hughes, whose fine book, *The Church in Early Irish Society* (London, 1966) was in some ways the last and already faltering fling of the old school, wrote a posthumously published paper, 'The Celtic Church: is this a valid concept?', *Cambridge Medieval Celtic Studies* 1 (1981), 1-20; her answer was No, and on the significant grounds that the Welsh Church was quite different from the Irish as normally envisaged. See also W. Davies & P. Wormald, *The Celtic Church* (Audio Learning Tapes, 1980), and the former's review article in *Journal of Religious History* 8 (1974-5), 406-11. But the revolution now overtaking this subject is best appreciated in two seminal papers by Richard Sharpe: 'Some problems concerning the organization of the Church in early medieval Ireland', *Peritia* 3 (1984), 230-70; and 'Churches and Communities in early medieval Ireland: towards a pastoral model', *Pastoral Care before the Parish*, ed. J. Blair & R. Sharpe (1992), pp. 81-109.

[4] F. M. Stenton, *Anglo-Saxon England*, 3rd edn. (Oxford, 1971), pp. 119-20, 125-6.

[5] W. Levison, 'Die Iren und die fränkische Kirche', repr. from *Historische Zeitschrift* 109 (1912) in his *Aus rheinischer und fränkischer Frühzeit* (Düsseldorf, 1948), pp. 247-63. See Campbell (as n. 7), pp. 64-5.

[6] *Jonas, Vitae Columbani abbatis discipulorumque eius*, ed. B. Krusch (MGH, SRM IV, 1902) i 18-19, pp. 86-90; tr. of these passages in E. Peters, *Monks, Bishops and Pagans* (Philadelphia, 1975), pp. 94-5.

[7] *Adomnan's Life of Columba*, ed. A.O. & M.O. Anderson, 2nd edn. (Oxford Medieval Texts, 1991). J. Campbell, 'The First Century of Christianity in England', *Ampleforth Journal* lxxvi (1971), 12-29, repr. in his *Essays in Anglo-Saxon History* (London, 1986), pp. 49-67, (pp. 60-1).

[8] *HE* iii 14, pp. 156-7; *Jonas* i 19, p. 87.

[9] *HE* iii 22, pp. 173-4; *Baedae Opera Historica* II, p. 260.

[10] *Adomnan* Pr., pp. 186-7, and Anderson's note ad loc.; cf. the introduction, p. 23: Adomnan also drew on Gregory's *Dialogues*.

[11] *HE* iii 4, p. 124: '*ordine inusitato*'. See the papers of Hughes and Sharpe (as n. 3); and further for Wales, W. Davies, *Wales in the Early Middle Ages* (Leicester, 1982), pp. 158-64.

[12] *HE* iii 4, p. 134. A. A. M. Duncan, 'Bede, Iona and the Picts', *The Writing of History in the Middle Ages: Essays presented to R. W. Southern*, ed. R. H. C. Davis and J. M. Wallace-Hadrill (Oxford, 1981), pp. 1-42, (pp. 9-10).

[13] *HE* iii 19, pp. 163-4; *Vita Sancti Fursei*, ed. B. Krusch (MGH, SRM IV, 1902) i 6, p. 437. But, for a rather more positive evaluation of Irish missionary enterprise, together with an instructive account of its secular legal context, see T. M. Charles-Edwards, 'The social background to Irish "*Peregrinatio*"', *Celtica* 11, *Studies presented to M. Dillon* (Dublin, 1976) 43-59.

[14] *HE* iii 5, pp. 135-6; iii 26, pp. 190-1; iv 3, pp. 210-11; iv 27, pp. 269-70 (together with Bede's *Life of Cuthberht*, ed. & tr. B. Colgrave, *Two Lives of Cuthberht* (Cambridge, 1985) ix, xvi, pp. 184-7, 206-13.)

[15] A. Thacker, 'Bede's Ideal of Reform', in *Ideal and Reality in Frankish and Anglo-Saxon Society: Studies presented to J. M. Wallace-Hadrill*, ed. P. Wormald, with D. Bullough & R. Collins (Oxford, 1983), pp. 130-53, (pp. 133-46). *Ep. Ecgb.* 3, p. 406, tr. *EHD I*, p. 800; *HE* iii 5, p. 136.

[16] *HE* iv 27, pp. 270-1, *Life of Cuthberht* xvi, pp. 208-9, and cf. Gregory's Response I to Augustine, *HE* i 27, pp. 48-9.

[17] *HE* iii 5, pp. 136-7; cf. Gregory's letter to Augustine, *HE* i 30, p. 65: '*Nam duris mentibus simul omnia abscidere impossibile non dubium est, quia et is, qui summum locum ascendere nititur, gradibus vel passibus, non autem saltibus elevatur*'.

[18] J. Campbell, 'Bede', *Latin Historians*, ed. T. A. Dorey (London, 1966), pp. 159-90, (p. 182); repr. in his *Essays in Anglo-Saxon History* (London, 1986), pp. 1-27, (p. 25).

[19] The best account of these matters remains the introduction by C. W. Jones to his edition, *Bedae Opera de Temporibus* (Cambridge, Mass., 1946), pp. 55-104; but see also Duncan, as n. 12, together with the introduction by M. Walsh and D. Ó'Cróinín to their edn. and trans. of *Cummian's Letter De Controversia Paschali* (Toronto, 1988).

[20] *HE* iii 25, pp. 181-9; iv 5, pp. 214-17.

21 *Eddius' Life of Wilfrid*, ed. & tr. B. Colgrave (Cambridge, 1985) x, pp. 20-3; *Cummian*, pp. 56-97.

22 *HE* pr. ad Albinum, p. 3. Bede's founding abbot, Biscop, had been abbot at Canterbury: *Historia Abbatum auctore Baeda* 3, ibid., p. 367.

23 P. Meyvaert, *Bede and Gregory the Great* (Jarrow Lecture, 1964), pp. 16-18.

24 *HE* iii 25, p. 184; cf. *Cummian*, pp. 72-5.

25 I Cn. Pr, II Cn. 1, 62, 65, ed. F. Liebermann, *Gesetze der Angelsachsen*, 3 vols, (Halle, 1903-16) I, pp. 278-9, 350-3; tr. *EHD I*, pp. 454-5, 464. The usage derives increased, not reduced, significance from the fact that '*Dena*' and '*Dena lage*' are envisaged as entities distinct from their 'English' counterparts.

26 *EHD II*, pp. 119, 125. This is the 'D' version, probably reflecting the outlook of Ealdred, from 1061 the (southerner) archbishop of York, but drawing for 1052 on 'C', a southern text).

27 *Ælfric, Lives of the Saints*, ed. & tr. W. W. Skeat, Early English Texts Society 76, 82, 2 vols., (Oxford, 1881-5) xix lines 16-17, I, pp. 414-15.

28 F. Kluge, 'Fragment eines angelsächsischen Briefes', *Englische Studien* viii (1885), 62-3; translated *EHD I*, pp. 895-6. See N. P. Brooks, *History and Myth, Forgery and Truth* (Univ. Birmingham Inaugural Lecture, 1986), p. 3, who points out that the hairstyle, presumably that of Cnut's court, is sported by Normans on the Bayeux Tapestry.

29 See (among much else), K. F. Werner, 'Les nations et le sentiment national dans l'Europe médiévale', *Revue Historique* 244 (1970), 285-304, (pp. 292-4); H. Fuhrmann, *Germany in the High Middle Ages* tr. T. Reuter, (Cambridge, 1986), p. 19.

30 F. J. Byrne, *Irish Kings and High Kings* (London, 1973), pp. 46-69; D. Ó'Cróinín, 'Nationality and Kingship in pre-Norman Ireland', *Historical Studies XI*, ed. T. Moody (Belfast, 1978), pp. 1-35, (pp. 5-8).

31 *Cartularium Saxonicum* 488-9, ed. W. de G. Birch, 3 vols, (London, 1885-99), tr. *EHD I*, p. 528; *Select English Historical Documents of the Ninth and Tenth Centuries*, ed. & tr. F. Harmer (Cambridge, 1914), pp. 14, 48.

32 *H. Sweet's Anglo-Saxon Reader* rev. by D. Whitelock, 15th edn. (Oxford, 1967), pp. 4-7, tr. Whitelock, *EHD*, pp. 888-9.

33 Stenton, *Anglo-Saxon England*, pp. 33-6, drawing upon his celebrated paper, 'The Supremacy of the Mercian Kings', *English Historical Review XXXIII* (1918), 433-52, repr. in his *Preparatory to Anglo-Saxon England*, ed. D. M. Stenton (Oxford, 1970), pp. 48-66.

34 P. Wormald, 'Bede, the *Bretwaldas*, and the Origins of the *Gens Anglorum*, in *Ideal and Reality* (as n. 15), pp. 99-129; S. Fanning, 'Bede, *Imperium* and the Bretwaldas', *Speculum* 66 (1991), 1-26; S. Keynes, 'Rædwald the Bretwalda' (forthcoming); this scholar admits to encouraging his students to wear T-shirts with the logo 'BAN THE *BRETWALDA*'.

35 *Ælfric's Catholic Homilies, the Second Series* ed. M. Godden (Early English Texts Society, Supl. Ser. 5, 1979) ix, p. 74.

[36] W. Goffart, *The Narrators of Barbarian History* (Princeton, 1988), pp. 240, 250-3; Fanning (as n. 34), 20-22. In what follows, I am of course indebted to the invaluable P. F. Jones, *A Concordance to Bede's Ecclesiastical History* (Cambridge, Mass., 1929), pp. 29-31, and the following citations are given, as in Jones, by page and line number of Plummer's edition.

[37] 125:14, 142:7, 142:16, 30:24, 348:13. Other 'secular' usages: 33:4, 42:19, 45:2, 82:4, 85:16, 89:10, 89:22, 114:1, 196:4, 201:16, 205:5, 325:6, 327:20, 351:25, 352:28, 353:14. 'Ecclesiastical' meanings (* denoting a papal letter): 5:3, 6:25, 42:11, 42:22, 42:30, 46:10, 48:6, 48:9, 48:29*, 49:26*, 49:32*, 51:17*, 52:7*, 54:2*, 63:22*, 65:6*, 66:18*, 67:25*, 67:28*, 73:7, 76:33, 78:26, 79:19, 80:25, 83:20, 83:30, 87:9, 88:14, 88:22, 88:26, 89:6, 94:4, 116:29, 125:18, 139:13, 196:7, 196:10, 196:15, 201:17, 202:5, 204:10, 204:17, 204:22, 205:13, 238:28, 241:34, 242:28, 270:33*, 294:12, 295:3, 327:4*, 347:1, 347:8, 347:10, 347:12, 353:16, 357:1.

[38] Possible 'Northumbrian' (or other 'Anglian'): 26:26, 82:22, 84:2, 97:16, 117:25, 118:20, 128:21, 129:20, 132:10, 133:30, 145:10, 164:14, 184:17, 245:2, 253:25, 259:1, 284:4. 'Non-Anglian': 9:11, 11:14, 21:26, 45:6, 81:13, 85:22, 90:12, 138:6, 237:10, 331:11.

[39] 30:29, 31:15, 31:22, 31:28, 42:4, 80:13, 296:13. Perhaps to be added here are the two cases where 'Angle' is used for the East Anglian kingdom: 107:2, 167:29.

[40] Æthelfrith etc.: 71:8, 71:11, 71:17, 83:34; Edwin etc.: 89:25, 97:12, 97:16, 100:23*, 100:24*, 109:9, 119:1*, 124:14; Oswald: 131:12, 132:15, 137:31; Oswiu: 180:9, 229:26; Aldfrith: 315:18. Perhaps the best case is the 'apostate kings': 128:12, 145:2.

[41] 323:31; cf. 132:22, 134:31 & 191:26, 135:18, 170:20, 171:14, 179:26, 190:11, 205:18, 205:19, 299:16, 324:34.

[42] 133:20, 267:10, 267:12, 267:16, 267:20, 267:21; cf. 72:4, 97:7, 266:17, 332:22, 345:28.

[43] Mayo etc.: 213:2, 213:6, 213:20, 213:30, 214:1, 214:5; '*Angli*' in Ireland etc.: 192:10, 192:20, 195:27; relations with neighbours: 351:6, 351:9, 351:11, 351:16; Caedmon: 259:5. Cf. 137:4, 189:21, 195:29, 213:10, 269:28, 315:25, 347:20.

[44] *HE* v 2 - 6, pp. 282-92; v 12, pp. 303-10; v 15 - 17, pp. 316-19; v 19, pp. 322-30; v 21, pp. 332-46: this accounts for forty out of sixty-eight pages of Plummer's edition, excluding the two summarizing chapters.

[45] *HE* v 23-4, pp. 348-56.

[46] For the record, '*Angli*' are a singular '*gens*' fifty-three times, a *genus* thrice, but plural '*gentes*' only thrice, and '*populi*' five times. They belong to a single '*ecclesia*' ten times, and to plural '*ecclesiae*' nine (especially when Bede is discussing unification).

[47] See Gregory's prefatory dedication of his *Moralia in Job* to Bishop Leander of Seville: ed. M. Adriaen (*CCSL* CXLIII, 1979) 4, p. 6.

[48] *Aliquot Quaestionum Liber* viii, *PL* 93, cols 460-1; on its authenticity as a work of Bede, see H. Mayr-Harting, *The Coming of Christianity to Anglo-Saxon England*, 3rd edn. (London, 1991), p. 207, with reference. See, in similar vein: *In Regum Librum XXX Quaestiones*, ed. D. C. Hurst (*CCSL* CIX: Bedae Venerabilis Opera II:2, 1962), pp. 296-322.

[49] *Bedae Explanatio Apocalypsis*, praef., *PL* 93, col. 134.

[50] *HE* i 1-23, pp. 9-43; cf. v 23, p. 351, and *Ep. Ecgb.* 4-13, pp. 407-17 (*EHD I*, pp. 800-7).

[51] See n. 32, and cf. especially *HE* iv 2, pp. 204-5.

[52] Af. El. 49:6-9, ed. Liebermann, *Gesetze* I, pp. 26-47 (the last part tr. *EHD I*, pp. 408-9, but for a full translation, one must turn to B. Thorpe, *Ancient Laws and Institutes of England* (London, 1840), pp. 20-7). The legal consequences are a central theme of my forthcoming book, *The Making of English Law* (Oxford, 1994/5).

[53] 'Sermon of the Wolf': *EHD I*, pp. 933-4 (and samples of Wulfstan's laws, pp. 442-52, 454-67). Alcuin's letter: S. Allott, *Alcuin of York* (York, 1974) no. 48, p. 62.

[54] C8th/9th *HE* MSS remaining in England: H. Gneuss, 'A preliminary list of manuscripts written or owned in England up to 1100', *Anglo-Saxon England* 9 (1980), 1-60, nos. 367, 377, 863; Latin MSS c. 900-1066: Gneuss, nos. 75, 181, 555, 630, 759, with BL Egerton MS 3278 (Mynors, 'Textual Introduction' to the Colgrave-Mynors edition (above, n. 1), p. xlvii); Old English MSS: Gneuss, nos. 22, 39, 330, 357, 668, 673. In addition, two Latin MSS are datable 1066-1100: Gneuss, nos. 238, 487 (the same goes for c. 5 of the 25 Ælfric MSS). MSS of Pope Gregory's *Pastoral Rule* are 16 (two post-1066); of the *Rule of St Benedict*, 14 (one post-1066).

[55] R. H. C. Davis, 'Bede after Bede', in *Studies in Medieval History presented to R. Allen Brown*, ed. C. Harper-Bill (Woodbridge, 1989), pp. 103-16, (pp. 104-14). Exact totals from Mynors (as n. 54) are: Benedictine, 14; Augustinian, 8; Cistercian (Jervaulx, Newminster, Sawley), 3; secular cathedral, 1; unprovenanced, 9.

[56] *The Chronicle of Battle Abbey*, ed. & tr. E. Searle (Oxford, 1980), pp. 178-81; E. van Houts, 'The Ship List of William the Conqueror', *Anglo-Norman Studies* X (1987), 159-83.

[57] On William, see A. Gransden, *Historical Writing in England c. 550 - c. 1307*, pp. 166-85, especially pp. 173-4; and on Orderic, further to the 'General Introduction' in Vol. I of the superb edn. trans. by M. Chibnall, *The Ecclesiastical History of Orderic Vitalis*, 6 vols, (Oxford, 1969-80), Davis (as n. 55), pp. 103-16, especially at p. 116.

[58] E. Tatnall, 'John Wycliffe and *Ecclesia Anglicana*', *Journal of Theological Studies* 20 (1969), 19-43, especially at 34-6.

[59] Cf. P. Corrigan and D. Sayer, *The Great Arch. English State Formation as Cultural Revolution* (Oxford, 1985), pp. 57, 59.

[60] C. Hill, *Milton and the English Revolution* (London, 1977), especially pp. 279-84.

SIR RICHARD SOUTHERN

Anselm and the English
Religious Tradition

DOES ANSELM have a place in a book about the English religious tradition? He was not English after all, and he spent only a short period in England as a reluctant Archbishop of Canterbury for the last sixteen years of his life; and half of these were spent in exile, where he was much happier than he was in England. Nevertheless, I believe that he has a real and permanent primacy among those who laid the foundations of an English religious tradition at a moment when, such as it then was, it was threatened with almost complete demolition. So, without more ado, I shall mention the two features of this tradition to which Anselm made an essential contribution.

The first is a strong attachment to local forms of worship and Church organization, combined with a not unlimited recognition of papal authority. His balance in this matter, in combining a strong personal loyalty to papal authority with an unflinching provinciality, displeased almost everyone in some degree and certainly exposed him to papal disapproval, only mitigated by admiration for his personal sanctity.

The second feature of the English tradition in which Anselm plays an important part is his strong emphasis on private prayer and meditation outside the regular liturgy, practised initially by individuals and by small groups of like-minded friends, and then made available for use by everyone, clergy and laity alike. This feature of the tradition will be observed in several of the subjects of later chapters, and I shall hope to show that Anselm has a position of unique importance in establishing private prayer as a distinct part of the English tradition.

In order to understand his significance in these two areas of local tradition and private prayer, I must begin with a brief outline of his life, for the precise nature of his contribution is shaped by the fact that his life-span covered a period of fundamental change in the social and political organization, and in the intellectual outlook, of Western Europe; and, for England in particular, it brought the most brutal, complete, and permanent conquest by a foreign invader that was suffered by any European country after the barbarian invasions of the fifth to seventh centuries.

To begin then with the general scene: he was born in 1033, when Western Europe was nearing the end of a long period of economic and political immobility, beset by Vikings in the North, Magyars in the East, and Islam along the whole Mediterranean front. It was barely holding its own in any of these areas, and it was exhibiting no signs of growth in population, productivity, or prosperity, and very little sign of any important developments in thought. The most important innovations were found in an increasing elaboration of monastic life as a specialized form of corporate strength, making (as one may crudely say) full use of Christendom's supernatural resources in disciplined expiation for sin.

Rigour, discipline, concentration of resources, were the keynotes of Europe in 1033, and very necessary they were. But, if we go on to the time of Anselm's death in 1109, we find a scene that is dramatically different. The threats from external enemies have been replaced by a whole series of successful counterthrusts against Scandinavians and Slavs in the north and centre, and against Islam along the whole length of the Mediterranean. Then too, more important even than this external transformation, the static society of the early part of the century was being rapidly transformed by a continuing growth of population, by an immense diversification of social life, by an increasing variety of economic activities, and by profoundly important new developments in government and in thought; and all these features were destined to continue for the next two hundred and fifty years.

The change represented the most important transformation in European society before the Industrial Revolution. The growth in population and productivity was accompanied by an unparalleled development in administrative complexity in every area of government, and by an increasing diversity of new initiatives in art and architecture, in systematic knowledge and in religious experience.

Most conspicuous of all was the developing complexity of institutions, and this was particularly evident in ecclesiastical government, which by 1109 was developing the most elaborate system of unified law and administration under papal direction that had ever existed in Europe at any period — not excluding the period of the Roman Empire.

Anselm's life and thought reflected all these developments in varying degrees. To put his position in the most general terms, we can say that, in his personal attitudes and ideas, he was one of the great stimulators of the intellectual and spiritual diversification of the new age; but, in his political and governmental attitudes, he continued to the end of his life to belong to the earlier age into which he had been born. It is important to emphasize — and I shall try in the course of this lecture to illustrate — this double-sidedness in his legacy to the future. On the one hand, his political conservatism led him to insist on the preservation of local traditions and local powers and to comply with the rights of kings in ecclesiastical affairs. On the other hand, his spiritual legacy to the future is chiefly conspicuous in the intensity of his expressions of personal friendship, in the intimacy of his spiritual correspondence, in the independence of his theological speculations, and in the passionate introspection of his Prayers and Meditations. All these characteristics are of course to be found in varying degrees in other contemporary writers and scholars, but Anselm's words and works have a unity of impulse and a warmth of passion and individual energy spread over a wide range of activities, which mark him out from all his contemporaries.

II

THESE REMARKS MUST suffice as a preliminary sketch of his place in the general developments of his time. But we still have to ask how he became associated with England at all and how he reacted to this unexpected association. There was nothing in his origins or early life to make this connection at all likely. He was born in Aosta (the last town in Italy for a traveller coming northwards before crossing the St Bernard Pass), the only son of a fairly impoverished branch of a Burgundian noble family. His mother, whom he loved, had died when he was young. He hated and quarrelled with his father, and finally he left home at the age of about twenty-two in total uncertainty about his future. He was an eleventh century drop-out, and he spent about three years in his mid-twenties, between about 1055 and 1059, wandering through France without finding whatever it was he was looking for. His lack of reaction to his surroundings during these years is rather surprising because the parts of France through which he passed were beginning to show very conspicuous signs of renewed intellectual activity. But this was evidently not what he was especially looking for, and he wandered through the whole length of France as far as Avranches in Normandy without finding anything to arrest his attention or to bring his journey to an end.

At this point it was hard for him to know where to go next. For a man with his background, he had reached the end of the civilized world: beyond was only the already well-known barbarity of England. But in Avranches he got one new impulse. About fifteen years earlier, Lanfranc, another North Italian wanderer who had broken away from diminishing prospects in his home town of Pavia, had come to Avranches and set up a school. He had then gone on to become a monk at Bec, about sixty miles away, and there he had prospered enormously, creating a new school of grammar and dialectic that was attracting pupils from all parts of Europe. He had moreover recently become the chief adviser in ecclesiastical affairs to the Duke of Normandy.

Anselm went to Bec to see this phenomenon, and when he got there, something happened that was to happen on several occasions in his later life: he formed an instant, lasting and devoted friendship with the man he met. Lanfranc gave him all the personal inspiration that he had so far sought in vain, and Anselm gave Lanfranc the help that he badly needed. Anselm had had a good classical education at Aosta, though he had not made much use of it; and Lanfranc (who had many other things on his hands) set him to work teaching in his school. Anselm found it utterly exhausting. Who doesn't? As he told the disciple who later became his biographer, he had scarcely time to sleep, and he felt he was wearing himself out — for what? Like most of us he was torn in different directions, and he weighed up his options thus: he might become a hermit; or he might use his small inheritance to found a hospital; or he might enter a monastery — but where? Perhaps Cluny? But there he would be so busy with the heavy routine of corporate worship that he would have no time for thought. Or Bec? There he would be only Lanfranc's shadow. In the end he left it to Lanfranc to decide; and Lanfranc left it to the Archbishop of Rouen, who decreed that he should become a monk at Bec.

So the course of his life was settled for him, and for the next ten years he threw himself into the life of prayer, monastic discipline, and theological study, with an intensity and eagerness that later bore fruit in some of the most impassioned Prayers, Meditations, theological speculations, and letters of religious friendship in Western history. This body of writings, small in bulk though it is, and written in all its most important parts between 1070 and 1097, forms one of the most vivid personal legacies of the Middle Ages to the modern world. Every item in it points to an expanding world, and almost no item has lost its freshness by the passage of time.

The beginning of his personal transformation goes back to his becoming a monk at Bec. For four years, in addition to the long daily liturgical routine, he worked in Lanfranc's school. Then, in 1063, Lanfranc left Bec to become Abbot of a new monastery at Caen, and (to put it bluntly) this obstacle to Anselm's unfettered development was removed. The school for external students ceased to exist, and Anselm gave himself up to prayer, meditation, and to talk with like-minded companions.

One of the remarkable features of his development is that nearly everything that he wrote had its origin in talk with his intimate friends among the monks at Bec and elsewhere. We have an account of the impression he made on one of his companions who had become a monk of Bec at about the same time. He described the two of them talking together, each inciting the other to increasing efforts of self-abasement and higher and higher thoughts of God. Anselm did most of the talking, and at last he complained: 'You are sharpening your knife on my skin, but you never give me a chance of doing likewise; I beat myself black and blue in recalling the multitude of my sins, while you rise up to heaven in contemplating God.'

This flow of intimate highly charged talk is both unprecedented and significant: unprecedented, because talking was something that the Rule of St Benedict explicitly discouraged: it required *silence* as a foundation for the disciplined, corporate, liturgical routine of the whole community. Anselm simply broke away from this fundamental principle of the Rule, and his flow of talk with like-minded members of the community laid the foundations for all his later theological and devotional writing. It also made so great an impression on those to whom he talked that several of them went off at once to write accounts of what he had said. It was, moreover, in his talking that Anselm made his first impact on the English Church.

To understand this, we must go on several years and notice the changes caused by Duke William's conquest of England. His victory in 1066 had been miraculously complete, and by 1070 the country had been more or less finally redistributed between the followers of the Conqueror. King William then turned his attention to the Normanization of the Church. He made Lanfranc Archbishop of Canterbury, and Lanfranc set to work bringing the English Church into conformity with Continental discipline and organization. The English Church, like the country as a whole, had preserved a life-style conspicuously different from that of northern France, particularly in its vernacular literature and in many of its liturgical observances; and Lanfranc set to work with immense vigour and ability to change all this. Quite ruthlessly he cut out all local eccentricities and established a firm uniformity along northern European lines. He rebuilt Canterbury cathedral on the model of his abbey church at Caen; he restocked the library with the classics of Western theology, which were only meagrely represented in what remained of the pre-Conquest library; he mercilessly destroyed all insular peculiarities of liturgy, personal piety and learning. He threw out a whole heap of Anglo-Saxon religious customs and observances, as well as the relics and Feast Days of uncouth unpronounceable Anglo-Saxon saints. In order to carry through this plan of reform against the united opposition of the numerous Anglo-Saxon monks who still formed the main part of the monastic community at Canterbury, Lanfranc imported a small group of monks from Bec and Caen, to whom he gave all the important positions in the community. Anselm's early correspondence was mainly with these Norman exiles in Canterbury and naturally he imbibed from them their tales of English barbarity.

The English survivors among the Canterbury monks, however, were numerous and doggedly uncooperative; and — in order to silence their criticisms and complaints, and weaken their resistance — Lanfranc posted off their ringleader, a certain Osbern, to Bec to be disciplined by Anselm.

It was this action which first brought Anselm into close contact with an Englishman. He had so far accepted the gloomy accounts of English barbarism which he received from his friends, but the arrival of Osbern gave him a new view. From him he first heard about the Anglo-Saxon saints whose bodies Lanfranc had thrown out of his cathedral, and whose commemoration he had cut out of the liturgy. He heard too about the existence of a Rule of St Dunstan, which had regulated the lives of the Canterbury monks before Lanfranc's arrival. Most surprising of all, he got to know the ringleader of the Anglo-Saxon opposition whom he was expected to discipline, and he wrote glowing accounts of him to Lanfranc: their souls (he declared) had become so intertwined that he would find it hard to part from him. Further, he asked Lanfranc to send him a copy of the Rule of St Dunstan, which he had scrapped with all the

other insular peculiarities without (it would seem) so much as reading it, or perhaps even knowing that it existed. And, at the end of
Osbern's visit, he sent him back to Canterbury with letters of commendation to those to whom Lanfranc had given positions of authority at Canterbury.

It must strike any reader of these letters as extraordinary that
Anselm — coming from an entirely alien environment in northern
Italy, and then being firmly rooted in the Benedictine tradition as
represented by Lanfranc and the community at Bec — should at
once, from the single impression made on him by an offender sent
to him for reformation, have felt the force both of his personality
and of the way of life which he represented, and should have so unambiguously expressed his view to Lanfranc and his group of supporters.

On any ordinary reckoning it must seem a bit unbalanced.
But, whether it is or not, it lies at the very centre of Anselm's personality and of the contribution which he made to the religious tradition, not only of England, but more generally of Western
Christendom as a whole. In the heavily corporate society into
which he had been born, and of which he himself accepted all the
rules in their main features, he stands out, conspicuous and alone, in
the immediacy of his reactions to others, and in the unfettered live-
liness and ready availability of his impressions, and the freedom with
which he expresses them. With whatever situation or person he was
confronted, he seems always to have reacted with complete assurance to the experience with which he was faced.

This spontaneity has a wider importance in considering his
theological judgements. He arrived at these judgements, not by the
lengthy processes of collection, comparison, refinement and sys-
tematization, which produced the body of scholastic thought now
emerging as a new force in the intellectual life of Western Europe,
but spontaneously and — in appearance at least — impulsively. In
the whole body of his writings and his widely recorded spoken
words, he scarcely mentions a single authority; nor does he dissect
the words of his great forerunners. His problems all come from
within his own mind or from the questions of his friends; and he
reaches his conclusions, and expresses them in sharply pointed
terms, as if there were no earlier footprints in the sand.

Of course, from one point of view, this impression is illusory:
Anselm knew intimately the capital authoritative texts, the Bible,
the Rule of St Benedict, the creeds and the liturgy, and the works of
St Augustine especially. His conclusions are sustained by a total
commitment to the established orthodoxy of the Church. But he

brought a fresh eye to every personal contact, to every event or argument, to every problem. Everything he thought came from a new personal scrutiny, and the result — whether in defending the old or announcing the new — is as firm and fresh today as it has ever been.

We find these qualities exemplified at every stage of his life and in every area of his experience, but they appear with a peculiar spontaneity and clarity in this first meeting with the recalcitrant representative of what we may call the persecuted and defeated English monks of Canterbury.

III

ABOUT A YEAR after his meeting with the English rebel at Bec, Anselm paid his first visit to Canterbury. The year was 1079, and the purpose of his journey was purely practical. He had recently become Abbot of Bec, and one of his first duties was to visit the Abbey's recently acquired properties in England. Naturally his first stop was Canterbury. And, equally naturally, the group of English monks, who would have heard of him from their ringleader Osbern, gathered round him, and he talked. On this occasion, as on many others, one of his listeners kept a record of his words, and we know what he talked about. His main theme was quite simple: *It is more blessed to give than to receive.* And he developed this contrast in comparing the eternal rewards that await those who give, whether gifts or love, with the merely temporal rewards of those who receive such gifts. This simple dichotomy between things temporal and eternal was a subject on which he was always finding new similitudes and illustrations, and one of his listeners made a compilation of his *Similitudes,* which later had a very wide circulation. But, on his visit to Canterbury in 1078, the English monks offered him a new problem on which he could exercise his peculiar talent for seizing the general significance of an individual case. Their problem was this:

Among the many Anglo-Saxon saints whom Lanfranc had thrown out of the liturgy, there was one, Elphege, a former Archbishop of Canterbury in the early years of the eleventh century. Very little was known about him except that he had been murdered by Viking pirates in 1012 for refusing to tax his tenants in order to pay Danegeld. Not unreasonably, this had seemed to Lanfranc insufficient grounds for venerating him as a martyr, and he had thrown Elphege out of the Canterbury calendar together with all the other rejects.

The English monks had resisted in vain, and they asked for Anselm's view. He replied with great firmness: a martyr is one who has died for the Truth, whereas Elphege died for Justice. But — Anselm went on — Truth and Justice are the same substance exhibited in different situations: Truth is 'Justice in discourse'; Justice is 'Truth in action'. So Elphege, in suffering for Justice, had suffered equally for Truth; and, since this is the requirement for being venerated as martyr, Elphege was properly venerated as a martyr.

Remarkably enough, Lanfranc accepted Anselm's explanation and his conclusion without demur. He at once ordered Elphege to be restored to the Canterbury calendar and commissioned Osbern, the English monk whom he had sent to Bec for discipline, to write the necessary *Life* for the saint's Feast Day.

A trivial incident, you may think, over-simplifying on Anselm's part, and scarcely worthy of a place among the features of an English religious tradition. But we are touching the hem of a great subject. In persuading Lanfranc to reverse his decision about Elphege, Anselm was responsible for the first step in the revival of the observances and pieties of the English past which Lanfranc had aimed at sweeping away. Anselm's judgement in the case of Elphege bore fruit over the next two generations, when at Canterbury and other great churches with pre-Conquest roots there were many resuscitations of Old English observances and pieties. So Anselm's intervention in favour of the English rebels against Lanfranc's policy of integrating the practices of the English Church with those of continental Europe provided a general impetus for the whole movement of English revival during the next two generations; and — more important still — it enunciated a principle, endangered by the Conquest, that, in matters of worship, practices established by the pieties of the past, in however local a setting, are not to be cleared away in a rage for uniformity.

There is no need to follow further the process of reviving old cults, of writing lives of Old English saints, and of restoring Old English liturgical celebrations to the calendar. Many of the details are well known, though they deserve an up-to-date treatment, for they left a lasting impression on the English ecclesiastical calendar. And yet, it is relevant to ask: was Anselm right in his extraordinary intervention? Even if Truth and Justice have the same essence, does it follow that death for just any form of Truth or Justice qualifies the sufferer for the status of martyr? And, even if it does, may there not be some doubt about an incident that had taken place more than fifty years earlier and had never been recorded in writing? Is there not something simply impulsive in Anselm's answer?

These questions deserve a brief notice if we are to understand Anselm's mind. He seems very generally to have been content to accept the corporate memory and continuing practice of a community, in some ways uncouth and illiterate, as a sufficient basis on which to build a whole system of pious commemorations, liturgical practices, and even claims to a widespread jurisdiction. Corporate memory and a continuity of tradition seemed to him sufficiently decisive testimonies despite the absence of written records and the lack of any general, still less any universal, observance. Indeed it is obvious that a great deal in Christian devotion and doctrine has at some stage depended on the validity of this principle, and it is clear that Anselm was very ready to allow it a continuing place in the development of faith, worship, and ecclesiastical organization. Beginning with this case, the principle was extended to a large variety of Anglo-Saxon practices and claims during the next two generations.

Anselm's association with this reversal of Lanfranc's initial policy of enforced uniformity with Continental practice is one of the most challenging aspects of his character and outlook. Although — or possibly because — he was the most precise and exacting logical thinker of his time, he was content to accept the corporate experience of the past as a sufficient foundation for faith and practice. His famous principle of theological inquiry, *Faith seeking understanding*, implies that we must begin with what we have received.

To unravel the meaning of this programme would require many more and better lectures than I can give. For the moment it must suffice to say that Anselm's theological programme can be exemplified at many levels of sophistication in his life and works. With all his powers of logical refinement, he was willing to use the corporate experience of the Church, in its local members as well as in its universal testimony, as a sufficient basis for faith, piety, and jurisdiction alike. The *existence* of God he held to be convincingly established on a self-authenticating definition of the word God. But, beyond this, all the conclusions of theological argument can at best only clarify a long continuing tradition of corporate doctrine and practical piety. In this sense, therefore, his supporting local traditions of worship and organization is consistent with the whole of his theological programme.

To understand him it is important to recognize the extent of his commitment to ancient local practices. For him, the tradition mattered more than a wealth of documentary evidence, and to some degree at least he thought that the past could not be abrogated by new legislation. Hence, while most of the younger generation of reformers were prepared to sweep away long established usages,

Anselm adhered to the practices of the past not only with regard to religious practices and venerations, but also with regard to the jurisdiction and authority which had been entrusted to him on assuming his Archbishopric. Even the inherited rights of the king in episcopal appointments and investiture were not offensive to him, and he only desisted from observing them when he was expressly forbidden by a papal prohibition delivered in his presence.

IV

THERE IS NO SPACE to examine further the extent to which Anselm was prepared to recognize the validity of local custom — for example in his refusal to recognize any papal legate in the British Isles except the Archbishop of Canterbury — for I must too belatedly turn to another aspect of Anselm's influence in England arising from the dissemination of, and additions to, his collection of Prayers and Meditations, which helped to break down long-established barriers between monastic and secular, and clerical and lay, forms of religious devotion.

To understand Anselm's contribution to the future in this field, it is necessary to remember that nearly all his theological treatises arose from talk about God, Sin and Redemption, among groups of friends, generally within, but sometimes on the margins of, the monastic life. I have mentioned already the extent to which he broke through the Benedictine injunction of silence in the large use which he made of talk within the community. He did not, as the Benedictine Rule required, 'study to be silent'. He talked much in private. Similarly at meals, the Rule clearly envisaged that — although the abbot might speak occasionally — this would be a rare event. But Anselm talked often and freely. The spiritual life for him was a life of collaboration with others, certainly in stimulating devotion and confessing sins, but also in analysing and exploring the meaning of difficult concepts, such as Justice, Truth, Sin, Nothingness, God. Communication and freedom were central features of Anselm's spiritual life, and he extended this freedom also to Prayer, the most intimate of all forms of communication. When in the last years of his life he made a collection of his prayers to send to the great Countess Matilda of Tuscany, he enclosed a preface describing the way in which he wished them to be used:

These Prayers and Meditations were written to inflame the minds of their readers to self-examination in the love or fear of God. They are not to be read in tumult, but in quietness; not cursorily or quickly, but slowly and with intense and painful meditation; and there is no need to start at the beginning or to go on to the end, but to read only so much as may excite a desire to pray.

Here we get the outline of a new programme of devotional life, equally applicable to monks, clergy and laity, tied to no texts or times, freely moving as the spirit stirs the individual in approaching God. Anselm indeed was not alone in his time in thus stretching out to a new freedom outside the liturgy for those outside the monasteries, and for the laity as well as the clergy. But when you read his words and those of others who displayed similar tendencies, you see the difference at once. The most adventurous of his contemporaries stretched out only tentatively, whereas Anselm broke through at once into a new world in which individuals of all kinds probed the depths of the soul and sought a new understanding — even in some way an experience — of the divine nature.

What all the evidence of Anselm's relations with other people makes clear is that his friendships at every period of his life, from the time of his arrival at Bec in 1059 until his death in 1109, were an engagement in prayer, repentance, and the study of God's being and modes of operation. These efforts provided the stimulus for his Prayers and Meditations and for his theological treatises on the nature of God, Truth, Sin, and Free-will. The relationship between the treatises and his earliest prayers and meditations and his later theological treatises may be summed up by saying that the former sought self-knowledge as a means of carrying out God's purpose for mankind, and the latter were concerned with the nature of God, first in Himself, then in relation to the individual soul, and finally in relation to the divine plan for the universe.

The *Prayers and Meditations*, therefore, were preparatory steps towards a full knowledge of God, and one of the main ways in which Anselm influenced the future was through their circulation. They were by far the most widely distributed of his works in the Middle Ages, and it is a symptom of the importance of his disciples at Canterbury that they were chiefly responsible for making and circulating the fullest collection of them. These disciples in England also had, from a scholarly point of view, the more dubious distinction of having made the earliest and most numerous apocryphal additions to Anselm's genuine pieces. By the mid-thirteenth century about a hundred and twenty-one Prayers and Meditations circulated under Anselm's name, and they all continued to be read as genuine works of Anselm until about fifty years ago. Recent criticism has reduced the number of genuine pieces to about twenty, and we can now see that there is a pretty wide gap between the intensity of the genuine pieces and the diffuseness of the later additions. But, in judging the extent of Anselm's influence, and his place in the English religious tradition, the spurious pieces (of which many are of English origin) are quite as important as the genuine, because they are expressions of discipleship, and (since their 'inferiority' was not discovered for nearly nine hundred years) they evidently had enough of Anselm's spirit in them to satisfy a long succession of readers.

V

IN CONCLUSION, let me sum up the two sides of Anselm's personality and writings which give him a special place in the English religious tradition.

First, at a critical moment for the survival of distinctive English traits in ecclesiastical organization and habits of piety, Anselm put the whole weight of his influence and powers of critical thought on the side of the preservation of local traditions which were in imminent danger of extinction; and his work survived in the preservation of ancient pieties, and in the continuing existence of the Primacy of Canterbury, though at a level of authority much less than he desired. Second, he provided models of Prayer and Meditation which continued to influence the piety of the English Church until the seventeenth century and to some extent until the present day. As for his general view of the universal Church under the authority of the successors of St Peter, he was certainly very old fashioned by the time of his death in the wide scope for local peculiarities, local disciplines, and the exercise of an independent local jurisdiction which he strenuously defended. His main aim was the creation and maintenance of a world-wide society of souls knit together in faith and living in the presence of God.

And there we may leave him. Everything that he said, wrote, or did, was based on the two props of an unchanging body of established doctrine and a growing and diversified experience of its meaning. It was the function of his Prayers and Meditations to turn the statements of Faith into the inner convictions and personal experiences of each individual. It was the function of the monastic Rule to provide a routine of life which would give systematic order to these convictions and experiences, not only to those within the monastic communities but also to the friends, patrons and supporters of these communities in the outside world. What Anselm contributed to this continuing process was a brilliance of definition, a refinement of sensibility, and an intimate affection for those who were engaged in this activity which make his letters more like love-letters than the stern invitations to extreme self-renunciation which they also were.

To everything that he touched, and to all with whom he discussed these problems, he brought a warmth and passion in which it is hard to say whether reason or faith predominates. The more we look into writings, the more we see him, not just as a theologian with deep insights into the truth of the Christian revelation, not just as the defender of local privileges and devotional practices, but also as a pilgrim in company with all others who had made, were making, or in future would make, the same journey. In this context his defence of local rites, pieties and privileges is not a political or organizational programme, though it has political and organizational consequences. It is simply one part of his vision of a world-wide, age-long, communion of souls linked together in a common service.

NOTE

Most of the details mentioned in this chapter are more fully elaborated in my volume, *St Anselm: A Portrait in a Landscape* (Cambridge University Press, Cambridge, 1990).

SISTER BENEDICTA WARD

Lady Julian and Her Audience: 'Mine Even-Christian'

THE FOURTEENTH-CENTURY writer known as Julian of Norwich has been called 'the first English woman of letters' but even more striking is the fact that she is also the first English theologian in the sense that her two books, called by her first editor in 1670 'Sixteen Revelations of Divine Love', are the first serious piece of theology to be written in English. Perhaps it takes a long time for a people to become accustomed to articulating their thoughts to God and about God in a new language. In the eighth century Bede created the concept of the English and in his day English first began to be a written language, but he himself wrote in Latin and his theology is contained in the Latin commentaries and homilies on the Scriptures which made him the most renowned scholar of his times.[1] Four centuries later, the Italian-born, Norman-trained Anselm gave new direction to English Christians both in the sense of continuity and change in worship and in the private devotion which was affected so dramatically by his *Prayers and Meditations*[2]; but he also wrote in Latin. Both men moved on a wider stage through their use of the international language for talking to God and about God; but by the fourteenth century Latin was becoming a block rather than the communicating medium it had always been; vernacular languages were beginning to be the vehicle for prayer, praise and poetry. The other English mystics used English for their devotional works either partly as with Richard Rolle or entirely as with the author of the *Cloud of Unknowing*, Walter Hilton and Margery Kempe. But it is Julian of Norwich who used the English language first for the analysis and exploration of true theology, that is, for talk about God. In lively, humorous and vigorous prose, she explored the love which is the Trinity and its relationship to man in Jesus Christ, combining the loving and serious following after Jesus of Bede with the theological eagerness for truth of Anselm; like them both, in Julian 'faith is seeking understanding', compunction of heart is combined with rigour of intellect in an unassuming and practical religion which can be called English. The surprising thing is that Julian, like Bede and Anselm, can be English without being in any way insular. These writers began where they were, and by accepting and loving their limitations of time and space, made them not limits but contacts. 'Home is where we start from', or to quote Traherne,

> All creatures in all nations and tongues and people praise God infinitely and the more for being your sole and perfect treasures. You are never what you ought until you go out of yourself and walk among them.[3]

This sense of one place as the matrix of love is especially evident in the author of the *Shewings of Divine Love*. On 13 May 1373, when Julian was thirty and a half years old, she was so ill that she was thought to be dying; a crucifix was held before her eyes and for a few hours only out of a long life in one time and one place she saw what she called 'a revelation of the love of Jesus Christ' shewn to her in the extreme of pain and dereliction. After her recovery, she wrote down her perception of these moments in two books: the fifteen chapters of the 'Short Text', and the 'Long Text', her meditation on the shewings over the next twenty years which expanded her original insights into eighty-six chapters which was finished about 1393.[4]

It is useful to remember that the original text of the *Revelations of Divine Love* is lost; her own manuscripts, written or dictated by her, have not so far been found. There are no known copies of the complete Long Text earlier than three hundred years after her death. It is known through three manuscripts now in Paris and London, with some selections in a manuscript at Upholland and one in the Westminster Cathedral Archives.[5] All are in difficult seventeenth-century hands and differ significantly from one another. The Benedictine Serenus de Cressey first edited the text of the Long Version in 1670 which was reprinted in 1843 and appeared in a modernized version in 1877; Grace Warrack's thorough modernization did not appear until 1901; and the first attempts at the very difficult job of making a critical edition of the Long Text was begun fairly recently and the process is by no means complete. Moreover, between the writing of the texts and the twentieth century, almost no references have been discovered to either versions of the *Revelations* in contemporary literature and perhaps none were made. Knowledge of this work which now seems so important was very rare indeed before this century. The fact is, while it is clear that the Long Text is a major work of theology we do not now know exactly what its author wrote; the text is a difficult one to establish let alone interpret; and few people seem to have read it.

The case is a little different however with the Short Text, Julian's first book. There is only one known manuscript of it, a section in a larger book, but it differs from the versions of the Long Text in two significant ways: first, it is legible, being written in a clear and beautiful hand, and secondly, the scribe claims that it was written in the early fifteenth century while Julian was still alive. This oldest surviving copy of her work is part of a collection of devotional works bought by the British Museum at a Sotheby's sale from the library of Lord Amherst in March 1910,[6] where it occupies nineteen pages of a beautifully written fifteenth-century manuscript, which had been in the possession of the Yorkshire Catholic family. The Short Text was printed two years after its discovery, and more recently has been translated into modern English.

I am interested in the *Revelations* first of all as a historian and not as a theologian, and it is therefore not the Long Text with all its extraordinary flights of sublime theology that most concerns me but the older manuscript of the Short Text. It is there that I most of all meet its author and make contact with the overflow of love towards others that coloured all her relationships in person or in writing. It seemed to me when I gave the annual Julian lecture in Norwich two years ago[7] that who Julian was can affect the reading of her work, perhaps not in any major way but in some details and I therefore looked at Julian herself and challenged the usual assertion that she was a nun; I proposed a very different background for her as a north-country woman living in Norwich. She was, I suggested, a wife and mother, then a young widow, and only later an anchoress. I found that my reading of the *Revelations* was enhanced by having re-evaluated her life and background; she speaks more truly and consistently, and many of the minor difficulties of the text disappear. I did this of course in direct opposition to Julian's own preference, that no attention should be given to herself but only to her message:

> I pray you all . . . that you disregard the wretch to whom (this) was

[49]

shewn and that mightily, wisely and meekly you contemplate God.[8]

My excuse is that attention had already been given to her to make her out to have been a nun and the picture presented was proving a block to her message, by putting her into the little world of professionally religious people. I would like today to take my arguments in this matter for granted and expand an area upon which I touched, that of those connected with Julian and her work and continue this liberation of Julian by seeing first of all who in fact knew and talked with her, who read her books, for whom did she intend them and what does she have to say not only about the love that is God but about the love between human beings. For she did not think of love of others as peripheral; it was an integral part of the revelation of God as love. She understood the two commandments as inextricably linked, and the love that is God as both the pattern and the uniting force for all he has created:

> For God is everything that is good, and God has made everything that is made, and God loves everything that he has made and if any man or woman withdraws his love from any of his even-christians he does not love at all because he has not love towards all. . . . Anyone who has general love for his even-christians has love for everything that is[9]

From the Short Text itself it is possible to see other people who were near to Julian. In her illness she sent for 'the parson, my curate', a phrase suggesting either a chaplain to a private household or the parish priest, and he came with a little boy and a cross, the focus of her visions.[10] In her illness her bedside was crowded with friends; her mother was also there and they were all prepared to laugh heartily. Julian approved of their laughter provided it was a positive happiness but she says she wanted to warn them to love God more and leave earthly vanity.[11] This sense of being involved in a matter of ultimate seriousness which was not quite understood by those near her recurs when she says that her mother, supposing her to be dead, tried to close her eyes at just the moment when Julian most wanted them open. 'I did not want to be hindered from seeing because of my love for Him'.[12] Later, she mentions a conversation with a cleric at her bedside, again involving laughter, but also an incident which is revealing in another way:

> I said the cross that stood at the foot of my bed bled profusely and

when I said this the religious I was speaking to became very serious and surprised. And at once I was very ashamed of my imprudence.[13]

The shewings were not to become incidents that made her famous or respected; and she reacted against her mistake at once.

I wish to make one other suggestion in exploring the relationships in Julian's background and suggest that she had been married, widowed early and had borne at least one child. If this is so, all the language she uses about the attitude of God towards us being like that of a mother then takes on a natural meaning:

> The mother's service is nearest, readiest and surest, readiest because it is most loving and surest because it is truest . . . Our bodily bringing to birth is only little, humble and simple . . . still it is he who does it in the creatures by whom it is done . . . A kind, loving mother who knows and sees the need of her child guards it very tenderly as the nature and condition of motherhood will have it. And always as the child grows in stature, she acts differently but she does not change her love; and when it grows older she allows it to be chastised to destroy its faults so as to make the child receive virtues and grace.[14]

These are passages which show warmth and care but also a woman of independent mind, lacking in sentimentality, full of discretion and wisdom. And above all they show her in a family context, already moving from the centre of Christ within her in the following of 'our courteous Lord'.

Do we know of any other contemporaries who had contact with Julian? There was not only one Julian in Norwich. There are many wills of the fourteenth and early fifteenth centuries leaving money or goods to solitaries as well as to religious, to monks presumably for them to offer masses, to the solitaries for their prayers. A number of wills made in Norfolk in the fourteenth century contain references to money left to 'Julian, the anchoress at Conisford' and these are direct bequests. In 1394, when Julian was fifty one, there was a bequest of two shillings by Roger Reed, a parish priest, rector of St Michael's Coslany in Norwich to 'Julian the anchorite' and Thomas Edmund of Aylesham, a chantry priest of Aylesham in Norwich in 1404 left one shilling to 'The anchorite Julian at St Julian's in Norwich' and some pence to her servant Sara. In 1415, John Plumpton of Norwich left forty pence to 'the anchoress in the church of St Julian at Conisford in Norwich' and twelve pence each to her maid Alice and her previous maid, additions which suggest that John Plumpton had at various times consulted the anchoress and had been received with kindness by her servants. Isabel Ufford, the devout daughter of Thomas Beauchamp, Earl of Warwick, who after the death of her second husband entered a house of canonesses in Suffolk, died in 1416 and left forty pence to 'Julian a recluse in Norwich.'[15] It seems that the Julian of these wills may well have been the 'devout woman' of the Short Text, in which case Julian had two, perhaps three girls as her handmaids: one called Sara, another Alice; and had in some way helped either by prayer or advice, two men of Norwich, one of Aylesham and a devout lady. It was the ordinary but serious Christians of her own area who were her companions and friends and benefactors.

There is one other direct reference to Julian living at the end of her life as a respected anchoress in Norwich and that is in Margery Kempe's account of her visit to Norwich where she was specifically advised to consult Julian. The married visionary of Lynn spoke with William Southfield, a friar of Norwich, himself known as a visionary, and afterwards was 'commanded by our Lord' to go and see 'an anchoress in the same city who was called Julian'. This was in 1413 when Julian was in her seventy-first year, having completed both versions of her revelations, and already known for her wise advice in matters concerning the inner life. Perhaps it is significant that it seemed appropriate for Margery to go to consult Julian about her inner experiences at a time when she had borne another child and decided it should be her last; Julian commended her choice of chastity, 'for all chaste livers are temples of the Holy Ghost' and urged her to have confidence in her own experience of God and not to be swayed by criticism. They seem to have had more than one conversation, in which Julian took seriously Margery's account of her revelations, so different in style from those of Julian herself:

> great was the holy conversation that the anchoress and this creature had through talking of the love of our Lord Jesus Christ for the many days that they were together.[16]

Margery was no nun but another part of the network of spiritual individualists in England at the time and someone the content of whose visionary experience if not their style was similar to those of Julian. Margery, who irritated many other people, and was resentful enough of the lack of appreciation shown towards her ecstasies, was received with serious interest by Julian who reminded her that God willed her to do what was for the 'worship of God' and also for 'the profit of her fellow Christians'; she added some friendly if perceptive advice:

> I pray God grant you perseverance. Set all your trust in God and do not fear the talk of the world. Patience is necessary for you in that shall you keep your soul. [17]

Julian can be glimpsed within her world of family and friends, visitors and acquaintances, but she was also keenly aware of a great cloud of witnesses, the familiarity with the saints of God. St Mary, St Cecilia, St John of Beverley, St Peter and St Paul, St Veronica, St Mary Magdalene, are all mentioned with warmth and affection. Three times Julian was shown the saint nearest to Jesus, that is Mary, first as 'a simple, humble maiden young in years of the stature which she had when she conceived',[18] then as the lover of Christ and sharer in his passion 'Christ and she were so united in love that the greatness of her love was the cause of the greatness of her pain'[19] and finally 'as she is now in delight honour and joy . . . more pleasing to him than all creatures'.[20] Here is no idolatry but as she says 'all who take delight in him should take delight in her . . . to see Mary and pass on to God in prayer'.[21] John of Beverley, the Northumbrian saint who ordained Bede to the diaconate and the priesthood and about whom Bede wrote with affection and humour in the *Ecclesiastical History of the English People* was to Julian a fellow northerner: 'exalted yet a familiar for our comfort and he brought to my mind how he is a kind neighbour and of our acquaintance'.[22] There is the same restraint about the saints together with an easy, familar love of them which was there in Bede and also in Anselm:[23] they are for her dear neighbours, a part of that great cloud of witnesses all of whom like her had learned to 'choose Jesus for my heaven: meliked no other heaven but Jesus which shall be my bliss when I come there'.[24]

Julian became through her books more than an isolated individual; it is possible to see her being read most of all in her own day in the close-knit network of solitaries throughout England. Her readers were not many it seems, but it is possible to identify a few. The first contemporary of Julian's who both knew of her and had read her first book is the scribe who copied the Short Text in the fifteenth century. He describes the author as

> A devout woman and her name is Julian that is a recluse at Norwich and she is still living in this year of our Lord 1413.[25]

The Short Text then was written down and copied out again during Julian's life-time, by someone who had either met her or known someone who had. Julian is described as a recluse and a devout woman but not a nun. She is referred to as a recluse 'of Norwich', a town, not of a nunnery; and she is called Julian, the name of the saint to whom was dedicated the church near which she lived. The scribe who copied this text into his book had read it and knew at least so much about Julian. The Amherst manuscript is now a large book, perhaps originally much smaller, and the first texts which include Julian's book were copied by one scribe, the text being corrected by another but contemporary hand; most of the corrections are in fact in the Julian text which perhaps indicates either that the original was hard to read or that its northern dialect of Middle English was unfamiliar to an East Anglian scribe. It has been most carefully corrected, indicating a reader anxious to have an accurate text of a book which he valued. The other pieces copied into this book indicate others who at any rate had a copy of Julian's book. The first two texts are translations into English of Latin works by the Yorkshire hermit Richard Rolle, the first of which ends thus:

> Thus ends the twelve chapters of Richard Hampole into English translated by Brother Richard Misyn to the information of Christian souls in 1434

The second is more specific: it begins

> At the reverence of our Lord Jesus Christ to the asking of thy desire, Sister Margaret, coveting ye say to make for increase of ghostly comfort . . . who of Latin understandeth naught.[26]

At the end it reads

> Here is the book of the *Fire of Love* by Richard Hampole hermit translated into English at the request of Margaret Heslyngton a recluse by Brother Richard Misyn bachelor of theology and prior of Lincoln of the Carmelite Order, on the feast of the translation of St Martin July 4th 1435.[27]

Two other readers of the book appear here: the Carmelite Richard Misyn and the recluse Margaret Heslyngton. It may be that Margaret Heslyngton was aware of the fact that Rolle had originally directed his treatise on *The Form of Living* to another recluse called

Margaret, and had asked for it simply because of a coincidence of names. The third piece which is headed

> This pistill made St Bernard unto his cousin the which is called the golden epistle for the great abundance of ghostly fruit that is contained in it.[28]

It ends with the pious wish that 'He of my sins will have mercy. amen. Jesu mercy, lady help' with the monogram I.S. though the hand indicates the same scribe as the previous pieces. The text of Julian's revelations is next, headed

> Here is a vision shown by the goodness of God to a devout woman and her name is Julian which is a recluse in Norwich and is still alive ad 1413 in which vision are very many words of comfort greatly moving for all those who desire to be Christ's lovers.[29]

It is followed by translations of other texts of a similar nature, that is, a piece called *Of the Perfection of the Sons of God*, a translation of a treatise by Ruysbroek, some more material by Rolle and a text by Suso, until another scribe took over with *The Mirror of Simple Souls* and perhaps began another book. The first treatises are in English and may all have been made for Margaret Heslyngton, an English-speaking lady who was one of the many devout men and women living as solitaries throughout England at the time, of whom Julian was also one. These are texts directed to helping people to understand the love of God and respond to it. Richard Misyn was a Carmelite friar and prior of the Lincoln Carmel, a man well acquainted with Norfolk, who may have succeeded the eccentric Norfolk hermit Scrope in his Irish bishopric. It seems that he knew and read Julian's text and prized it enough to include it in the works he was translating for the recluse Margaret. Julian's book was therefore influencing other Christians in her own day, and in one particular way: the scribes' notes to the works in this collection present the texts as words in English which will draw non-Latinate readers more deeply into the love of God and desire for him, using words like 'ghostly fruit', 'deepening of desire', 'ghostly comfort'. Julian's book therefore was offered among texts which were all meant for the increase of love among English men and women who knew no Latin but were able to read, or have read to them, classics of spirituality.

It is possible to see Julian among her contemporaries and to glimpse some of those who in the past have read her works. The

Short Text seems to have fallen into the hands of the Carmelite James Grenehalgh of the Sheen Charterhouse, an assiduous collector of spiritual texts.[30] On the first folio there is the name 'Vincent Winge', a sixteenth-century owner, and it has also the book-plates of two north-country owners, William Constable (d.1791) and Lord Amherst. Other readers of Julian include the English nuns in exile in Cambrai in the sixteenth century where the Long Text was preserved and copied. It is little enough. The two books by Julian seem to have been little known in her own time and then virtually ignored until this century. But the real audience of Julian's works was not in any case her contemporaries alone; like Bede and Anselm, home was only where she started from. Her words were not directed like so much religious writing in the form of a letter to a specific person or group of people; they were from the first for her 'even-christians', that is for those who are as much in Christ as herself; and who they are in any age only Christ really knows. She disclaimed fiercely any idea of being a teacher of others; she says she wrote only what she has been shown so that everyone might also contemplate 'Jesus who is every man's teacher'. At the end of the Short Text it is Julian's even-Christians that still occupy her mind:

> God wants us always to be strong in our love and peaceful and restful as He is towards us, and He wants us to be for ourselves and for our even-christians, what He is for us. Amen.[31]

She wrote always for these 'even-christians', a phrase she seems to have invented. A simple woman herself, it was not nuns, monks, friars, nor priests, not especially clever or religious persons that she thought might read what she had written, but those who also are in the hand of God as she had discovered herself to be. Christians, yes, but she makes no decisions about whom God loves in his Son; it can be those covered by Mark Frank's phrase, 'his dear humankind'. In fact, her audience is: ourselves.

What does Julian tell us then? First and foremost, that she has been shown the reality of God's love for her, and since it is for her it is therefore for all. She is identified with all whom God loves, and there is of course no-one else. For her, this love which is the Trinity is the pattern and source of all love for others. This fact is central to understanding the *Revelations of Divine Love*: it is not a book about how we love God, but a true theology, about how God loves us and in loving us communicates love through us to all creation. The fact that one result of what she was shewn was that she withdrew from contact with her even-Christians as an anchoress is no contradiction to her understanding of that love as intimately concerned with others: what mattered essentially was that here was one human being really able to understand that she was loved by God; and so since one frail human being is able to stand in one place upon earth steadily holding up towards God all the broken edges of her life, all that inner sense of alienation, of being unloving and unlovable, without self-pity, impatience or shame, one part of humanity has made this life-giving encounter and all creation therefore has done the same: 'This vision was shown for all men and not for me alone'[32] 'for we are all one in love'.[33]

From the centre of Julian's vision the love that is the Trinity, there is a wonderful and astringent pursuit of what it means for God to love us, and she pressed this home after the few hours of startling realization during many years of faith seeking understanding and that is the glory of the Long Text. But from the beginning hers was not a selfish or static vision of glory. She saw at once how from that centre also arises true love of others and indeed of ourselves.

All that I say of myself I mean in the person of all mine even-christians . . . the sight was shewed for mine even-christians in general and not only me in particular. We are one in endless love to ourselves our Lord Jesus Christ. Let us pray for all our even-christians and for all manner of men as for ourselves.[34]

I would like to conclude by indicating three aspects of Julian's understanding of this love as applied to others, under the headings of discretion, suffering, joy. It is her conclusion that mankind is not left to work out how to love but is given both the example and the ability to do it: 'He wants us to be for ourselves and for our even-christians what he is for us'.[35]

First, there is in Julian's books the theme of discretion, the ability to act appropriately, which was for Bede as for Gregory the Great the controlling power which regulates all the virtues. Other English mystics also exhibited and recommended this trait of common sense and restraint so that zeal never outruns strength; at its worst it is mediocrity, at its best discretion. 'Love was our Lord's meaning' for Julian but love applied wisely. God shewed her the respect he has for his creatures, so that in her account of redemption in the parable of the Lord and Servant she can say that God 'sat upon the ground awaiting human nature'; so for her, right relationship between people must include that same respect for their freedom. Also, God is not the subject of our exploration in a way which would destroy and annihilate Him; there is, Julian says, a right

[57]

eagerness to know God and a wrong curiosity about God: all shall be well, she says, and a great deed shall be done, but what it is we do not know:

> It is God's will that we should know in general that all shall be well but it is not his will that we should know it now.
> We ought to rejoice in him for everything that he reveals and everything that he conceals.[36]

This is a dimension therefore of our knowledge of others: in particular she was shown that we do not know and cannot know anything about the mystery of God's judgement of other people. She was herself given a practical instance of this when, she says,

> I wished to know concerning a certain person whom I loved what her future would be; and by wishing this I impeded myself for I was not then told this.[37]

This reverence before the mystery of God in each person is fundamental to Julian's conception of her even-Christian: all are equally loved by God and therefore as He has respect for each, so each must respect the freedom, the secret at the centre, of the other.

Secondly, just as Julian was shown with minute detail and realism the sufferings of Christ on the cross, so she did not advocate illusion in relationship to others, or avoidance of suffering by any notion of romance, niceness or hypocrisy. She was above all realistic; what other mystic has used as an example of the wonder of God's creating love the fact that

> A man walks upright and the food in his body is shut in as in a well-made purse. When the time of his necessity comes, the purse is opened and shut again, in most seemly fashion.[38]

She lived in a time and a place where the sufferings occasioned by the recurrent plague called the Black Death, as well as by insurrections and wars made pain and death a commonplace, with daily horrors on a scale unmatched until the twentieth century. Can one suggest that her child, loved and watched and guarded had died, perhaps in the recurrent onslaughts of plague? In 1361, when Julian would have been nineteen, a form of plague occurred which was especially fatal to children. The imagery of one passage which occurs soon after her use of the image of motherhood at least suggests a memory of such a thing, with its wistful conclusion:

I saw a body lying on the earth which appeared heavy and horrible, and without shape and form, as it were a swollen pit of stinking mud, and suddenly out of this body there sprang a most beautiful creature, a little child, fully shaped and formed, swift and lively and whiter than a lily, which quickly glided up to heaven. . . . It is more blissful that man be taken from pain than that pain be taken from man, for if pain be taken from us it may come again.[39]

No wonder she was most deeply concerned to understand how suffering and love can exist together. Her repeated question to Christ in His shewing of love, is how can love be reconciled with a world of pain, suffering, death, damnation, loss? And she is shewn that in Christ there is such a reconciliation; and so there must be between human beings. The centre of Julian's understanding of pain and love is the cross which Bede recorded as the first image carried into Canterbury by the missionaries who brought Christianity to this island; the same cross which Anselm made central to his discussion of Atonement as it was to his prayers.

All creatures that might suffer pain suffered with him . . . he suffered more pain than would all men together from the first beginning to the last day[40]

In her own time with eyes open to such sin, pain and death, in the cross and in her own life, she discovered that in this also 'Love was his meaning'.

But thirdly, pain, death and darkness were not the end. In her hard-won theology of the cross there is continually woven into that austere fabric the bright threads of delight, laughter and glory, and this glowing joyfulness comes directly from all the delight of Christ in us. He has no blame towards anyone; guilt is not what he wants from us but thankfulness; for Him, even our sins are seen 'not as wounds but as worships'. In her contemplation of the details of the passion Julian does not hear Christ blaming sinners or urging them to repent for causing such pain but saying

Are you well satisfied that I suffered for you? If you are satisfied, Our Lord said, I am satisfied. It is a joy and a bliss and an endless delight to me that ever I suffered my passion for you for if I could suffer more I would.[41]

For Jesus has greater joy in all the deeds which he has done for

[59]

our salvation . . . we are his bliss, we are his reward, we are his honour, we are his crown.[42]

It is not the wit that cuts people down that Julian offers to her even-Christians but joy, the generous delight of God in us. As God delights in all his creation, so each should rejoice in the other, without blame to anyone, but with compassion and love.

Just as I was before filled full of pain and compassion on account of Christ's passion, so I was now in a measure filled with compassion for all my even-christians and then I saw that every kind of compassion which one has for one's even-christian in love is Christ in us.[43]

The English tradition of which Julian's works form part is not special in the sense of being different from the whole pilgrimage of Christian living. Her life was plain in every sense yet she understood in her time and place the central fact of the Gospel that God was in Christ reconciling the world unto himself and for her that central indwelling of love was expressed and communicated to others first in her acceptance of it for herself and then in her discreet, realistic and happy love of all God had made, the people she knew and those who would know her works. She herself, who saw so clearly and wrote so truly about the love the Crucified has for each creature, was not burnt up by a few ecstatic moments of vision before entering heaven at once. On the contrary, she lived for many years after those moments of revelation and in the silence of a room in Norwich who knows what anguish and longing, what prayer and compassion, what patience and waiting, followed on from the *Revelations of Divine Love*?

The trivial round, the common task,
Will furnish all we ought to ask,
Room to deny ourselves, a road
To bring us daily nearer God

Julian was no finished and complete saint; throughout the Revelations she makes it clear that she was as stupid and selfish and unresponsive and tempted as anyone; but she held steadily to the central fact shewn her that in all things 'love was his meaning' in the conviction that 'all shall be well':

He beholds his heavenly treasure with so great love on earth that

He will give us more light and solace in heavenly joy, drawing us from the sorrow and darkness we are in. Thanks be to God. Here ends the book of the revelations of Julian the anchorite of Norwich on whose soul may God have mercy. amen.[44]

NOTES

[1] Bede, *Ecclesiastical History of the English People* ed. and trans. Colgrave and Mynors, (Oxford University Press, Oxford, 1968). For an introduction to his commentaries, see Benedicta Ward, *The Venerable Bede* (London, 1991).

[2] For a discussion of the influence of Anselm on prayer see R. W. Southern, *Saint Anselm: a Portrait in a Landscape* (Cambridge, 1991). For a translation of Anselm's *Prayers and Meditations*, see *Prayers and Meditations of St Anselm* trans. Benedicta Ward, (Penguin, Harmondsworth, 1979/88).

[3] Thomas Traherne *Centuries of Meditation* (London, 1960), The Second Century, 79, pp. 91-2.

[4] The most recent critical edition of both texts is *A Book of Shewings to the Anchoress Julian of Norwich* ed. E. College and J. Walsh, (Pontifical Institute, Toronto, 1978). Quotations are taken from *Julian of Norwich: Shewings* trans. E. College and J. Walsh, (Paulist Press, New York, 1978), hereinafter referred to as either 'Short Text' or 'Long Text'; I have however preferred 'even-Christian' to the 'fellow-Christian' of this translation.

[5] Dates for manuscripts and printed texts of her works:
1413 Short Text MS British Library Additional MS 37790
1500c Selections from Long Text (Westminster Cathedral Archives MS)
1640c Selections from Long Text (St Joseph's College, Upholland MS
1650c Long Text (Paris MS Bibliothèque Nationale Fonds Anglais 40
1650c Long Text (British Library, Sloane 2499)
1700c Long Text (British Library, Sloane 3705)
1670 Long Text printed in London from text by Dom Serenus Cressy; reprinted 1843. 1877, a modernization printed by H. Collins, 1901, Grace Warrack's version.

[6] The Short Text was purchased unrecognized and was only noticed after two years in the British Library and printed in a modernized edition by Dundas Hartford in 1911.

[7] K. Leach and B. Ward, *Julian Reconsidered* (Fairacres Press, Oxford, 1988). The dates I there proposed for Julian of Norwich are:
1342: Born prob. in North of England.
Moved to Norwich, (perhaps after marriage?).
1348-9: The Black Death.
1361: children affected by the Black Death; In this period, married, widowed, bore a child/children, one or more of whom died.
1373: Illness and Showings in her own home at 'thirty and a half years old'.
Dates for Showings: P reads: 'the xiii daie of May'; SS both read 'viii daie of May'. 8 May 1373 was after Feast of St John of Beverley (cf. Cap. 38) also the third Sunday after Easter. 13 May was a Friday. Time is given as four in the

morning; there was a clock that struck the hours on Norwich Cathedral by 1325.

Julian enclosed as an anchoress at St Julian's in Norwich in this period.

1393: Long Text completed.

1393: Bequest by Roger Reed of Norwich to the anchoress at Norwich 1404; Bequest of Thomas Edmund; 'Juliane anchorite apud St Juliane in Norwico' with money also to her servant Sarah.

1413/15: Visit of Margery Kempe. See *The Book of Margery Kempe* cap. 18. Margery lived in Bishop's Lynn (now King's Lynne) 40 miles from Norwich. The *Book* was written in 1436 'twenty years or more' after Margery's conversion, which must therefore be placed about 1416. She visited Norwich soon after the birth of her last child.

1413: Short text reference: 'Here is a vision shewn by the goodness of God to a devout woman whose name is Julyan. She is a recluse at Norwich and is yet alive in this year of Our Lord 1413' (aged 71).

1415: Bequest by John Plumpton of Norwich to the anchoress Julian at Norwich and also to her maid Alice and to her former maid.

1416: Bequest by Isabel Ufford of 20 shillings to 'Julian recluz of Norwich'.

1429: Bequest to 'an anchoress in the churchyard of St Julian's'. Therefore perhaps still alive at 87.

Death: date unknown.

[8] Short Text VI, p. 135.

[9] ibid. VI, p. 134.

[10] ibid. II, p. 128.

[11] ibid. VII, p. 136.

[12] ibid. X, p. 42.

[13] ibid. XXI, p. 162.

[14] Long Text LX, pp. 298-99.

[15] N. P. Tanner, *Popular Religion in Norfolk with special reference to the evidence of wills, 1370-1532*, unpublished D.Phil. Thesis, 1973.

[16] *The Book of Margery Kempe* trans. B. A. Windeatt, (Penguin Classics, Harmondsworth, 1985), pp. 76-79.

[17] ibid. p. 78.

[18] Short Text IV, p. 131.

[19] ibid. X, p. 142.

[20] ibid. XIII, p. 146.

[21] ibid.

[22] Long Text 38, p. 243.

[23] Cf. Anselm's 'Prayer to St Peter' and 'Prayer to St Mary Magdalene' op. cit.

[24] Short Text XI, p. 43.

[25] ibid. chapter 1, p. 125.

[26] British Library Additional MS. 37790, f. 18r.

[27] ibid. f.18v. For further information about English solitaries in the Middle Ages, see R. M. Clay *The Hermits and Anchorites of England* (Methuen, London, 1914), especially appendix C, pp. 203-283.

[28] British Library Additional MS 37790, fol. 95v.

[29] ibid. f. 97r.
[30] ibid. f. 33r. for his monogram.
[31] Short Text XXV, p. 170.
[32] ibid. VI, p. 133.
[33] ibid. XVII, p. 154.
[34] ibid. VI, p. 133.
[35] ibid. XV, p. 152.
[36] ibid. XIV, P. 150.
[37] ibid. XVI, p. 153.
[38] Long text VI, p. 186.
[39] ibid. LXIV, p. 306.
[40] ibid. XX, p. 213.
[41] Short Text XII, p. 144.
[42] ibid. XII, p. 145.
[43] ibid. XII, p. 149.
[44] ibid. XIV, p. 170.

ANNE HUDSON

John Wyclif

JOHN WYCLIF, it seems, is a figure about whom it is almost impossible to be dispassionate — Beryl Smalley described him in 1984 as the most controversial of all Oxford's sons. Reviled, if not formally condemned, by the end of his own lifetime by the ecclesiastical hierarchy as the originator of the first English heresy, he came to be regarded by John Bale, John Foxe and other writers of the Edwardian and Elizabethan church as 'the morning-star of the Reformation'.[1] Catholics around the time of the Council of Trent were understandably less than enthusiastic about this distinction, but both they and their reformed opponents stressed the extent to which the ideas of Luther, Calvin and other sixteenth-century radicals can be traced back to the teaching of the late fourteenth-century Oxford academic.[2] In the ecumenical climate of the mid-twentieth century Wyclif has tended to disappear from ecclesiastical discourse, relegated to the decent obscurities of the academic world; Wyclif the medieval schoolman has taken the place of Wyclif the reformer, and the issues he discussed are held to be the dusty minutiae of medieval debate, irrelevant to our more sophisticated concerns. Only in Bohemia is Wyclif remembered as a potent social, and indeed political figure as John Hus's revered mentor — and in the aftermath of the 1968 occupation of Prague many historical scholars paid with the loss of their jobs for the realization that their Hussite concerns offered a potential model for a new revolt against a foreign and hostile power. For this same reason, the name of John Wyclif is still a more emotive one, and one more central to medievalists' preoccupations, in Prague and the Czech lands than it is in England.

Can a balanced judgement be reached? It seems to me doubtful, because a number of the issues which Wyclif broached seem likely to remain central to human concerns, at least in the Western world. Christians may now be more willing to compromise on matters such as the precise way in which Christ is present in the eucharist, Last Supper, memorial meal (call it what you will), or at least to allow that others may honestly hold differing opinions and not for that reason be automatically dangerous to the community; Pope and Archbishop of Canterbury may be happy to exchange both courtesies and meaningful dialogue on various issues; the necessity for scripture to be in the vernacular of the community may now be conceded by all. But some of Wyclif's ideas remain contentious, remain issues whose implications are so far-reaching that compromise cannot be reached. Perhaps the central matter here is one which, by a distinguished historian of medieval philosophy, was dismissed as an idea of no practical consequence and one that was forgotten, even if ever understood, by Wyclif's followers: that of dominion.[3] Wyclif took the view that dominion, that is the authority to wield power over material things and over human beings, was dependent upon the state of grace of the person attempting to use that power. Authority only rightly inhered in the person who was in a state of grace — it could not properly be used by anyone in a state of mortal sin. This was not just a rod to beat the avaricious claims, as Wyclif and many others of his time saw it, of the contemporary Church to a disproportionate amount of the wealth of England. It implied that the authority of *all* office-holders, and the legitimacy of all acts that they might initiate, could only be justified if the holder himself was out of mortal sin; office could not legitimate law, an act that in itself was good or at least neutral could be invalidated by the sinful state of the actor, legitimacy inhered if at all in the officer, not in the office. The implications of this view could hardly be more far-reaching, whether in Church or in State. And it is clear that we are far from having found a consensus on it today: should the sexual immorality of the cabinet minister impose a duty of resignation? And what is the correct relation of private vice with public knowledge of it? Many would regard Wyclif's view of dominion as authorization for no form of state other than anarchy, even if Wyclif himself certainly did not countenance such a far-reaching shift in the secular kingdom. It is hard for most to be coldly dispassionate about such a question. In one regard, at least, related to this is the issue of authority in the Church: do the advantages of unity outweigh the problems of allegiance to an office whose holder may not be in a state of grace? The other dimension to this particular question is, of course, the extent to which the Bible is to be taken as the sole source of law in the Church. And again this is a question on which most find it hard to be impartial.

As this brief introduction may imply, debate about John Wyclif and his views is not likely to go away. But it would be reasonable at this point to look at the historical facts of his life, though facts are in short supply for certain important matters even in this.[4] The date of his birth is unknown, and even the year can only be guessed from the first mention of him as a probationary fellow of Merton College in 1356; from this it seems reasonable to think that he was born between 1330 and 1335. He seems to have come from the North Yorkshire family of Wyclif, and this may indicate that when he became Master of Balliol in 1360 he was returning to the college where he had first studied. He did not stay there long, and for his long periods of residence in Oxford from 1363 to 1381 he apparently lodged at Queen's. His lecturing followed the traditional pattern: first in logic and on Aristotle's *Physics*, then on philosophy and theology; he incepted as Doctor of Theology in 1372 or 1373. His tenure of a series of relatively unimportant benefices from 1361 on does not, despite his later teaching on the duties of a resident clergy, seem to have kept him away from Oxford for any long period until 1381. But from 1371 onwards Wyclif was called on by the King, the King's Council and later by John of Gaunt, for advice, opinions and on one occasion for participation in an embassy to Bruges; in the period between 1375 and early 1379 it seems plain that he must have spent considerable time in London or in the entourage of court and Parliament. His opinions, expressed both verbally and in writings during this period, aroused increasing hostility amongst the ecclesiastical hierarchy, and gained him notoriety as far distant as the papal court. Pope Gregory XI in 1377 condemned 18 conclusions, and demanded Wyclif's arrest and condemnation;[5] the Bull containing these was published in England but, possibly because of his standing in the regard of Gaunt and others at the court, Wyclif at this stage escaped judgement. He was again used by the court in October 1378 to argue the claim against the Abbot of Westminster in a case involving the arrest of two men within the sanctuary of the Abbey. Evasion of ecclesiastical anger became more difficult when Wyclif lectured on the eucharist, probably in 1379, revealing his dissension from the accepted teaching of transubstantiation, especially since it became clear that his followers were not content for this dissension to remain in the decent obscurity of a

Latin academic debate but intended to preach it outside the university and in English. Lecturing on the eucharist in the spring of 1381 in the schools of the Austin Friars, on the site of the present King's Arms pub, Wyclif was interrupted by a messenger who came to announce the condemnation of his views by a committee of twelve under the Chancellor William Barton. The lecture, despite the intrusion, continued and Wyclif claimed that it would not change his opinion.[6] It did, however, change his position — and later that year Wyclif withdrew from Oxford, evidently under strong pressure, to his living at Lutterworth. He did not, as far as we know, return to the university; but he continued writing, almost frenziedly, in defence of his opinions from Lutterworth until his death on 31 December 1384.[7] To that final period in Lutterworth I will return later. The formal condemnation which Wyclif had escaped in 1377–8 was finally issued in May 1382, when ten of his opinions were deemed heretical and a further fourteen erroneous (albeit without mention of his name in the body of the text).[8] But no attempt seems to have been made to bring Wyclif himself to trial, or finally to silence him: his followers came under pressure from 1381 onwards, but for some reason persecution passed by the originator of the heresies. It was, however, as a direct result of his teaching that the death penalty for heresy was introduced into England in 1401, and that Archbishop Arundel between 1407 and 1409 brought into force his *Constitutions*, legislation that laid severe restraints upon the freedom of speech and writing, whether within the universities or in preaching or in the translation of scripture.[9] Largely because of Wyclif's perceived responsibility for much of the dissent in Bohemia, his views were condemned along with those of Hus at the Council of Constance in 1415; in 1428 Bishop Flemyng of Lincoln, an alleged favourer of Wyclif in his early years, finally carried out the edict issued there, exhumed Wyclif's bones, burned them and scattered them into the river Swift.[10]

The 1377 condemnation centred on the view that I described earlier as perhaps the most continuously troubling of Wyclif's ideas, that of dominion. The 1382 Council at Blackfriars in London assembled a wider collection, and one that must have seemed at the time a group with more immediately practical implications: the first three heresies concerned the eucharist, one denied the need for anyone contrite to make oral confession, one denied the authority of any pope not in a state of grace (hence taking up the dominion issue), and another stated that it was against sacred scripture for the clergy to have temporal possessions; a further heresy went on to the interesting claim that after Urban VI none was to be accepted as pope, but that the Church was to live, *more Graecorum, sub legibus propriis*, this last obviously anticipating an implicit claim of the Henrician and later Church in England. The ensuing errors largely represent deductions or implications from these major ideas: excommunication by a prelate was immaterial unless validated previously by God, that the legal powers of the State should override those of the Church in regard to temporal matters, but that none, secular or religious, held dominion in a state of mortal sin, that secular rulers can legitimately remove temporalities from erring clergy and can correct them, that tithes are alms and not obligatory payments, that private prayers are less useful than general prayers, and that all private religions (that is orders that remove the individual from the normal communal Christian life) are sinful and should be abandoned; more positively, preaching is the primary obligation on all clergy and cannot be prevented by any human prohibition.

Although the list is deliberately extreme in its format, as opposition lists of 'heresies and errors' are bound to be, in only one case (the seventh heresy, that God must obey the devil) do the terms unfairly represent Wyclif's views. Of course, in many respects the context modifies the extremity of the opinion: Wyclif's views on oral confession, for instance, were supported by citation of a section of canon law which confirmed that for the person truly contrite God's forgiveness was available without confession to a priest[11] — though certainly Wyclif generalized this, interpreted habitually as covering the emergency in which no priest was available, to the norm and added to it his own more far-reaching claim that, since God alone could know the state of a man's soul, God alone could pronounce absolution so that the priest's formal statement was, depending upon its agreement with God's judgement, either merely confirmatory or arrant blasphemy.

Would Wyclif, had he lived in the late sixteenth century or later, have been an Anglican? In 1608 Bodley's Librarian, Thomas James, addressed precisely this question in a modest book entitled *An Apologie for Iohn Wickliffe, shewing his conformitie with the now Church of England; with answere to such slanderous obiections, as haue beene lately vrged against him by Father Parsons, the Apologists and others.*[12] James declared on the title page that he intended to carry out this demonstration by extensive quotation from Wyclif's own writings found in the Bodleian Library. By modern critical standards James's evidence is less than perfect: many of his citations derive from English texts almost certainly by the followers of Wyclif and not by the heresiarch himself.[13] But the book represents, as Kenny observed, the beginnings of a scholarly analysis of Wyclif's opinions and writings.[14]

The obscurities concerning the source of a few of James's quotations are not relevant to the present purpose. More interesting are the topics on which James sought to demonstrate Wyclif's 'conformitie with the now Church of England in the chiefest points controverted, thence to descend vnto questions not altogether so material, and last of al to answere al such obiections as haue beene mooued by our late Popish writers.' (p. 2) The seven main matters were, in order, The Scripture, Traditions, The Pope, The Church, Justification, Merits, and The Blessed Sacrament of the Lord's Supper. Whilst there are perhaps no surprises amongst these, from the viewpoint of an early seventeenth-century Anglican, it is interesting that James left till last the issue that had both finished Wyclif's own public teaching career and proved a touchstone in later Reformation theology, and also that he had the discrimination to put first the matter that arguably formed the positive lynchpin of Wyclif's teaching, the primacy of scripture. The eucharist seems to have involved no difficulties for James: Wyclif's 'opinion of the Sacrament was the same with the Church of England; *that the body of Christ was really and truely in the Sacrament, in his kind, that is sacramentaliter and figuraliter, by way of Sacrament,* and figuratiuely, *so Iohn Baptist figuratiuely was Helias, and not personally*; and *as Christ was together God and man so the consecrated host* (for so he calleth it) *was at the same time Christs very body, and very bread* not by waie of Consubstantiation, as the *Lutherans* teach, for it was *Christes body in figure, and true bread in nature; or which is all one, true breade naturallie, and Christs body figuratiuely'* (p. 29, the material in italics is referred to Wyclif's *Confessio de sacramento altaris* from MS Bodley 703, f.58 quoted by James in translation). Interestingly James does not raise the question of the availability of the sacrament in both kinds to the laity, a question that Wyclif, to the best of my knowledge, never raised, but which certainly marked off the Anglican church (as it had done the Hussite sect) from Rome. James was right in understanding Wyclif to have denied the accepted view of transubstantiation, and the various theories advanced to provide a physical explanation of this, at the end of the fourteenth century; the language he uses, with its parallels, derives ultimately from Wyclif's own writing, and was repeated by Wyclif's enemies. He was also right in asserting that Wyclif held that the corruption of eucharistic doctrine had begun after a thousand years of church history, and that Wyclif attributed the corruption particularly to the evil influence of the friars.[15] In all of this James could claim Wyclif's anticipation in outline of the Anglican doctrine, and even of the murky language in which that doctrine was framed, just as Archbishop Parker in his *Testimonie of Antiquitie* of 1566 had claimed a greater antiquity for the doctrine in the Paschal homily of Aelfric.[16] James spent more time on the first issue of scripture (pp. 6-14): there was no difficulty in proving Wyclif's differentiation between the 22 canonical books of the Bible and the Apocrypha, and equally no problem in demonstrating Wyclif's support for translation of the Bible into the vernacular — even if James's claim that Wyclif himself had translated the whole Bible may seem chronologically difficult, despite the continued attraction of the idea to all popular writers on Wyclif and to some whose scepticism might be expected.[17] More central to this section are the questions of whether 'Holy Scripture containeth althings necessarie to Saluation, and that whatsoeuer is not read therin, nor may be proued thereby, is not to be required of anie man that it should be beleeued as an Article of the faith, or bee thought requisite or necessarie to Saluation' (p. 7), and of the limits of interpretation and the control of that interpretation. James produces citations to back up his assertions. But it is not surprising that the dispassionate modern reader may remain somewhat confused at the end of his analysis, both about Wyclif and perhaps also about the Anglican position, at least in James's outline of it. Whilst Wyclif certainly regarded the New Testament as a mirror for the contemporary Church, and because of the defects of the latter as a rod to beat it with, his precise position in regard to *scriptura sola* is decidedly unclear, or more accurately fluctuating: whether scripture was to be a positive model, against which the modern Church was to be reformed to restore the lineaments of the early Church, or whether scripture was be a straitjacket that could negatively rule all change off limits — Wyclif moved between the two views, often it seems according to the adversary in his sights at the moment.[18] Equally Wyclif repeatedly grappled with the problems of biblical interpretation, and his own practice was far from the naive fundamentalism that his emphasis on the literal sense of scripture might lead a modern reader to expect; and Wyclif, in my view, never resolved, or indeed fully argued, the dilemma of the limits of legitimate interpretation — or perhaps was over-optimistic in his assumption that others would share his own intelligence and expertise.[19] But, as I have said, it is interesting that James should place Wyclif's attitude to scripture in first position: I would certainly want to argue that, if the inspirational centre of the Hussite movement was the access of the laity to the chalice, and of the Lutheran church was salvation by faith alone, then the equivalent centre of Wyclif's message, to which his followers remained true right through to the 1530s, was scripture as the touchstone of Christian religion and the corollary of this, the availability of scripture in the vernacular.[20]

In the second section of his book, James reviewed 25 subsidiary matters: some, such as the 14th *Of Divorces*, he dismissed abruptly 'He held against vnlawfull divorces, so doe we' (p. 36) with no further definition and a single marginal quotation from the *De mandatis*; others, such as the 21st *Of the Discipline of the Church*, covered a number of issues in rather more detail (pp. 38–40). But nearly half of the book was devoted to refuting the slanders of Parsons and others, and it is here that some of the most interesting material is to be found, for whilst some of the slanders were mere personal abuse (7th 'He was more giuen to scoffing, and prating, then became a sober Diuine' p. 66), others were more tricky for an Anglican to refute. Thus Parsons is cited in the 6th objection as averring that Wyclif had taught that 'Tythes are meere almes, and may be detained by the Parishioners, and bestowed where they wil at their pleasures' (p. 52). This is in fact a repetition of the eighth error condemned by the Blackfriars Council in 1382; it is a fair, if cursory, summary of an opinion that Wyclif taught fairly consistently from *De civili dominio* onwards.[21] James has to admit the truth of the allegation: 'That Tythes are meere almes, hee holdeth eueriewhere, it was his errour' — an error Wyclif came to, according to James, by trusting too much to 'the Common Lawyers' (pp. 52–8). What James tries to demonstrate is that Wyclif's view was coupled first to his concern for the reform of the parish clergy, and second to his desire for a ministry living in evangelical poverty. His evidence does not quite allow him to demonstrate that Wyclif thought tithes must be levied, but might be directed by ecclesiastical authority to a recipient other than the parish priest — but he has a good try to suggest that this was what Wyclif meant to say.[22]

But, it may fairly be objected, is it fair to use one critic of no standing even in the Church of his time as a judge of Wyclif's anticipation of the Anglican dispensation? Would a modern Anglican recognize Wyclif as foreshadowing his Church? I have argued elsewhere that his early followers had developed a set of teachings that went considerably beyond the changes introduced by Henry VIII and Elizabeth I into English public religion: their demand for a clergy living from immediate alms and from the labour of their hands runs counter to the retention of tithes in the post-Reformation established Church; their insistence upon the complete separation of the clergy from the secular administration of the State is still more radical than the presence of some bishops in the House of

Lords; their rejection of images, pilgrimages, all visual and aural ornamentation of churches and their services has been only fluctuatingly implemented in the mainstream Anglican Church.[23] Whilst his followers may have been more simplistic in their formulations than their master, only in the last of these matters were the Lollards perceptibly more extreme — and it may be reasonably suspected that, had Wyclif had time to write at length on these issues in his retirement at Lutterworth, the brief indications of his more moderate opinions in his early works might well have been superseded by positions much like those of his disciples.[24] Wyclif would, I think it can fairly be said, have had more in common with the views of Thomas James, or of Edmund Grindal, Elizabeth's Puritan Archbishop of Canterbury, than he would have found in the position of John Keble or of post-Oxford reform movement Anglicanism, even of the less 'high' variety.

One of the most obscure areas of Wyclif's thought is indeed the question of the Church. This does not affect the metaphysical Church: this to Wyclif was the *congregatio predestinatorum*, those predestined by God to salvation. But this Church, whilst it might be the referent of all Christ's promises, was invisible to human sight: only God could know its members — though it might be legitimate to identify from the manifest activities of many in the existing ecclesiastical hierarchy some of those who would *not* belong to it. A second form of the church was the physical building — this was of no significance, useful given the English climate, but otherwise not worth discussion save to deplore the diversion of the patrimony of the poor to frivolous decoration. More difficult was the organization of the earthly *ecclesia*, the mixture of those predestined to salvation and those foreknown to damnation.[25] Here, I think, it is possible to see how Wyclif's thought was circumscribed by his date: to see his apparent inability to go beyond a fervent desire for the total reform of the contemporary Church in head and members to a concept of a new Church in this world over against that corrupted contemporary Church. For Wyclif certainly saw a value in some community for Christians in this world, one perhaps without any designated unifying head, certainly under the authority of the secular ruler, perhaps with a clergy little differentiated from the laity, since, by the new understanding of the eucharist and by abandonment of oral confession coupled with the duty for all Christians to proclaim the Gospel, few distinguishing marks remained. Yet Wyclif never moved beyond the continued existence of the clergy, and seems to have thought to the end in terms of priests and bishops, terms legitimized by New Testament indications of the primitive Church. The fact that he spent time in his retirement in Lutterworth putting together, partly from earlier materials, three sets of model sermons is equally revealing: these sermons provide preaching material on the Epistle and Gospel for each Sunday and major feast, together with material for saints' days.[26] There is a very revealing contradiction here: of radicalism in the reduction of the *Proprium Sanctorum* to a few largely biblical saints, and in the repeated condemnation within the sermons of the whole contemporary ecclesiastical institution, but of conservatism in the retention of the entire Sarum liturgical framework both of lections and of occasions. This contradiction is perpetuated in the activities of his followers: to take an example, in the provision of, and insistence upon, vernacular scriptures, but the traditional inclusion of calendars within those books and of guidance in the use of the vernacular Bibles for liturgical occasions. Equally, the format and layout of many of the Wycliffite Bible manuscripts suggest that they were designed for use on a lectern and within public services.[27] It is possible that Wyclif and his followers, were they alive today, would *not* be members, or at least not active members, of the mainstream Church of England. But would Wyclif have thought house-churches an adequate form of Christian witness, or been prepared to tolerate the lack of cohesive authority that the existence of such fragile groups implies? The question, as anachronistic, is perhaps not significant; but, because it points up in acute form what seems to be an obscurity in Wyclif's own thought, it is not one easily put aside.

If Wyclif can only with hesitation, if at all, be included within Anglicanism, is it possible to define more closely what he contributed to the English religious tradition? Here, it seems to me, he cannot be separated from his immediate followers, whether Wyclif himself closely organized these or not. Wyclif's *direct* influence was for the most part on the academic world of Latin theological and political debate, and, following a period of some thirty years' attack by his opponents, this direct influence came to an end, with the decline of dispassionate enquiry in fifteenth-century Oxford. But *indirectly*, through the preaching and writing of his followers, predominantly in English and outside the university world, Wyclif's contribution was much greater and, despite the efforts of the ecclesiastical hierarchy, was never entirely suppressed. This contribution was, I would suggest, in two main areas. The first, and more tangible, was in the completion of the first full English translation of the Bible. Though, as I have indicated, I do not believe that Wyclif himself participated in the work of translation (if only because I do not see how he could have fitted such endeavour into an already overcrowded writing life), it does seem clear that his declared views encouraged or even inspired the work and that the translation was associated with his name from the last decade of the fourteenth century onwards.[28] England, after an early start in the Anglo-Saxon period, had been slow to produce a vernacular Bible;[29] but the Wycliffite versions, despite the hysteria of pre-Reformation detractors, were careful renderings of the Vulgate, without polemical twisting or indeed, apart from a few copies in which extra glosses or prologues had been added, clear signs of their origins. The account of the steps taken that appears in the final chapter of the so-called General Prologue gives evidence of a scholarly and collaborative endeavour, almost certainly undertaken in Oxford. The later, more idiomatic, version was widely disseminated in the fifteenth century; and ownership by such entirely orthodox people as Henry VI or by religious houses such as Syon, makes it clear that its honesty, despite the prohibitions of Archbishop Arundel, was apprehended.[30] The extent to which it was utilized by Tyndale and later translators is still to be fully assessed, though the fact that most were working from originals in Hebrew and Greek, not from the Vulgate, inevitably means that divergences may not indicate a deliberate rejection of the earlier English renderings.

The other contribution of Wyclif to the English religious tradition is less easy to measure, though it is not wholly to be dissociated from the first. This is the encouragement offered partly through the availability of vernacular scriptures to the involvement of the laity in theological and ecclesiastical matters. At the end of the fourteenth century any attempt by the laity to advance ideas or to argue about theological matters was regarded with deep suspicion: theology was the preserve of the clergy, conducted in Latin, advanced to the laity for their consumption and direction, not for their comment. To Wyclif and to his followers this was not acceptable, either in theory, since scripture did not preclude the responsibility of the laity for the faith, or in practice since the contemporary clergy was so evidently corrupted by temporal power and temporal wealth. The duty to spread the Gospel was placed by Christ on all Christians, and for this duty to be effected all needed education and understanding. This encouragement to secular involvement was paradoxically *forwarded* by the very persecution that sought to eliminate it: cut off from any supply of new academic teachers, self-help and self-education became the only possibility for Lollards. In the schools which they organized in private houses scripture was read, tracts heard and discussed, issues debated — from surviving texts and from episcopal registers this is clear. It is possible to trace here the antecedents to the later tradition of family Bible reading, devotions and religious instruction, not peculiar to England, but characteristic nonetheless. That the tradition of lay concern with theological and ecclesiastical issues fostered by Lollardy fed into the English Reformation is now, thanks to the efforts of scholars investigating the language of men such as William Tyndale and Hugh Latimer, in their own writings rather than in their translations, coming to be acknowledged.[31]

Wyclif then, unlike some of the other figures celebrated in this series, offers little that the twentieth-century Anglican is likely to find instantly attractive either for devotional or for ecumenical purposes. His own writings are tough, written in language by turns opaquely philosophical or strongly polemical, often evidently part of an ongoing academic argument within the Oxford schools. Near contemporary portraits of him, none of them done by an artist likely actually to have seen him, present a medieval cleric without individualizing traits;[32] later portraits, whether on the Bodley frieze planned by Thomas James or of the kind represented by that in the hall at Balliol, model him after the style of their own time as a patriarchal pastor.[33] Neither is perhaps helpful today. But equally we should do well to remember Wyclif's role in the religious tradition in Bohemia as well as in England; and if Anglicanism is a part of the Protestant movement, then Wyclif must surely be counted England's first true pro*test*ant.

NOTES

[1] See Beryl Smalley's introduction to the catalogue of the Bodleian exhibition *Wyclif and his Followers* (Oxford, 1984), p. 5; sixteenth-century views are conveniently summarized in M. Aston, 'John Wycliffe's Reformation Reputation', *Past and Present* 30 (1965), 23–51.

[2] See A. Kenny, 'The Accursed Memory: the Counter-Reformation Reputation of John Wyclif', in *Wyclif in his Times*, ed. A. Kenny (Oxford, 1986), pp. 147–68.

[3] G. Leff, *Heresy in the Later Middle Ages* (Manchester, 1967), ii. 545–9; for a more recent and balanced evaluation of the view see A. Kenny, *Wyclif* (Oxford, 1985), pp. 42–55.

[4] The standard biography remains that of H. B. Workman, *John Wyclif* (Oxford, 1926), though details are corrected in A. B. Emden, *A Biographical Register of the University of Oxford to A.D. 1500* (Oxford, 1957–9), iii. 2103–6.

[5] These are printed in Walsingham's *Chronicon Angliae*, ed. E. M. Thompson (Rolls Series, 1874), pp. 181–3.

[6] For these events see my paper 'Wycliffism in Oxford 1381–1411', in *Wyclif in his Times* (above n. 2), pp. 67–9.

[7] See the listing of his writings by W. R. Thomson, *The Latin Writings of John Wyclyf* (Toronto, 1983); the datings given there are open to some modifications.

[8] Set out in *Fasciculi Zizaniorum*, ed. W. W. Shirley (Rolls Series, 1858), pp. 277–82.

[9] The process leading to the introduction of the death penalty is surveyed by H. G. Richardson, 'Heresy and the Lay Power under Richard II', *English Historical Review* 51 (1936), 1–28; Arundel's legislation is printed by D. Wilkins, *Concilia Magnae Britanniae et Hiberniae* (London, 1737), iii. 314–19.

[10] For proceedings at the Council of Constance see Kenny (1986), pp. 150–6 and references there given.

[11] See E. Friedberg (ed.), *Corpus Iuris Canonici* (Leipzig, 1879–81) i. 1159; for Wyclif's views see, for instance, *Sermones*, ed. J. Loserth (Wyclif Society, 1887–90) ii. 62/26, 138/24.

[12] *A Short-Title Catalogue of Books printed . . . 1475–1640*, ed. A. W. Pollard and G. R. Redgrave, revd. W. A. Jackson *et al.* (London, 1976–90), no. 14445. For James and his importance in the early Bodleian Library see I. Philip, *The Bodleian Library in the Seventeenth and Eighteenth Centuries* (Oxford, 1983), pp. 10–37, and W. D. Macray, *Annals of the Bodleian Library Oxford* (Oxford, 1890), pp. 25–55.

[13] For instance, the *Vita sacerdotum* and the *Regula S. Francisci* cited p. 35 are almost certainly the English texts extant in MS Bodley 647, ff. 57v–62, 71–83 respectively. Thomas James's interest in Wyclif was continued by his nephew Richard James, as is clear from Bodleian MS James 3 in which he transcribed extracts from Wyclif's works.

[14] Kenny (1986), pp. 167–8.

[15] See the material in Leff pp. 549–58, and Kenny (1985) pp. 80–90.

[16] *STC* 159.

[17] See the references given in my *The Premature Reformation* (Oxford, 1988), pp. 228–47.

[18] The problems of the issue are expertly set out by H. A. Oberman, *The Harvest of Medieval Theology: Gabriel Biel and Late Medieval Nominalism* (revd. edn., Grand Rapids, Mich. 1967), pp. 361–93.

[19] Wyclif discussed the issues most fully in *De veritate sacre scripture*, ed. R. Buddensieg (Wyclif Society, 1905–7), but at an earlier stage had debated questions of biblical interpretation with the Carmelite John Kenningham (see the surviving texts from both sides printed in *Fasciculi Zizaniorum* pp. 4–103 and 453–80).

[20] See *Premature Reformation* pp. 273–7, 461–6, 470–2, 483–94.

[21] *Fasciculi Zizaniorum* pp. 280–1; see for instance *De civili dominio*, ed. R. L. Poole and J. Loserth (Wyclif Society, 1885–1904), i. 310/15ff.

[22] For the views of Wyclif's followers, some of whom were nearer to James than their master on this issue, see *Premature Reformation* pp. 342–5.

[23] *Premature Reformation* pp. 508–9.

24 In *De civili dominio* iii. 7/6 Wyclif commented on ' . . . differencia vestimentorum vel aliorum rituum, que sunt accidencia ad observaciam legis Christi', but did not develop the view further.

25 See Leff ii. 516–46, Kenny (1985) pp. 68–79, *Premature Reformation* pp. 314–27.

26 *Sermones* i–iii, ed. J. Loserth (Wyclif Society, 1887–9); the period at which they were put together is indicated by the preface to the first set, but work by Dr Pamela Gradon makes it increasingly clear that they incorporate material that goes back a long way in Wyclif's career.

27 See the material in *Premature Reformation* pp. 198–9.

28 For one early testimony see Henry Knighton *Chronicon*, ed. H. R. Lumby (Rolls Series, 1889–95) ii. 151–2.

29 G. Shepherd has reviewed the earlier material in *The Cambridge History of the Bible vol. 2 The West from the Fathers to the Reformation*, ed. G. W. H. Lampe (Cambridge, 1969), pp. 362–87.

30 *Premature Reformation* pp. 238–47.

31 See D. D. Smeeton, *Lollard Themes in the Reformation Theology of William Tyndale (Sixteenth Century Essays and Studies* vi, 1986), and D. S. Dunnan, *The Preaching of Hugh Latimer: A Reappraisal* (unpub. Oxford D. Phil. thesis, 1991).

32 There are two fifteenth-century portraits in Prague manuscripts of his works, University Library VIII. C.3, f.2 and Metropolitan Chapter Library C.38, f. 119v; the first of these appears on the cover of the catalogue mentioned in n. 1.

33 For the first see J. N. L. Myres, 'Thomas James and the Painted Frieze', *Bodleian Library Record* iv (1952–3), 30–51; the second is reproduced on the dustjacket of Kenny (1986).

PATRICK COLLINSON

Thomas Cranmer

A FULLER TITLE FOR this chapter might be 'Thomas Cranmer and the Truth': but not anything as presumptuous as 'the Truth about Cranmer', for what is that? The partial truth of outward appearance is shrouded, not least by that composed, uncommunicative portrait by Gerlach Flicke, emblematic and not intended to reveal the man beneath the rochet. What do we know of anyone to whom we are first properly introduced in middle age? Cranmer's modern biographer devotes more pages to his last twenty-four hours than to the first forty years.[1] By the end of his life, those years were so remote from Cranmer himself that he could not remember whether his first wife's name was Black or Brown, although he did remember marrying 'one Joan'.[2]

What little was written by contemporaries contains only fragments of apparently authentic description: few flies in this amber.[3] We hear about Cranmer's total baldness in old age, offset by a free-flowing, snow-white beard, full enough to offer some protection to his chest. We are told that he never used spectacles; and that 'my lord bitt his lippe, as his maner was when he was moved'. So his secretary reported, no doubt as reliable a witness as Cardinal Wolsey's gentleman usher and biographer, George Cavendish. What was that meant to tell us? Apparently something about a capacity for self-control unusual and remarkable in the sixteenth century. Such a man was perhaps more liable to do violence to himself than to others. Contemplating Cranmer, John Foxe wondered whether over-much patience might not be a vice.[4] But then we remember that

Thomas More described King Richard III 'knawing on hys lippes' (according to Polydore Vergil, Richard 'dyd contynually byte his nether lyppe'), so we finish up wondering whether we have learned anything truthful about the man, Thomas Cranmer.[5]

Cranmer *and* the truth is another matter, the subject, in effect, of almost everything that posterity has ever had to say about him. There is, of course, but one truth, not a Protestant truth and a Catholic truth, nor may God help us, an Anglican truth. But if posterity had been able to agree on what that truth is, Cranmer might have been allowed to sleep in peace, instead of being so regularly disturbed, not least by centenary occasions. 'Truth' was a word which the Archbishop often invoked. We are told that as a young arts graduate at Cambridge 'considering what great contraversie was in matters of religion . . . [he] bent himselfe to trye out the truthe herin'. In that momentous encounter at Waltham with the King's servants, Edward Fox and Stephen Gardiner, a conversation which not only made Cranmer's career but changed the history of England, the future Archbishop, having already confessed his substantial ignorance of the King's great matter, nevertheless declared with startling confidence: 'This is moost certeyne . . . that there ys but one trueth in it'[6] — a theological rather than legal truth. (We now know that Cranmer exaggerated his ignorance: that he had been interested for some time in the precedents and texts which would soon be stockpiled by others, notably by Edward Fox, in order to buttress the ideological claims summed up in the royal supremacy.)[7] When many eventful years later, Henry committed to Cranmer himself the investigation of a conspiracy to bring the Archbishop to ruin, the King told him: 'For suerlie I reken that you will tell me the trueth'.[8] Writing about a certain heretic, a man who was about to die for his beliefs, Cranmer remarked that he had denied transubstantiation, and therein 'I think he taught but the truth'.[9]

As late as 1548, Cranmer endorsed the view that to deny the real presence in the eucharist (not necessarily by the mode of transubstantiation) was 'deceitfull'. 'Suche men surely are not trew Christyans.'[10] Yet it appears that Cranmer himself had abandoned all belief in the real presence two years earlier. Presently, arguing the eucharistic toss with Bishop Stephen Gardiner, Cranmer asked 'Doth not God's word teach a true presence of Christ in spirit? . . . Was it not a true presence that Christ in these places promised?'[11] So Dr Peter Brooks has identified Cranmer's mature, post-1546 doctrine of the Lord's Supper as one incorporating the true presence, something other than Christ's literal, carnal presence.[12] Yet, as he wrote in his final recantation, when Cranmer was 'come to the last end of his life' 'whereupon hangeth all my life past': 'Now is time and place to say truth', whereupon he renounced his heretical doctrine of the sacrament; only to reaffirm it in the renunciation of his recantations, with remorse for having acted 'contrarye to my conscience and the truthe'.[13]

It would not be right to say that Cranmer was the only Archbishop of Canterbury in all history to have been addicted to the truth, or even to have set so much store by the truth: only that an almost obsessional concern with the value of truth was the hallmark of Cranmer's century. Never, perhaps, in all history was the possession of the truth more fiercely contested, or regarded as so precious a prize. No doubt the challenge to the once-received truth of custom, Luther's challenge, made it so, together with all the counter-challenges that followed. Truth without the provocation of falsehood is inert and lifeless. Bishop Latimer declared from the pulpit: 'It is a goodly word "Peace", and a fair thing Unity . . . [But] peace ought not to be redeemed . . . with the loss of the truth; that we would seek peace so much, that we should lose the truth of God's word'. (The Elizabethan Catholic scholar and controversialist Thomas Stapleton made the same point more pungently, quoting, I suppose, some old adage: 'Truth purchaseth hatred'.) 'Therefore,' pronounced Latimer, 'whereas ye pray for agreement both in the truth and in uttering of the truth, when shall that be, as long as we will not hear the truth, but disquiet with crafty conveyance the preachers of the truth, because they reprove our evilness with the truth. And, to say the truth, better it were to have a deformity in preaching, so that some would preach the truth of God': seven 'truths' in one peroration.[14]

Sixteenth-century historians, in the heat of controversy about the truth of every kind of thing, from the origins of the British peoples to the fate of the little princes in the Tower, constantly invoked the old trope about truth the principal adornment of history, truth the daughter of time. William Camden wrote: 'Which Truth to take from History, is nothing else but, as it were, to pluck out the Eyes of the beautifullest Creature in the World'.[15] The Protestant ecclesiastical historian and martyrologist John Foxe claimed to 'open the plain truth of times lying long hid in obscure darkness of antiquity'. So it was that Foxe's Protestant readers took it as axiomatic that his *Book of Martyrs* was true, 'a book of credit': whereas by the same token Catholics found it a tissue of lies, 'so many lines, so many lies'. The merits of the book were discussed on the basis of truth and on no other basis, there being no half-truths.[16] Bishop John Aylmer made an audacious claim for the English Reformation.

Our countryman and brother John Wyclif begat Hus, who begat Luther, who begat truth. Since Christ was truth, that was as much as to say that Christ had been 'as it were' born a second time in England, and Aylmer was not afraid to state explicitly this ethnocentric heresy.[17]

The century had turned before Francis Bacon in his essay *Of Truth* wrote his famous line: 'What is truth? said jesting Pilate; and would not stay for an answer'. But the sixteenth century already knew Pilate's answerless question. It appears that when Thomas More turned historian he found that history could not be easily made to square with the truth, or to serve the purposes of truth. For in the tragical history of Richard III, what was true and what was false amidst so much hearsay, so much treachery, some of it benign, as when More's old master, Bishop Morton, suborned the Duke of Buckingham? George Cavendish sat down to write what he claimed would be the true history of his master Cardinal Wolsey ('therfore I commyt the treuthe to hyme that knowyth all truethe'), but to have confronted the truth, not least about his own falsehoods, seems to have alarmed and disgusted Cavendish.[18] Later in the century, Sir Philip Sidney found that only fiction, not 'true' history, could be trusted to vindicate and exemplify those ultimate truths which are moral and fruitful. The historian was hopelessly tied 'not to what should be, but to what is, to the particular truth of things'. If one wished to see virtue exalted and vice punished, 'truly that commendation is peculiar to Poetry, and far off from history'.[19] Neither the historian of the sixteenth century nor the biographer of Thomas Cranmer is likely to disagree.

The divines knew these things. Having first defined truth as 'Christ himself, the word of God', Thomas Becon added: 'There is also a civil truth or verity, . . . and that is when with that which is said the thing agreeth, and when we find words agreeing with the thing itself': in other words, there is the truth of what is, a mundane thing, and there is the higher truth of what ought to be, not at all one and the same thing.[20] Meanwhile those living (and dying) in the real world of what is (and they included that author of poetic fictions, Thomas More) found that often the survival not only of themselves but of the truth which they professed to hold and advance depended upon economies with the truth so drastic as to leave little of the truth intact: to such an extent that a recent book on these agonies of the sixteenth-century conscience is called not Valiant for Truth but *Ways of Lying*. To lie might be the only way to hang on to the truth.[21]

And always there was Pilate's question, asked not in a mocking and cynical spirit but with desperate and conscientious urgency, and by no inhabitant of the sixteenth century with more urgent conscientiousness than by Thomas Cranmer. A few years after his violent death, Bishop Jewel would pen some disturbing sentences:

> The philosopher telleth us, truth and falsehood are nigh neighbours, and dwell one by the other; the utter porch of the one is like the porch of the other; yet their way is contrary; the one leadeth to life; the other leadeth to death; they differ little to the shew . . . Thereby it happeneth that men be deceived; . . . they call evil good, falsehood truth . . .[22]

This was the world inhabited by the mind and conscience of Thomas Cranmer, not least in those last twenty-four hours. Only that branch of improving fiction which is hagiography would describe Cranmer as an utterly true man or even (the height of modern aspirations) a consistent man. Was he true to his own self? Few men have made their ends with so many undefended, unexplained, unresolved inconsistencies as this Archbishop who stood so much upon the truth. At his consecration he took a solemn oath to the pope preceded by a protestation that the oath would not be binding. At his trial, Cranmer said that that was routine procedure. Perhaps so. Cranmer dissolved Henry VIII's marriage to Ann Boleyn referring to an impediment, involving Henry's relations with Ann's sister, that he had known all about when he blessed the union in the first place. He abandoned colleagues and friends when all his pleas on their behalf (which are not to be overlooked) failed, and it became necessary to abandon them. At Thomas Cromwell's downfall, we are told 'there would have byn laied thousands of powndes to hundrethes in London, that he shoulde have . . . byn sett upp in the Tower beside his frende the Lorde Crumwell'.[23] But while Cromwell and others died, Cranmer lived, the Archbishop expressing less regret for all that spilled blood than the poet Wyatt — but perhaps biting his nether lip.

Cranmer was one of that small minority in any generation to change their religion, denouncing as error what had been stoutly maintained as the truth, and in Cranmer's case not as an innocent child or a half-formed adolescent but as a middle-aged archbishop. Dr Diarmaid MacCulloch will tell us that in his late thirties Cranmer still believed in the pope, and even more in the catholic doctrine of the magisterial authority of church councils. Reading the attack mounted on Luther by Bishop John Fisher, he filled the margins with observations which leave us in no doubt about the loyal and traditional catholic sentiments which moved the future Protestant Archbishop in the 1520s.[24] In the 1530s the pope had been expunged from Cranmer's creed (by law), but not yet the doctrine of the real presence of Christ's body and blood in the sacrament of the altar, which he would discard in the 1540s.

So on sleepless nights, if there were any, Cranmer may have remembered that he had consented in the death of a man who believed only what he himself now believed. He would know that St Paul shared this experience. But at his trial the prosecutor was careful to remind him of that embarrassing circumstance. The trial ended in a series of recantations, no less than five, followed by renunciation of the recantations, leading his modern biographer to speculate, without justification: 'Perhaps if he had lived for another hour, he would have recanted again'.[25] Less dramatically, Cranmer's first Prayer Book of 1549 presented 'the truth' so artfully that it was almost a piece of equivocation in itself, as in the very title of its communion rite, 'commonly called the Mass'. That may have been intended to deceive 'the simple sort', although they were not deceived down in Cornwall. Someone as lacking in simplicity as Bishop Stephen Gardiner *chose* to be deceived, declaring that 1549 was 'not distant from the catholic faith in my judgment'.[26] So in our own age learned scholars have been misled into believing what is most unlikely: that Cranmer changed his doctrine of the eucharist (which is to say, his religion) between 1549 and 1552.[27] To explain, or even to comprehend, these apparent inconsistencies it is necessary to know the sixteenth century and to know it well; but to know the twentieth century also helps, not least in order to have some insight into the meaning of those sad recantations. To have served with the Gloucesters in Korea might be a significant item on the CV of a would-be biographer of Cranmer.

It is the moment to ask what this Archbishop, the founder of the Church of England and of Anglicanism as we have known it, had and has to do with truth? It is a question which looms a little larger than would the same question if if were to be asked of you or me. For to enquire what Cranmer had to do with the truth (rather than with a series of compromises with the truth) is in effect to ask whether the Church of England is indeed a true church. Bishop Stephen Gardiner was not one to mince his words. He told Cranmer that by his example it would be learned that 'our religion is nothing but an agreement made for the time being, and then changeable as occasion arise'.[28] Well, one has heard something like that before, and not long ago. Cranmer is the ghost of the present Church of England, not merely its remote founding father.

In his 1962 biography, Jasper Ridley sliced through these problems with a surgical instrument, his cutting tool the sixteenth-century principle that to be a true man it was sufficient to be a true subject, obedient to one's lawful prince. Truth consisted in obedience. When Cranmer told Henry VIII that he had always believed the best of his wife Ann Boleyn until obliged to believe otherwise, when he assured the King that he had always believed Thomas Cromwell to be the truest servant he ever had, he was not saying that he had changed his intellectual opinion of those great persons with whose active assistance the cause of religious reform had been advanced. He meant that he now had no choice, in all conscience and obedience, but to alter his opinion and to join in the general denunciation. To repeat a point already made, modern Chinese students of history would have less difficulty in understanding and perhaps condoning his actions than ourselves. Cranmer made no attempt to resist the *coup d'état* of the summer of 1549 which toppled Somerset and brought Northumberland's conciliar regime to power, although at the time it must have appeared that this political upset would strike a fatal blow at everything in which Cranmer most profoundly believed. When under Mary he recanted it was less from intellectual wavering, still less for mere fear, than in the conviction that perhaps the prince could constrain mind and conscience, even in matters of faith. Ridley writes:

> If the known facts of Cranmer's life are impartially examined, nearly all the apparent contradictions disappear and a consistent personality emerges. Like most of his contemporaries . . . Cranmer believed in royal absolutism. He believed that his primary duty as a Christian was to strengthen the power of the King, and was prepared if necessary to sacrifice all his other doctrines to accomplish this.

Thus far Jasper Ridley. Obedience simplifies everything for the historian and biographer, just as it simplified nearly everything for Thomas Cranmer.[29]

No one should underestimate the force of obedience in the reign of Henry VIII as not only a constitutional but a theological necessity. Notoriously, William Tyndale wrote in his book on the subject (a book written as a disaffected exile) that the King was 'in this world, without law; and may at his lust do right or wrong, and shall give accounts but to God only'; that princes were 'in God's stead' and 'may not be resisted: do they never so evil, they must be reserved unto the wrath of God'. Only if princes were to countenance evil must the subject disobey and say 'we are otherwise commanded of God'. But they must on no account offer resistance.[30] And who was to say, with authority, what was evil, or what was error, since truth and error were such close bed-fellows? Cranmer went further. 'All Christian princes have committed unto them immediately of God, the whole cure of all their subjects, as well concerning the administration of God's word for the cure of souls, as concerning the ministration of things political, and civil governance.'[31] What happened to Tyndale's principle of passive, principled disobedience where matters of faith were concerned if your king was also your bishop, the curate of your soul? One might almost say that if the leitmotif of the Lutheran Reformation was salvation by faith alone, the corresponding principle for the Henrician Reformation was salvation by obedience alone.[32] Consciences were placed, as it were, in the royal bank vaults. It was obedience rather than faith which Henry's Great Bible of 1539 aroused in those exposed to its text, according to the graphics of its engraved title page. Where preaching wanteth, Archbishop Grindal later advised Henry's daughter, obedience faileth.[33]

Nevertheless, this scalpel was too sharp, the surgery too neat. In reviewing Ridley on Cranmer, Dr Peter Brooks made use of Sir Isaiah Berlin's fable of the hedgehog and the fox.[34] According to Ridley, Cranmer was one of history's hedgehogs, possessed by one commanding idea; according to Brooks, a fox, an improbable survivor who owed his survival to his political dexterity. Witness the adroitness with which, with more than a little help from Henry VIII, he turned the tables on his accusers in Kent in the so-called Prebendaries' Plot of 1543, which could so easily have unseated him.[35] At that dangerous moment rather more than a hedgehog-like obedience was needed. If the Kentish evidence sifted in the course of Cranmer's own investigation of this conspiracy[36] proves his political talents it also, in the estimation of another Cambridge colleague, Dr Eamon Duffy, speaks volumes for Cranmer's pastoral ineptitude. If Cranmer were to be classified as popes are traditionally divided, he would seem to have been a political rather than a religious Archbishop. But how many Archbishops of Canterbury have had the leisure to be effective pastors in East Kent? The problem concerns the Canterbury diocesan synod to this very day.

But Dr Brooks's fox is not the solution to all our problems. The sixteenth century knew all about foxes, of course. Almost the only thing known on the Continent about England was that there were no wolves in England, which was the subject of the only recorded conversation in which Sir Philip Sidney took part. But if no wolves, or so the saying went, all the more foxes. Everyone, in the age of the Renaissance, knew about crafty, foxy Ulysses, not least William Shakespeare when he wrote *Troilus and Cressida*, a play badly misrepresented by E. M. W. Tillyard when he credited that character with a hedgehog-like obsession with cosmic order and degree. Dr Andrew Perne, the famous (or infamous) Elizabethan master of Peterhouse, told Gabriel Harvey when they met at Sir Thomas Smith's funeral that he was a fox. Not while you are still around, said Harvey. I can't claim to be more than a mere cub.[37] The ecclesiastical fox *par excellence* was Perne's patron and Cranmer's arch-rival and theological opponent Stephen Gardiner, the principal target of polemical pamphlets with titles like *The Hunting of the Romish Fox*. For foxes symbolized covert popery. However, Dr Glyn Redworth believes that that was to do Gardiner, a doughty champion of catholic orthodoxy, a considerable injustice.[38]

But no one in the sixteenth century seems to have called Cranmer a fox. Rather, unless Henry VIII was himself lying like a fox, Cranmer was the youthful George Washington, constitutionally incapable of telling lies. Henry told his political enemies: 'I accompte my Lord of Canterbury as faithfull a man towardes me as ever was prelate in this realme.' 'O Lord', he is supposed to have said to Cranmer at his moment of supreme danger, 'What manner of man be you! What simplicity is in you!' Cromwell remarked: 'You were borne in a happie howre I suppose, ... ffor, do or sey what you will, the kyng will alwaies well take it at your hande . . . [His majestie] will never give credite againste you . . .'[39] It is of course possible that Henry saw in Cranmer an Israelite indeed in whom there was no guile, when there was considerable guile. The wisdom of serpents can coexist with the harmlessness of doves. The Bible says so. And what Dr Brooks meant when he identified Cranmer as a fox was that, far from succumbing in passive and unthinking obedience to Henry VIII, he worked resourcefully with the vast and capricious power of that monarch, not merely to survive but in order to promote his cause of reformation, tapping the huge energy of the royal supremacy to erect a reformed Church of England.

II

So MUCH FOR CRANMER the politician, the survivor, the teflon prelate. But theological infidelities, theological falsehoods are presumably less venial than political. What do we say of an Archbishop who must have knowingly authorized, if he did not himself expressly effect, the deft conjuring trick which altered in a small but critically important respect the sense of the more or less official *Cat-echism*, published in the second year of the reign of Edward VI, three editions within the one year? This *Catechism* was a translated adapt-ation of a Latin text of German provenance, deriving from Martin Luther's *Little Catechism* and associated with Cranmer's wife's uncle, the Nuremberg reformer Andreas Osiander, but linked with another German name, that of Justus Jonas.

In the first English edition of the *Catechism*, the account of the Lord's Supper was faithful to its Lutheran original. 'For he doth not only, with his bodyly mouthe receave the bodye and bloude of Christ, but he doth also beleve the wordes of Christ, whereby he is assured, that Christes bodye was gyven to death for us, and that his bloude was shed for us.' In the third edition, which appeared within weeks of the first, the Lutheran doctrine of the real presence was deftly jettisoned in favour of a formulation consistent with South German-Swiss, proto-Reformed doctrine, dispensing with the real presence as either Luther or Catholics affirmed it. This was done by omitting the two words 'only' and 'also'. Now no longer 'he doth not only with his bodyly mouthe receave the bodye and bloude of Christ . . . but he doth also beleve the wordes of Christ' but 'he doth not with his bodyly mouthe receave the bodye and bloude of Christ but he doth believe the wordes of Christ'.[40] Was this honest? More-over it was not the case that Cranmer had changed his mind on the subject of the real presence in the summer of 1548, between two editions of the *Catechism*. If we combine his own testimony with evidence supplied by Bishop Nicholas Ridley and Sir John Cheke, it appears that Cranmer's conversion in this respect had happened two years earlier, in 1546.[41] An economist or Chancellor of the Ex-chequer who changed his position on, say, monetarism, so drasti-cally and yet so insidiously, would not retain much professional or political credibility, especially if he had lost his faith in monetarism two years before so shyly disclosing the fact. So why should we trust a theologian like Cranmer? Why should we buy a used church from such a churchman? Since the *Catechism* was addressed to children, his theological opponents could be forgiven for thinking in terms of millstones, and of being cast into the depths of the sea.

What needs to be said at this point is that Archbishop Cranmer was not the only prominent Tudor churchman to wonder, if not what he should believe, what it was proper and even feasible to con-fess. Truth and error were too close for comfort, and at moments of confessional instability they could look like nearly identical twins, or the two charming ladies of *The Beggar's Opera*. How happy, ac-cording to circumstances, one might be with either. In Cranmer's own University, the balance of judgement even in Edward's reign still tipped towards traditional, catholic belief. That was the ground on which the Lady Margaret Professor and first Master of Trinity, Dr John Redman, stood, and such was his intellectual authority that for minds and consciences less robust it was sufficient to believe as Redman believed. Even the King found himself in this position, for Redman was one of the authors, perhaps the principal author, of that authoritative theological statement of Henry's last years known as *The Kings Book*. Yet under the radically Protestant regime headed by the Duke of Northumberland, not even Redman was safe and it was not necessarily safe to stay with Redman. Redman chose this moment to die, and he was questioned about his belief on his deathbed by, amongst others, the schoolmaster of Westminster and future Dean of St Paul's, Alexander Nowell, and by the Master of Christ's, Richard Wilkes, a known supporter of the new learning.[42]

Asked by Wilkes whether we receive Christ with our mouth in the sacrament, Redman 'paused and dyd holde his peace a lytle space, and shortley after he spake, sayinge, I wyll not saye so, I can not tel, it is a hard question'. Pleased with this answer, Wilkes himself took a little pause and then said, 'Mayster Doctor yf I shulde not trouble you, I wolde praye you to knowe your mynde in transubstantiacion.' 'Jesu Mayster Wilkes sayeth he, wyll you ask me that?' 'Syr sayde I, not yf I shulde trouble you, no, no. I wyl tel you sayth he.' It appeared that both Redman and his Trinity colleague, John Young, also present, were wavering on transubstantiation, had perhaps already surrendered the point. Once they would have burned for the doctrine. Now they didn't know. Young said: 'A man shall knowe more and more by process of tyme, and readinge and hearinge of others'. Even what he had just heard fall from Redman's dying lips contained food for thought. So, in our own time, minds and consciences have squirmed in Eastern Europe and the former USSR. But under Mary it would be more or less officially stated by no less an authority than Bishop Cuthbert Tunstall, who was Redman's uncle, that he had died a Catholic; while Young became Mary's Regius Professor of Divinity, presided over the heresy trial of a King's man who was burned on Jesus Green, and after Elizabeth's accession would spend the last twenty years of his life in custody, as an unwavering catholic recusant.

All the books tell us that Cranmer charted his intellectual and spiritual course according to the principles propounded by Young: 'A man shall know more and more by process of tyme, and readinge and hearinge of others.' Usually we are told that Cranmer's glacially slow conversion was unusual, even unique. Everyone quotes the words he wrote to the Swiss reformer Vadianus: 'I have come to the conclusion that the writings of every man must be read with discrimination.'[43] And sometimes this is linked with what we are told in an anonymous near-contemporary account of the Archbishop's working practice: 'He was a slowe reader, but a diligent marker of whatsoever he redd, for he seldom redd without pen in hand, and whatsoever made eyther for the one parte or the other, of thinges being in contraversy, he wrote it out yf it were short, or at the least noted the author and the place, that he might fynd it and wryte it out by leysure; which was a great helpe to hym in debating of matters ever after.'[44]

When public office swallowed up the leisure for such intellectual pursuits, Cranmer's research assistants continued to apply these methods on his behalf, a good example of what is nowadays called 'the archaeology of reading practices', the particular practice in question being that whereby busy men had books read, extracted and annotated for them by their intellectual men of business. The evidence survives in copious quantity in Cranmer's theological commonplace books among the royal MSS of the British Library: 'Collectiones Ex Sancta Scriptura et Patribus', also including material abstracted from the modern theologians, Luther, Melanchthon and Brenz, Zwingli and Oecolampadius.[45]

And then an extraordinary coincidence of emergencies and opportunities brought some of these names to life and to England, enabling Cranmer to continue his dialogue with a spectrum of theological opinion, 'in ze meat', as a German chairman once said in introducing to his audience the late Professor H. H. Rowley of Manchester. For the political triumph of Protestantism in England coincided with the severe setback in Germany of a conservative religious settlement imposed by the Emperor after his victory over the political forces of Protestantism in the Schmalkaldic War. This drove into English exile many of the ranking theologians of the emergent reformed tendency: Martin Bucer and Peter Martyr above all, who were appointed to the two Regius Chairs in the Edwardian universities. It was not Cranmer's fault that their Lutheran counterparts declined all invitations to join the party (Melanchthon, who had received invitations since the mid-1530s, was to be offered the Cambridge Chair), so that the great debate on eucharistic doctrine and liturgy lost its Lutheran dimension and became a matter of fine-tuning important but somewhat narrower differences within the non-Lutheran camp of Bucer, Martyr and John à Lasco.[46]

These are usually represented as the footprints of a certain cautious cast of mind, filmed, as it were, in slow motion. But they are not evidence of Cranmer's chronic inability to make up his mind, still less of the kind of wavering instability allegedly manifested around John Redman's deathbed. Put to Cranmer the biblical question 'how long halt ye between two opinions?' and he might have answered: 'Just so long as it takes.' But it was another matter entirely, having persuaded himself of the truth of a matter, to profess it publicly, and yet another to impose it on the profession of others, and on their prayer life, under the constraint of fluctuating, unstable public policy. Hence the complexity of the Prayer Book problem: 1549 and 1552 as at once the expression of public policy, of a nation's belief, of Thomas Cranmer's own belief. His 1544 English Litany was devised, as he himself said, 'to the intent . . . your hearts and lips may go together in prayer.'[47] This was a conjunction not easily achieved outside and beyond well-worn, time-honoured, almost instinctive forms. As Bishop John Williams was heard to say in the following century, intending his words as criticism of Archbishop Laud: 'It is well known, how he that will bring a People from custom in God's Worship with which they have been inured, to a Change, must be more than wise: that is, he must be thought to be wise . . .'[48]

III

BUT IN ALL THIS complexity and amidst so much public and private camouflage, one thing is reasonably clear. From a relatively early date in his public career (albeit in middle age), Thomas Cranmer had heard, understood and internalized a broadly evangelical doctrine of salvation. No other prominent English reformer was more Lutheran: not because his views and emphases were precisely those of Martin Luther but because he shared Luther's sense of the utter centrality of the doctrine of salvation, the fundamental significance of the Gospel, not only for the individual Christian but for the Church. It was this which will prove to have been the most consistent thing about Cranmer, the automatic pilot which kept him on course towards that definitive statement of the English Reformation and of Anglicanism which was the Book of Common Prayer.

It appears that Cranmer's understanding of salvation moved within essentially Lutheran parameters no later than his German embassy of 1532, when he married his Lutheran wife (a remarkable and radical step in itself which he would hardly have taken if he could have foreseen the promotion to Canterbury which immediately followed) and had the opportunity to discuss the critical question of justification with his wife's uncle, the preacher Andreas Osiander. This was not the experience of many of his Cambridge contemporaries, or, indeed, juniors. Only the ex-Augustinian Robert Barnes, the theological diplomat of the 1530s, took on more of what was later called 'a Germanical nature'. John Young, who clashed in Edwardian Cambridge with Martin Bucer, said in 1551 (he was then thirty-seven to Cranmer's sixty-two) that 'he dyd repent him that he had so much strived against iustification by only fayth': but he would spend the rest of a long life continuing to strive against that doctrine. Redman, fifty-two years of age when he died in 1551, the principal author of *The Kings Book*, denounced Lutheranism posthumously in a book called *The complaint of grace*, written, it was claimed, 'not verie long before he left this transitory lyfe'. The dead Redman, yet speaking, declared that what was needed was not Luther's only faith but 'the pricke of spirituall ex-hortacions to charitie, humilitie, pacience, hope, godly vertue and wisedome'. Bishop St John Fisher had confronted Luther's heresy with the same medicine. As for Dr Andrew Perne, Master of Peter-house, the most notorious turncoat and weathercock of the mid-Tudor Cambridge scene, a mere thirty-two years of age in 1551, there is no evidence that he ever did agree with Martin Luther on the *ordo salutis*. Perne had already rejected transubstantiation and, for a while, continued to do so under Mary. But at heart he was no Protestant and never would be. For a Protestant must believe, at heart, that we are saved entirely of grace through the all-sufficiency of Christ's once-for-all sacrifice, appropriated by faith, and regard-less of any voluntary motion or effort.[49]

Biographers of Cranmer and historians of Anglicanism, for reasons partly understandable and allowable, partly of theological bias, focus on other issues and miss what is the most important of all the facts and circumstances concerning their subject: that he was the most Protestant of all the leading figures in the sixteenth-century Church of England, more Protestant even than Hugh Latimer, not in the sense that he was opposed to traditional religious belief and practice (although opposed he was, and with a blind vehemence hard for anyone sympathetic to traditional religion to stomach), but in the sense that, like Luther, he understood the matter of faith to be the mainspring of religion, in comparison with which almost noth-ing else mattered. We do not learn that from Latimer's remarkable sermons, which strike out in a number of directions but have no kernel, no sense that there is such a thing as *the* Gospel. It is some-thing we are bound to learn from Cranmer's *Homilies*, the 1547 Homilies of Salvation, of Faith, of Good Works, composed by the Archbishop and promulgated within months of Henry VIII's death.[50]

Cranmer's profound Lutheranism (in this most proper sense) was something half-concealed as long as Henry lived, just as his Lutheran wife was kept out of sight in a metaphorical if not literal box, especially in the last years of the reign, when the Church of which he was Primate was bound to Redman's *The Kings Book* and to the Act of Six Articles. On justification, *The Kings Book* taught:

> And albeit God is the principal cause and chief worker of this justification in us . . . yet so it pleaseth the high wisdom of God, that man, prevented by his grace, (which being offered, man may if he will refuse or receive) shall be also a worker by his free consent and obedience to the same, in the attaining of his own justification, and by God's grace and help shall walk in such works as be requisite to his justification . . .[51]

Hence Stephen Gardiner's indignation at the constitutional no less than the theological impropriety of so precipitately repudiating that doctrine in Cranmer's *Homilies*, published in the name of a nine-year old child and with his royal father hardly cold in the ground; and equally in Cranmer's version of the *Catechism* of Justus Jonas, which was in truth the work of Cranmer's wife's uncle, Osiander.

For repudiation the *Homilies* were, an unambiguously evangelical statement. This has sometimes been doubted, as if these sermons, which are made a kind of appendix to the Anglican Articles of Religion and so remain in some measure still in force, teach something other than justification by faith. The *Homilies* do, to be sure, contain evidence of Cranmer's sensitivity to that charge of antinomianism which the stark paradoxes of Lutheran solifidianism, and even of St Paul's doctrine in *Romans*, always attracts. In July 1537 he spent two days grilling the Vicar of Croydon, who had alleged in a sermon that those who trusted to be saved by faith and baptism had 'left all good works', such as prayer, fasting and alms deeds.[52] But Cranmer was not so scared of the antinomian bugbear as to compromise his understanding of the Gospel when the change of regime freed him from the constrained compromises contained in the Henrician formularies.

So those exposed to the Homily of Salvation heard that sinful man 'of necessity' was obliged to seek for a righteousness other than his own, embraced by faith, which was 'taken, accepted and allowed of God', 'for our perfect and full justification'. 'And therefore St Paul declareth here nothing upon the behalf of man, concerning his justification, but only a true and lively faith, which nevertheless is the gift of God, and not man's only work, without God.' 'What can be spoken more plainly, than to say, that freely without works, by faith only, we obtain remission of our sins.' Cranmer called this, as Luther might have called it, 'the strong rock and foundation of christian religion'. To be sure he declared that faith did not exclude good works, 'necessarily to be done afterwards of duty towards God'. But note the 'afterwards', and what follows: 'But it excludeth them, so that we may not do them to this intent, to be made just by doing of them.' Similarly, we should not be mis-led by Cranmer's rhetorical skill in the two succeeding Homilies of Faith, and of Good Works, particularly in the delicate rhetorical art of *concessio*. The Homily of Faith is all about good works, for a faith which brings forth no good works is idle, barren, unfruitful, dead. As for the Homily of Good Works, it is all about faith, for good works cannot be performed without faith. But the penitent thief on the cross, a compelling figure for Cranmer even as the moment of his own cruel death approached, provides what Americans call the bottom line. 'I can shew a man that, by faith, without works, lived and came to heaven; but without faith, never man had life.' 'Faith by itself saved him, but works by themselves never justified any man.'

For a full decade and more before this doctrine was made offi-cial, Cranmer had been promoting and protecting it in his advance-ment of evangelical preaching, as Dr Susan Wabuda has recently shown: in his own diocese, in his licensing of roving preachers, in those islands under his control in otherwise hostile dioceses which were the Archbishop's peculiars: parishes in London and Essex within Bishop Stokesley's diocese, Hadleigh in Suffolk, otherwise under the control of the fiercely conservative Bishop Nix, who was succeeded by the dogged and equally conservative William Rugg. In 1537 the Vicar of Croydon named Robert Barnes, Edward Crome, Richard Champion 'and many other soo', who preached that 'faith which justifieth of necessitie bringeth forth good workes'. At Harwich, the conservative curate closed his pulpit to one of the Archbishop's protégés, complaining of 'new learned fel-lows and teachers of new doctryne'. Cranmer's evangelical thrust had its negative, even cruel flip side. The curate of Hadleigh, the ex-Observant Hugh Payne, whom the Archbishop's formidable trou-bleshooter Rowland Taylor thrust aside, had taught that one paternoster said by the injunction of a priest was worth a thousand paternosters said voluntarily. He had also supported Katherine of Aragon. Cranmer pursued this man until, bound in irons and deprived of warm clothing, he died in the Marshalsea Prison.[53]

By the time the *Homilies* were read in the parishes, Cranmer had applied the full implications of evangelical doctrine to that good work which was the public worship of God and his sacraments. Cranmer knew that sacraments were God's ways of working, not man's; that the only appropriate human response was one of reception, with the organ of faith, itself a gift of God; that the only acceptable sacrifice was a sacrifice of praise and thanksgiving, coupled with the sacrifice of our selves, our souls and bodies. And he had been persuaded that the doctrine of a real presence in the eucharist was not only not true, as a statement of the case, but not answerable to the nature of true religion. Stephen Gardiner understood all this, pronouncing: 'It is evident to anyone that these things are so joined and interdependent that whoever has admitted the doctrine of "only faith" in justification is compelled to reject the Sacrament of the Eucharist in the way we professs it'.[54]

Nothing could be more clear, nothing less clear, initially, than Cranmer's great work of liturgical simplification and reconstruction which came to its first fruition in 1549. Gardiner was partly responsible. From motives which were less than candid, Gardiner chose to endorse the 1549 service as 'not distant from the catholic faith in my judgment'. Things precious to this continuing Catholic were 'so catholically spoken of', as in the words of the 1549 prayer of consecration, sanctifying these creatures of bread and wine 'to be to us the body and blood of Christ'.[55]

But Cranmer was equally responsible for having constructed a service of which a 'catholic' construction could be made, at least superficially. The Holy Communion was said to be 'commonly called the Mass'. Words and formulae consistent with real presence belief were retained: 'The body of our Lord Jesus Christ, which was given for thee, preserve thy body unto everlasting life'. Unlike any other Protestant liturgy, Cranmer's service retained the great prayer of consecration, to all appearances, especially in its 1549 construction and setting, the canon of the Mass, still punctuated in the printed text with those small crosses at 'bless' and 'sanctify' which called for the traditional manual acts. Nothing explicitly forbade the habitual elevations. But the effect was not that those 'creatures' of bread and wine should 'become' the body and blood of Christ but that they should 'be' unto us Christ's body and blood. As Cranmer insisted in his book against Gardiner: 'We do not pray that the creatures of bread and wine may be the body and blood of Christ; but that they may be to us the body and blood of Christ; that is to say, that we may so eat them and drink them [sc. those 'creatures'], that we be partakers of his body crucified, and of his blood shed for our redemption.'[56]

If Cranmer's eucharistic liturgy was unique in its retention of a kind of canon, it was equally distinctive in the strength of its Protestant insistence on the once-for-allness of Christ's sacrifice, 'who made there by his one oblation of himself once offered a full, perfect and sufficient sacrifice, oblation and satisfaction for the sins of the whole world'.[57] A careful reading of the 1549 consecration prayer will confirm that Christ's sacrifice is brought to remembrance, not repeated; and that the only sacrifices spoken of as enacted in the service are the sacrifice of praise and thanksgiving and the sacrifice of the communicants themselves, their souls and bodies, to be 'a reasonable, holy and lively sacrifice'.

In 1549 Cranmer was constrained: constrained by the need to carry with him his episcopal and other clerical colleagues; constrained politically by the theologically moderate regime of Somerset; constrained by the objection to putting into people's mouths sentiments which were not yet wholly theirs; and, moreover, constrained to an extent which cannot now be exactly measured by his own veneration for traditional structures and language, a conservative liturgical instinct in tension with the reformist thrust of his theology. This last difficulty has led some authorities to the opinion that 1549 was Cranmer's preferred liturgy, because closer to traditional forms; others to insist that 1552 was a plainer, truer expression of what he intended. In 1552 the possibility of reading the real presence into the communion service was no longer available. Now it was 'these thy creatures of bread and wine', 'take and eat this', 'drink this'.[58]

IV

SO FAR, SO GOOD. But as an assessment of Cranmer and of Cranmer's contribution to 'the genius of Anglicanism', not far enough. It has been suggested that on the centrality of the Gospel, Cranmer was temperamentally at one with Luther from an early date in his public career, and that his understanding of the Gospel moved within essentially Lutheran parameters, not that he was exactly a Lutheran in his account of justification and of the relation of faith to works, any more than many German theologians of the sixteenth century whom we nevertheless do not hesitate to call some kind of Lutherans taught exactly what Luther had taught. And how theologically consistent was Luther himself, who always wrote for the occasion, producing little that was systematic?

The issue is somewhat technical and concerns whether Cranmer believed that we are saved by a wholly other, extrinsic righteousness, merely imputed to us, the doctrine theologians call 'forensic'; or by the *imparting* of that righteousness to us so that it becomes an indwelling righteousness, in a sense our own righteousness, although not originally or properly ours but Christ's. The latter possibility resembles the position adopted by the Nuremberg and Königsberg preacher and Cranmer's adoptive uncle, Osiander, which landed him in a full-scale 'Osiandrist' controversy around 1550.[59] The prime evidence is contained in certain notes on justification which survive at Lambeth Palace, in Cranmer's own handwriting: commonplaces collected, according to the Archbishop's habitual method, from Scripture, the Fathers, certain Schoolmen.[60] Unfortunately these notes are undated and we cannot be sure that they represent the rough work for the great Homilies, as some have assumed. In that they are in Cranmer's hand rather than a secretary's they may be very much earlier, representing a transitional stage in his understanding of this subject.[61] Either on that account, or because of the ingestion of patristic and scholastic as well as biblical material, or because that was indeed his settled opinion on the matter which drew him to those texts, Cranmer wrote of a justification which continues and increases by means of charity as well as by faith, although the charity no less than the faith are ascribed only to Christ. There is also the 1548 evidence of the Justus Jonas *Catechism*, published on Cranmer's instructions three times in the year after the Homilies. The *Catechism* in its translated version fails to speak of justification by faith alone, even where *sola fide* appears in the original Latin, and it teaches that God both imputes and gives unto us the justice and righteousness of Christ. [62]

So it is rather more clear that Cranmer taught salvation by grace alone than that he advocated salvation by faith alone, with truly Lutheran starkness. It also appears that for Cranmer saving faith was not distant from what the scholastics had called *fides formata*. True, the dying thief on the cross had saving faith which had no time at all to work as *fides formata*. But, said Cranmer, if the thief had lived 'and not regarded faith, and the works thereof, he should have lost his salvation again'.[63] Seventy years later, that doctrine would have been called grossly Arminian: and yet it continued to stand in the Homily of Good Works, which is to say, in the Articles, into the seventeenth century and beyond.

Dr Alister McGrath, surveying this evidence in the course of his large book on justification in the history of Christian doctrine,[64] speaks of the general 'theological mediocrity' of the English Reformation and of Cranmer's inability to distinguish clearly between the Lutheran doctrine of imputed righteousness and a more properly

Augustinian concept of factitive righteousness, 'making righteous', to which, with the sole exception of that Germanical nature Robert Barnes, he believes the English reformers all leaned. However, it is not clear that Cranmer misheard Luther, and Dr McGrath may go too far when he says that the English doctrines of justification 'were quite distinct from those of the mainstream Continental Reformation'; for that is to make the Continental Reformation itself, even the Lutheran Reformation, altogether too monolithic. If Cranmer believed that justification embraced the inner renewal of the justified man, so did his wife's uncle, Osiander, and Osiander, while attracting the combined wrath of Melanchthon and the so-called 'Gnesio-Lutheran' hardliners, believed that his doctrine could be read legitimately out of the Lutheran premisses.

But it is certain that Cranmer placed a distinctive premium on those good works done afterwards, the works and fruit of faith, and that he even defined salvation as perseverance in those faithful works, amounting to personal union with Christ. And that is more than a technical point. It had profoundly practical and historical consequences. For Cranmer's Prayer Book is, as it were, marinated in that understanding of the salvation process, an exercise in the first instance in what it has become fashionable to call 'self-fashioning', but thereafter an instrument for the fashioning of others, indeed of an entire nation. *Credere est orare, orare credere.* This is especially true of the Prayer Book collects, those translated and filtrated adaptations of traditional and in no way Protestant prayers. In these supplications, the Prayer Book serves as a manual for a Christian life which must persist in faith and the good works which spring from faith if it is to come safely to its end and attain salvation.

Familiar phrases can make the point: 'that thou being our ruler and guide, we may so pass through things temporal, that we finally lose not the things eternal'; 'that we loving thee in all things may obtain thy promises'; 'that we, running to thy promises, may be made partakers of thy heavenly treasure'; 'grant . . . that we may so run to thy heavenly promises, that we fail not finally to attain the same'. 'Almighty and everlasting God, give unto us the increase of faith, hope and charity; and that we may obtain that which thou dost promise, make us to love that which thou dost command . . .'

If there was theological tension between these expressions of Cranmer's faith and other versions of Protestantism, soon to be nearly dominant in the later sixteenth-century Church of England, to such an extent that there are difficulties in calling Cranmer's account of the matter 'Anglicanism', the tension was equally one of tone, mood and proportion. The collects are all between thirty and sixty words in length, whereas the prayers in the Middelburg, Puritan Prayer Book of 1587, which is such a liturgy as many English Protestants of that generation would have composed without the prompting and restraint of Cranmer and the law, run to as many as two thousand words and more, forty times the length of the collects and so not prayers in the same sense at all.[65]

We should not forget that Cranmer's legacy was not simply one of the sublime, quasi-Shakespearian consensuality of the Prayer Book, which it is usual to celebrate on such an occasion as this; but a legacy of tension, division and the extreme bitterness of a civil war which, in part, was a war fought for and against the Prayer Book, for and against Archbishop Cranmer's continuing hand on the tiller of a nation's religious consciousness and sensibility.[66] That was a hand which, for all that it was itself guided by an essentially Protestant mind, could compose out of a time-worn original such a prayer as the second collect at Evensong, redolent of a cradle-to-grave, static and institutional religious structure, as timeless as the parish church where for generations it would be read; an 'edifying' prayer but not in the urgently Pauline sense of edification, revived in English Puritanism.[67] 'Give unto thy servants that peace which the world cannot give; that both our hearts may be set to obey thy commandments and also that by thee, we being defended from the fear of our enemies, may pass our time in rest and quietness.'

Cranmer himself can scarcely be said to have passed his time in rest and quietness; and at the end no man was in more need of that peace which the world cannot give. According to one possible reading of his recantations, this was a man who no longer knew which was the truth which would save him, which the error which would damn him. He was, in John Foxe's patterning of history, the most emblematic and representative of the English Protestant martyrs, the last of 'the learned sort' to go to the stake, burned 'about the very middle time' of Mary's reign, so that he was also 'almost the very middle man of all the martyrs'. But, as even Foxe conceded, no martyr needed martyrdom more, to resolve, heal and make amends, in Foxe's unforgiving words 'to purge his offences in this world', an interpretation of the meaning of martyrdom made of none of Foxe's other martyr characters.[68]

Just as it is hard to quarrel with suicide, so martyrdom removes the martyr beyond our reproach; even such a hesitant, unwilling martyr as Thomas Cranmer, although in the end he ran to the stake. Hence the inestimable value of martyrdom as apologetics. This chapter has pursued the theme of truth by twisting, labyrinthine paths. One symbol of truth and sincerity is the right hand, the hand which composed the Prayer Book. Few of us can be as proud of what our right hands have done, but since we are for the most part private rather than public men and women, we also have less to be ashamed of or to regret. In any event, none of us is likely to have the opportunity to hold that offending member, the right hand, in the consuming flames as Cranmer did, oftentimes repeating 'his unworthy right hand'.[69]

NOTES

1 Jasper Ridley, *Thomas Cranmer* (Oxford, 1962).
2 *Miscellaneous Writings and Letters of Thomas Cranmer* ed. J. E. Cox, Parker Society (Cambridge, 1846), p. 219.
3 J. G. Nichols, ed., *Narratives of the Days of the Reformation*, Camden Society (London, 1859) prints the anonymous 'The Lyfe and Death of Thomas Cranmer, Late Archebushop of Caunterbury' (from British Library, MS Harley 417), which was the martyrologist John Foxe's principal source; and the account by Cranmer's secretary Ralph Morrice (Corpus Christi College, Cambridge, MS 128). For Cranmer's total baldness and copious beard, observed at his martyrdom, see *The Acts and Monuments of John Foxe*, ed. S. R. Cattley, viii (London, 1839), 89.
4 ibid., viii. 15.
5 *The Complete Works of St. Thomas More*, ii. ed. R. S. Sylvester (New Haven, 1963), 47; *Three Books of Polydore Vergil's English History*, ed. Sir Henry Ellis, Camden Society (London, 1844), p. 227.
6 Nichols, *Narratives*, pp. 219, 242.
7 Peter Brooks in *Cranmer in Context* (London, 1989), pp. 18–22, provides evidence of Cranmer's possession and use of the 1524 Paris edition of Merlin's *Quatuor conciliorum generalium*, a source for the foundation prepared for the Henrician Reformation in the *Collectanea satis copiosa* of c. 1530, associated with Bishop Edward Fox, who seems to have known only the later, 1530 edition of Merlin.
8 Nichols, *Narratives*, p.252.
9 Cranmer to Thomas Cromwell, 15 August (1538), *Miscellaneous Writings of Cranmer*, p. 375.
10 *A Catechism Set Forth by Thomas Cranmer from the Nuremberg Catechism Translated into Latin by Justus Jonas*, ed. D. G. Selwyn (Appleford, 1978), p. 61.
11 *Writings and Disputations of Thomas Cranmer*, ed. J. E. Cox, Parker Society (Cambridge, 1844), p. 61.
12 P. N. Brooks, *Thomas Cranmer's Doctrine of the Eucharist: An Essay in Historical Development*, 2nd edn. (London, 1992).
13 *Miscellaneous Writings of Cranmer*, p. 566; *Acts and Monuments of John Foxe*, viii. 88.
14 *Sermons of Hugh Latimer*, ed. G. E. Corrie, Parker Society (Cambridge, 1844), p. 487; *The history of the Church of England compiled by the Venerable Bede*, tr. Thomas Stapleton (Antwerp, 1565), Epistle.

15 William Camden, *The History of the Most Renowned and Victorious Princess Elizabeth Late Queen of England*, abridged and ed. Wallace T. MacCaffrey (Chicago, 1970), p. 4.

16 Patrick Collinson, 'Truth and Legend: the Veracity of John Foxe's Book of Martyrs', in A. C. Duke and C. A. Tamse, eds., *Clio's Mirror: Historiography in Britain and the Netherlands, Britain and the Netherlands*, viii (Zutphen, 1985), pp. 31–54.

17 John Aylmer, *An harborowe for faithfull and trewe subiectes* ('at Strasborow' but *recte* London, 1559), Sig. Rl^v.

18 Alastair Fox, *Thomas More: History and Providence* (Oxford, 1982); Alastair Fox, *Politics and Literature in the Reigns of Henry VII and Henry VIII* (Oxford, 1989), pp. 108–27; Judith H. Anderson, *Biographical Truth: the Representation of Historical Persons in Tudor-Stuart Writing* (New Haven, 1984), pp. 27–39, 75–109; *The Life and Death of Cardinal Wolsey by George Cavendish*, ed. R. S. Sylvester, Early English Text Society no. 243 (1959), pp. 3–4, 182–8.

19 Sir Philip Sidney, *An Apology for Poetry or the Defence of Poesy*, ed. G. Shepherd (London, 1965), p. 107.

20 *Prayers and Other Pieces of Thomas Becon*, ed. J. Ayre, Parker Society (Cambridge, 1844), p. 604.

21 Perez Zagorin, *Ways of Lying: Dissimulation, Persecution and Conformity in Early Modern Europe* (Cambridge, Mass., 1990).

22 *The Works of John Jewel*, ed. J. Ayre, iv. Parker Society (Cambridge, 1850), p. 1167.

23 Nichols, *Narratives*, p. 249.

24 See Dr MacCulloch's forthcoming article on Archbishop Cranmer and Bishop Stephen Gardiner in the *Historical Journal*.

25 *Miscellaneous Writings of Cranmer*, pp. 218, 563–5; Ridley, *Cranmer*, p. 409.

26 Brooks, *Thomas Cranmer's Doctrine of the Eucharist*, pp. 112, 141.

27 Dr Brooks gives the best concise and critical account of the long-running debate about Cranmer's eucharistic doctrine.

28 J. A. Muller ed., *The Letters of Stephen Gardiner* (Westport, Conn., 1970), p. 330.

29 Ridley, *Cranmer*, p. 12.

30 *The Obedience of a Christian Man* (1528), in *Doctrinal Treatises . . . by William Tyndale*, ed. H. Walter (Cambridge, 1848).

31 Quoted, Gordon Rupp, *Six Makers of English Religion 1500–1700* (London, 1957), p. 41.

32 See the forthcoming book on the Henrician Reformation by Dr Richard Rex.

33 *The Remains of Archbishop Grindal*, ed. W. Nicholson, Parker Society (Cambridge, 1843), p. 379.

34 P. N. Brooks, 'Cranmer Studies in the Wake of the Quatercentenary', *Historical Magazine of the Protestant Episcopal Church*, xxxi (1962), 365–74.

35 A recent account of this episode is in G. Redworth, *In Defence of the Church Catholic: The Life of Stephen Gardiner* (Oxford, 1990).

36   Material largely printed (from Corpus Christi College, Cambridge, MS 128, pp. 5–359) in *Letters and Papers of Henry VIII*, xviii (2) as 'Cranmer and the Heretics of Kent'.

37   Patrick Collinson, 'Andrew Perne and His Times', in *Andrew Perne: Quatercentenary Studies*, Cambridge Bibliographical Society Monograph no. 11 (Cambridge, 1991).

38   Redworth, *In Defence of the Church Catholic*.

39   Nichols, *Narratives*, pp. 254–9. The most famous refractions of Henry's trustful relationship with Cranmer occur in Shakespeare's *Henry VIII*, Act V, scenes i and ii.

40   Selwyn, *A Catechism*, pp. 212 (Introduction), 80 (Text). See also D. G. Selwyn, 'A Neglected Edition of Cranmer's Catechism', *Journal of Theological Studies* n.s. xv. (1964), 76–91.

41   Brooks, *Thomas Cranmer's Doctrine of the Eucharist*, p. 38.

42   Collinson, 'Andrew Perne', pp. 3–4, and references in n. 13, p. 26.

43   Brooks, *Thomas Cranmer's Doctrine of the Eucharist*, p. 5.

44   Nichols, *Narratives* p. 219.

45   British Library, MSS Royal 7BXI and XII. Dr Peter Brooks pioneered the use of the *florilegia* in his *Thomas Cranmer's Doctrine of the Eucharist*. They are now being more fully exploited by Dr Brooks's pupil, Mr Ashley Null, with particular reference to Cranmer's doctrine of repentance. Mr Null has identified some collateral material in Lambeth Palace Library, MS 1107.

46   B. L. Beer, 'Philip Melanchthon and the Cambridge Professorship', *Notes & Queries*, ccxxxii (1987), 185; J. D. Alsop, 'Philip Melanchthon and England in 1553', ibid., n.s. xxxvii (1990), 164–5. I owe these references to Dr D. MacCulloch.

47   E. C. Ratcliff, 'The Liturgical Work of Archbishop Cranmer', *Journal of Ecclesiastical History*, vii (1956), 189–203.

48   John Hacket, *Scrinia Reserata* (London, 1693), ii. 103.

49   Collinson, 'Andrew Perne', pp. 3–4; John Redman, *A compendious treatise called the complaint of grace* (London, 1556), Preface and Sig. Gii; Richard Rex, *The Theology of John Fisher* (Cambridge, 1991).

50   Available in various nineteenth-century editions of the *Homilies*; in Cranmer, *Miscellaneous Writings*, pp. 128–49; and in *English Reformers*, ed. T. H. L. Parker, Library of Christian Classics, xxvi (London, 1966), pp. 253–86.

51   *A Necessary Doctrine and Erudition of a Christian Man*, ed. T. A. Lacey (London, 1895), pp. 144–5.

52   Cranmer, *Miscellaneous Writings*, pp.338–9.

53   S. M. Wabuda, 'The Provision of Preaching During the Early English Reformation: With Special Reference to Itineration c. 1530 to 1547', unpublished Cambridge Ph. D. dissertation, 1991, esp. 'Archbishop Cranmer's Patronage of Preachers', pp. 114–28. Reference to PRO, S.P. 1/115, fol. 89 establishes that Payne spoke of a thousand paternosters, not of a million, as Cranmer's Victorian editor mistakenly supposed.

54   Muller, *Letters of Stephen Gardiner*, p. 335.

55   Brooks, *Thomas Cranmer's Doctrine of the Eucharist*, pp. 141–3.

[56] ibid., pp. 146–7.

[57] Rupp, *Six Makers* p. 44.

[58] One may compare the views of C. W. Dugmore in *The Mass and the English Reformers* (London, 1958) and in *The English Prayer Book 1549–1662*, Alcuin Club (1963) with those of Dr Peter Brooks.

[59] On Osiander, see David Steinmetz, *Reformers in the Wings* (Philadelphia, 1971), pp. 91–9, and the references Steinmetz supplies to the literature in German.

[60] Printed in *Miscellaneous Writings*, pp. 203–11.

[61] I have been helped on this point by Mr Ashley Null.

[62] Selwyn, *Catechism*, pp.43–50 (Introduction), 115 (Text).

[63] Cranmer, *Miscellaneous Writings*, p. 143.

[64] Alister McGrath, *Iustitia Dei*, ii (Cambridge, 1986), chapter 8.

[65] The Middelburg Prayer Book was reprinted by Peter Hall in *Reliquiae Liturgica: the Middelburg Prayer Book* (Bath, 1847).

[66] J. S. Morrill, 'The Religious Context of the English Civil War', *Transactions of the Royal Historical Society*, 5th ser. xxxiv (1984), 155–78; J. S. Morrill, 'The Attack on the Church of England in the Long Parliament 1640–1642', in Derek Beales and Geoffrey Best, eds., *History, Society and the Churches: Essays in Honour of Owen Chadwick* (Cambridge, 1985), pp. 105–24.

[67] John S. Coolidge, *The Pauline Renaissance in England: Puritanism and the Bible* (Oxford, 1970).

[68] *Acts and Monuments of John Foxe*, viii. 90.

[69] ibid.

HENRY McADOO

Richard Hooker

FOR A SON OF THE Oxford Movement it is a privilege as well as a pleasure to be associated with this John Keble bi-centenary commemoration. More particularly is it so because it was Mr Keble's re-editing of the *Works* in 1836 which contributed to the reviving interest in Richard Hooker whose *Ecclesiastical Polity* had been a steady seller from 1611 onwards, though slow to sell in his own life-time. After numerous seventeenth-century editions there had been a gap of some seventy years when no new editions appeared from about 1723 until the Clarendon Press edition of 1793.[1] Keble's edition and those deriving from it were good and John Keble, so Georgina Battiscombe tells us, spent six years in its preparation,[2] placing us in his debt in this as in other spheres.

My problem in respect of an essay like this is best exemplified by the case of the commercial traveller in the West of Ireland just after the last war before the sign-posts had been replaced. Thoroughly lost in a wide expanse of bogland he espied an old man footing turf. Getting out of his car, he approached and asked 'How do I get to Roscommon?' The ancient leant on his spade and pondered. Then he replied, 'Roscommon is it? Now if I were going for Roscommon, 'tisn't from here I'd be starting.'

In my own case, I too know where I want to go. *I want to show, if I can, why Hooker matters to Anglicans today. What was he saying to his own time which was so important and why does it continue to be important?* But the difficulty is how to get there, *where to start?* Surveying the terrain, three points of departure suggest themselves. Indeed, though I know that it may sound a bit Irish, I think that one might profitably start from them all. Hooker's influence is everywhere in seventeenth-century Anglicanism. The list of his peers the form of whose thought and the method of whose presentation of the truths of faith owe so much to him reads like a latterday litany of the saints — Laud, Chillingworth, Andrewes, Morton, Potter, Hall, Field, Cosin, Bull, Sanderson, and Jeremy Taylor who called him 'the incomparable Mr Hooker'.[3] Moderns like C. J. Sisson and John S. Marshall assert that 'there is no figure of greater significance to the instructed mind than Hooker'[4] and 'it is hard to overestimate the importance of Hooker'.[5] F. J. Shirley said of him that he gave 'to Anglican theology a tone and a direction which it has never lost'.[6]

To get to the point from which I can attempt to evaluate Hooker's thrust and originality over against his contemporaries and at the same time to give some indication of the perennial quality of his work seems to me to require that exercise in gymnastics of starting from three places at once. These jumping-off places, as I see it, are marked by three dates: 1558, 1562 and 1572. When I remind you that in 1558 Hooker was four years old you may well fear the worst. But all I am aiming to do is to show by means of an impressionist *ébauche* the kind of mind-set with which Hooker would have to deal in the *Polity*; that this was active and militant from the accession of Elizabeth I in 1558 onwards; that the confrontation in which Hooker would be involved was then already forming in embryo. *That out of all this something time-defying was created for Anglicans is my theme.* That this permanent endowment emerged from a specific time and from a local situation is the mystery of our good fortune, or should I say *mysterium fidei*?

II

PEOPLE AND IDEAS were being prepared for liberation by event. That event was to come quickly with the end of Mary's five-year reign. The Marian exiles returned and the militants among them were more than ready in 1558. While abroad, after the fashion of *émigrés*, they had split into two factions, the hardly believable Cox and Knox set-up. The former, moderates who included John Jewel, supported the second Edwardian Prayer Book and the ecclesial structure as it was under Cranmer. The latter, root-and-branchers to a man, desired not only the Genevan type of worship but the abolition of the episcopate and the Prayer Book. Radical extremists, they have been said to out-Calvin Calvin. Thus we can see how, in the first year of Elizabeth's reign, circumstances were combining *to present in outline* confrontation between two sharply opposed views of polity and doctrine. This was the situation which was to develop and harden during Hooker's life-time and which was ultimately responsible for his *Ecclesiastical Polity*.

Elizabeth I, from the time of her accession in 1558, did much to preserve what one may call essential Anglicanism. Francis Bacon was to claim that during that first year 'she did so establish and settle all matters belonging to the church, as she departed not one hair's breadth from them to the end of her life'.[7] I sometimes think that there has been a tendency to canonize the phrases 'The Elizabethan Settlement' and 'The Elizabethan Compromise', reading into them more of our times and terms than historically they can bear. After the adulation of earlier writers such as Burnet there was a reaction among modern historians, particularly during the early part of our own century. The fashionable stance seems to have been to depict Elizabeth's ecclesiastical policy as that of a secular humanist, devoid of doctrinal conviction and with little personal religion, managing Church affairs with calculation. No doubt, that sibylline woman was expert at playing both ends against the middle in statecraft and diplomacy but on the evidence it would be simplistic so to characterize the ecclesiastical policy of the Queen whose private book of devotions is full of prayers for 'Thy Church my care'. Possibly Neale's *Queen Elizabeth I* was the first to give a more balanced picture and J. P. Hodges in *The Nature of the Lion* (1962) helped to set the record straight, using the prayers Elizabeth composed in French, Italian, Latin and Greek, 'that I should govern my people and nourish Thy Church'. Some concessions she had to make to the Puritan party but she engineered significant changes in the 1552 Prayer Book, notably the omission of the Black Rubric, the combining of the 1549 and 1552 words of administration at Holy Communion, and the loosely-worded Ornaments Rubric. She herself told de Silva, the Spanish Ambassador, that 'We only differ from other Catholics in things of small importance'. Yet she vigorously rejected the Papacy and Roman claims, informing the Council of Trent through her ambassador Cecil that the Pope was simply *primus inter pares* and that Anglican bishops were in the apostolic succession 'and not merely elected by a congregation like Lutheran and Calvinist heretics'.[8] She told Parliament in 1589 'that the estate and government of this Church of England, as now it standeth in this reformation . . . both in form and doctrine it is agreeable with the Scriptures, with the most ancient general Councils, with the practice of the primitive Church, and with the judgments of all the old and learned fathers'.[9] This is the classical Anglican appeal to Scripture and the

[107]

Primitive Church, enshrined, for example, in the Preamble to the Constitution of the Church of Ireland, and is precisely the position outlined twenty years earlier by one of the great theologians and controversialists of her reign.

This brings me back (am I being Irish again?) to my second starting point, the year 1562, in which John Jewel, Bishop of Salisbury since 1559, published his *Apology for the Church of England*, the first full-length essay in Anglican self-understanding. Scripture and the Primitive Church are the criteria by means of which the authenticity of a Church and the truth of its teaching are assessed. We can also discern in the book, as John Booty has suggested,[10] something of that 'aided reason' which the boy to whom Jewel gave his chance in life, Richard Hooker, would develop as an integral element in his theological method. *The Anglican threefold appeal to Scripture, tradition and reason, is there and at work but awaiting the advent of its great synthesizer.*

Probably, Jewel was 'the chief author' but the *Apology* clearly had an official aura for contemporaries. Cecil knew all about it before publication and Parkhurst, Bishop of Norwich, wrote '*In omnium nostrorum nomine edidit*'.[11] In his dedicatory preface to the Queen, Jewel had insisted that we had not 'changed anything taught and approved by the fathers, but only errors, superstitions and abuses . . . which lawful reformation of our Church . . . is so far from taking from us the name or nature of true Catholics . . . or depriving us of the fellowship of the apostolic Church or impairing the right faith, sacraments, priesthood and governance of the Catholic Church that it hath cleared and settled them unto us'. This is the line from which Anglicanism would never deviate and Jewel underscores it later in the *Apology*: 'We have returned to the Apostles and old Catholic fathers. We have planted no new religion, but only renewed the old that was undoubtedly founded and used by the Apostles of Christ and other holy Fathers of the primitive Church'. One recalls John Cosin's aphorism 'Protestant and Reformed according to the ancient Catholic Church'. In other words, my point is that already active on the scene which I am trying to sketch is a distinctive Anglican apologetic, a theological method for answering fundamental questions like 'Where is doctrine to be found?'; 'What establishes the Catholicity of a Church?'; 'How am I to know that this or that doctrinal formulation is consonant with the faith once for all delivered?' Richard Hooker would before long be taking that method and by means of his personal alchemy transmuting it into a flexible, versatile instrument for the seeking of truth, his avowed and constant objective: for 'the mind of man desireth evermore to know the truth according to the most infallible certainty which the nature of things can yield'.[12]

With my third starting point, the *Admonition* of 1572, the world into which Hooker would speak has arrived and the lines are being drawn for the confrontation in which he would be deeply involved. The document was the Puritans' opening salvo in a conflict which would continue. It was an aggressive document of all-out radicalism, clear, methodical, unequivocal and with considerable public appeal, its goal being 'a true platforme of a church reformed'. A platform was in fact what the *Admonition* gave to the Puritan party. The second *Admonition*, written by Cartwright, was repetitive. The *Admonition* was addressed to Parliament but the Queen vetoed it, being infuriated by its proposals to presbyterianize the Church: 'Now then, if you wyl restore the church to his ancient officers, this you must doe. In stead of an Archbishop or Lord bishop, you must make equalitie of ministers'.[13] Just as Elizabeth repudiated papal claims so she refused the abolition of the episcopate, characterizing it as 'newfangledness'.[14] Archbishop Parker asked Whitgift, a Cambridge scholar, to answer the *Admonition* which he did the following year in a book entitled *An Answere to a certen Libel*. Immediately Cartwright replied and the war of words went on up to 1577 with Cartwright's *The rest of the second replie*.

Now Hooker's hour was approaching when in 1585 Whitgift, Archbishop of Canterbury, appointed him Master of the Temple. There he would find, already ensconced as reader, Walter Travers, who has recently been described as 'second only to Thomas Cartwright in the shadow cabinet of Elizabethan Puritanism'.[15] Twelve years previously Travers, newly returned from Geneva, published a book called the *Explicatio* (1573). Based on a positive presentation of the *Admonitions*, it was an able production which became widely influential in advocating a narrow biblicism which denied the independent use of reason in discovering the moral and political aspects of life not revealed to us in the Scriptures and favoured 'a religion severed in every point from the Church of the Middle Ages'.[16] Travers had been trying to presbyterianize the Temple and endeavoured unsuccessfully to convert Hooker to his views. Thus was inaugurated their weekly contest when, as Izaak Walton recalled, 'The forenoon sermon spake Canterbury, and the afternoon, Geneva'. *It was a church of continuity versus a church of biblical radicalism*. Whitgift, who had answered the *Admonition*, had chosen one who would answer Travers whom he would after some time remove from the Temple on the grounds of non-episcopal ordination and erroneous doctrine.

Whether the *Ecclesiastical Polity* was a semi–official defence of the Church suggested by Whitgift, as some hold, or whether like Topsy 'it just growed' out of the Temple controversy and the encouragement of Hooker's friends George Cranmer and Edwin Sandys, as others think, hardly matters to us now because something timeless had been presented to Anglicans.

I trust then that I have up to this point been able to give some indication, however sketchy, of the theological method which Hooker inherited and immensely enhanced, and some sort of outline for the unfolding events and the opposing ideas which go to explain the title of the Preface to *The Laws of Ecclesiastical Polity*; 'A Preface to them that seek (as they term it) the Reformation of the Laws and Orders Ecclesiastical of the Church of England'. For despite the perennial impact of Hooker on Anglican thinking a true evaluation of his worth and stature could not be attempted in a theological and historical vacuum.

III

IN THE CLOSING decades of the seventeenth century, the Accountant General of Ireland, James Bonnell, had a great admiration for Richard Hooker 'whom he used to commend as an author who writ with a primitive spirit but modern judgment and correctness'.[17]

We do not often think of top civil servants as saints yet that is how his friend Bishop Wetenhall regarded Bonnell: 'I am truly of the opinion that, in the best age of the Church, had he lived therein, he would have passed for a saint'.[18] We are not dependent here on that hagiography in which distance lends enchantment. Bonnell's biographer knew him and collected written information from the Accountant's many friends in Ireland and England: bishops, professional men, gentry and the poor to whom he gave the eighth part of his yearly income. Hamilton thus claimed that his book pictured real religion 'not in notion but in life', but 'the principal materials for Mr Bonnell's *Life* are his own private papers . . . what he himself calls, the transcript of his heart'.[19] In them is revealed the typical Anglican spirituality of the period, prayers for different stages of each day, weekly Communion and twice daily churchgoing 'when the hurry of his business hindered this . . . he would use all his art to get prayers at some church or other'.[20] There is a warm affective devotion to Christ and a deliberate growth in the virtues through grace. It was no stained glass sanctity and people were instantly drawn to and attracted by him: 'Here we have an instance of one who reconciled a life of religion and business together'.[21] I refer to Bonnell, a cultivated amateur of music and mathematics, a linguist who left translations of St Francis de Sales and of Synesius, to indicate the kind of people, not simply clergy, who were reading and valuing Hooker. Indeed, in this connection one should not forget Bonnell's not so saintly fellow civil servant Samuel Pepys. He borrowed the *Polity* from a friend who 'chawed tobacco' for his health, and liked the book so much that he bought his own copy. But more than this, I feel that Bonnell got the real point of Hooker by emphasizing the 'primitive spirit' and the 'modern judgement' of the *Polity*.

Ours is the age of the acronym, the label and the ready-made tag, the hit-and-miss classification. To attempt to enclose Hooker in any such verbal capsule would be a lost cause. But if 'liberal' means 'an openness in the search for truth' rather than an accommodating and over-hospitable mind; if a 'conservative' is one who respects continuity, treasuring tradition's best and most durable gifts from the past, rather than being neurotically resistant to change, then, with some caution, one might say (anachronistically, I suspect) that Hooker is a liberal conservative.[22]

Structurally, then, the *Ecclesiastical Polity* is a carefully worked answer to seven Puritan propositions. Stemming from the *Admonition* and Cartwright, these are the general principles of Puritanism; that Scripture alone is the 'rule of all things which in this life may be done by men'; that Scripture contains of necessity an unalterable form of Church polity; that the English Church is corrupted by popish orders, rites and ceremonies; that our laws are corrupt in that we do not have lay elders, and that 'there ought not to be in the Church Bishops'. But it is in how he handles this that we see why Hooker is great and why and how there is an abiding quality in his work. If the *Polity* were only a rebuttal of the *Admonition*, a piece of learned negative polemics, it would have died the death in a generation as did so many of the controversial writings of the period. It is infinitely more *because it is in fact and at the same time a positive and organic presentation of Anglicanism*, a fusing into one instrument of the essential constituents latent in a philosophy and theology, an ecclesiology and a moral theology, which constitute a whole approach to religion. John S. Marshall put it this way: the *Polity* forms 'a continuous and coherent whole presenting a philosophy and theology congenial to the Anglican *Book of Common Prayer* and the traditional aspects of the Elizabethan Settlement. In Hooker, Anglicanism is no longer merely an apologetic, it has become a coherent theology'.[23] This, I would suggest, is the point at which Hooker brings a stage further the argument of the *Apology* of his patron Jewel and I would wish to add a further comment. It is that the *Polity* 'is in one sense a defence of reason, an attempt to establish . . . a liberal method which holds reason to be competent to deal with questions of ecclesiastical polity and to be in itself an ultimate factor in theology'.[24]

So how then does a Church, or an individual, approach those fundamental questions of faith and order to which I referred earlier? Hooker's method is crystallized in a couple of sentences: 'Be it in matter of the one kind or the other, what Scripture doth plainly deliver, to that the first place both of credit and obedience is due; the next whereunto is whatsoever any man can necessarily conclude by force of reason; after these the voice of the Church succeedeth. That which the Church by her ecclesiastical authority shall probably think and define to be true and good, must in congruity of reason overrule all other inferior judgments whatsoever'.[25] May I underline a comment on this by Egil Grislis and I would point out that his last sentence finds a clear resonance in the oft-quoted *Report* of the Lambeth Conference of 1948 (p. 85). This speaks of the 'organic relation' of these three elements (Scripture, tradition and reason) to each other and of the 'suppleness and elasticity in that the emphasis of one element over the others may and does change with the changing conditions of the Church'. Grislis, a Latvian and Professor of Historical Theology at Hartford, Connecticut, writes: 'When such guidelines are judiciously followed, an entire theological system can emerge. It will be neither exclusively a biblical theology nor merely a rational construct, but will have made use of both. Most important, while written by one man, it will not be narrowly his subjectivistic theology, but a devout offering to the Church to accept and to remold it, should it so choose, for its own'.[26] There is the reason why in a living Church in a changing society what Hooker is saying matters to Anglicans today and bears on the way we do theology, relate to other Christians. and seek to comprehend and, by grace, live the truths of faith. As F. Paget, the reviser of Keble's edition of Hooker's works, put it 'The distinctive strength of Anglicanism rests on equal loyalty to the unconflicting rights of reason, Scripture and tradition'. That was in 1899 and in 1960 Michael Ramsey wrote 'the times call urgently for the Anglican witness to Scripture, tradition and reason — alike for meeting the problems which Biblical theology is creating, for serving the reintegration of the Church, and for presenting the faith as at once supernatural and related to contemporary man'. It was a conviction he reiterated in lectures as late as 1979.[27] Speaking as one who did fourteen years hard at the coal-face of unity dialogue, it is a conviction I share, and endorse more than ever since the appearance of the Vatican *Response* to *The Final Report* of ARCIC I.

You may well ask, why is this criterion so important now? My answer, given recently elsewhere, is that this threefold dialectic 'is our insurance against a blindfold Christianity with earplugs. At the moment, and in more than one Church, a confident Christianity can be undermined by either or both of two trends. There is a fundamentalism of Scripture, a literalist interpretation of that which is seen by all as normative for the Church. There is also a fundamentalism of tradition which sees it much as a fly-in-amber rather than the living Church interpreting 'the faith once for all delivered' in the idiom and life-setting of each generation'.[28]

As I see it, there is all the difference in the world between traditionalism and tradition. The former means the dead hand, the latter means a life line. The one is a stance of adherence, the other is a living process of transmission. Hooker revered tradition: 'Neither may we in this case lightly esteem what hath been allowed as *fit* in the judgment of antiquity, and by the long continued practice of the whole Church; from which *unnecessarily* to swerve, experience hath never as yet found it safe' (V. vii. 1.). The controlling condition, of course, is the absolute sufficiency of Scripture for salvation and he warns against those who 'look for new revelations from heaven, or else dangerously add to the word of God uncertain tradition' (II. viii. 5). We find however that, unlike scripture, tradition is changeable by the authority of the Church: 'All things cannot be of ancient continuance, which are *expedient* and needful for the ordering of spiritual affairs: but the Church being a body which dieth not hath always power, as occasion requireth, no less to ordain that which never was, than to ratify what hath been before . . . the Church hath authority to establish that for an order at one time, which at another time it may abolish, and in both do well' (V. viii. 1-2). Here again the only exception is 'articles concerning doctrine'.

Is Hooker not implying that what we mean by 'tradition' is open to reassessment from time to time within the living continuity of the Church? His frequent use of the concept of 'aptness' or 'fitness', what is *expediens*, would suggest that all things pertaining to the life of the Church, i.e. its polity, are open to revision under the guidance of *the Spirit abiding in the Church*:

For this cause therefore we have endeavoured to make it appear, how in the nature of reason itself there is no impediment, but that the selfsame Spirit, which revealeth the things that God hath set down in his law, may also be thought to aid and direct men in finding out by the law of reason what laws are *expedient* to be

[113]

made for the guiding of his Church, over and besides them that are in Scripture. (III, viii. 18).

Hooker appears to me to be reminding us that tradition is not an ever-increasing accumulation of irreversibles but a transmission process in which reduction and change may have a place as well as acceptance within the Spirit-led community of faith:

> Lest therefore the name of tradition should be offensive to any, considering how far by some it hath been and is abused, we mean by traditions, ordinances made in the prime of Christian religion, established with that authority which Christ hath left to his Church for matters indifferent, and in that consideration requisite to be observed, till like authority see just and reasonable cause to alter them. (V. lxv. 2).

In the Advertisement to his poems *The Christian Year* Mr Keble spoke of the necessity of 'a sound rule of faith'. In a different context that is what Hooker does for us. Sensitively and splendidly he evolves an approach which relates the givenness of Christian faith to the total human experience: 'The whole drift of the Scripture of God, what is it but only to teach Theology? Theology, what is it but the science of things divine? What science can be attained unto without the help of natural discourse and reason?'.[29]

A warning to readers was issued when I very tentatively suggested that the term 'liberal conservative' might *just* help us to get inside the mind of Hooker, as could Bonnell's use of the phrases 'primitive spirit' and 'modern judgment'. Perhaps we shall better understand Hooker and his continuing relevance to our own times and situation if we try to unpack his methodology.

IV

WHEN I WAS A country rector a mountainy man said to me as we sat in his farmhouse kitchen, 'What do we want with all this theology? Sure, all we need is the simple Gospel'. I confess to a certain sneaking sympathy with this view-point, particularly when I think of the writings of some of our contemporaries. But honesty obliges me to ask 'Is the Gospel really so simple?' Seemingly, St Paul didn't think so when he wrote of 'the mystery of the Gospel'. The Gospel seems to be all theology, from Bethlehem through Calvary to the Empty Tomb and beyond to the Descent of the Dove. I am reminded of a phrase of Jaroslav Pelikan, 'the history of theology is the record of how the Church has interpreted the Scriptures'.[30] Hooker thought so too: 'By Scripture it hath in the wisdom of God seemed meet to deliver unto the world . . . many deep and profound points of doctrine, as being the main original ground whereupon the precepts of duty depend'.[31]

If there is one single vantage point from which one can have an overall view of Hooker's theological synthesis I think it must surely be his scriptural exegesis, the principles which he follows in scriptural interpretation. For here there come into view the degree of his use of Aquinas and his biblical presuppositions, his humanism, his qualified acceptance of tradition, the co-inherence of Church and Scripture and above all his judicious use of reason. The sharp contrast here between Hooker and his opponents is best captured by the word 'balance'. Marshall's comment is just, even if it fails to catch all the facets: 'A Thomism enriched by Renaissance insights, and by a great biblical revival and by the fresh developments of the law, became in Hooker's hand an old but new way of thinking'.[32] What strikes me as justifying Bonnell's term 'modern' and my hesitant use of the word 'liberal' is that I am conscious that Hooker is not apprehensive of change and one recalls his own words, 'Two things there are which trouble greatly these later times: one, that the Church of Rome cannot, another, that Geneva will not erre'. Truth has to be sought for through reason aided by grace and revelation.

So how does Hooker see Scripture and how does he relate it to his whole theological synthesis? (I am, of course, uncomfortably aware that this is not work for a single lecture so all I can do is give indications rather than expositions). For him, the 'sufficiency' of Scripture is inseparable from its main purpose and use. This implies that, unlike the Puritan position, reason has its office in religion where revelation does not speak. Similarly, when he affirms 'the absolute perfection of Scripture' he is saying, as against the then current Roman Catholic position, that tradition does not and cannot supplement Holy Writ. Hooker wrote 'The testimonies of God are *all sufficient* unto that end for which they were given. . . . What the Scripture purposeth, the same in all points it doth perform. Howbeit that here we swerve not in judgment, one thing especially we must observe, namely that the *absolute perfection* of Scripture is seen by relation unto that end whereto it tendeth'.[33] Here are asserted the sufficiency of Scripture for salvific doctrine and its perfection in respect of that end. It may not be used as a theological hold-all.

I think that as we try to evaluate Hooker's hermeneutics we have to be careful of two things. We blur the perspective if we oppose 'rational' to 'Scriptural' and we must not forget that Hooker's view of the Bible was a sixteenth-century view with the important rider that reason may be used in exegesis. This he develops in the third book of the *Polity*. Moreover, while appearing to accept verbal inspiration he makes certain distinctions in the levels of inspiration in Scripture and between what is central and what is peripheral. 'Here', writes Grislis 'the principle of selectivity is spelled out as Christocentric'.[34] For Hooker, Scripture is divinely inspired and necessary for salvation: 'Scripture indeed teacheth things above nature, things which our reason could not reach unto. Yet those things also we believe, knowing by reason that the Scripture is the word of God'. The question then is, *How do we know this?* Some answer that 'we have no other way than only tradition'. Hooker agrees that 'by experience we all know, that the first outward motive leading men so to esteem the Scripture is the authority of God's Church'. To refuse this, he says, is 'an impudent thing'. Nevertheless, even the Fathers were obliged to demonstrate to unbelievers 'the authority of the books of God by arguments'. His conclusion is 'Wherefore if I believe the Gospel, yet is reason of singular use, for that it confirmeth me in this my belief the more'. Here we are at the heart of Hooker's hermeneutics. Over against the view that Scripture is self-authenticating and contains all that is mandatory for every aspect of Christian living, his Thomism (if one can so call it), distinguishing supernatural knowledge from natural knowledge, allows him to treat reason as an interpreter of Scripture, 'an instrument which God doth use unto such purposes'.[35] In the second book he is making the same point: 'For whatsoever we believe concerning salvation by Christ, although the Scripture be therein the ground of our belief; yet the authority of man is, if we mark it, the key which openeth the door of entrance into the knowledge of the Scripture'.[36] This too is an approach confirmed by 'the manifest speeches of ancient Catholic Fathers'.[37] To sum it up: Hooker gives the primacy of value to Scripture and to reason in his hermeneutics and a secondary value to tradition which also has authority but only in so far as it is consonant with Scripture and with reason. In other words, Scriptural interpretation involves maintaining a balance between reason and grace, 'the special grace of the Holy Ghost' concurring 'to the enlightening of our minds'[38]; a balance between private and personal conclusions on the one hand and the corporate wisdom of the Church on the other.

I suggested that Hooker is not apprehensive of change and freedom. He asks 'Why should the later ages of the Church be deprived of the liberty the former had? Are we bound while the world standeth to put nothing in practice but only that which was at the very first?'[39] It is an element which the Anglican tradition still treasures but then as now there were boundary-markers: 'The Church hath authority to establish that for an order at one time, which at another time it may abolish, and in both it may do well. But that which in doctrine the Church doth now deliver rightly as a truth, no man will say that it may hereafter recall, and as rightly avouch the contrary. Laws touching matter of order are changeable, by the power of the Church; articles concerning doctrine not so'.[40] Here too is a permanent constituent in the Anglican ethos, the *hapax*, the faith 'once for all delivered', which runs through the entire corpus of seventeenth-century Anglican theology. Laud spoke for a Church when he wrote that it was the purpose of his *Conference* (1622/1639) 'to lay open those wider gates of the Catholic Church, confined to no age, time or place; nor knowing any bounds but that faith which was once (and but once for all) delivered to the saints'.[41] Without the control of the *hapax*, the Church is open to what R. P. C. Hanson called 'a virtually uncontrolled doctrinal space flight'.[42] We are back by another route to the appeal to Scripture and the Primitive Church which with the appeal to reason, constitute the criteria by which Anglicans today answer those basic questions and which guide them in inter-Church dialogue. Hooker still speaks to our situation and we see why Bonnell valued his 'primitive spirit' and 'modern judgment'.

When with all this is juxtaposed the view of Scripture set forth in the *Admonitions* and then by Cartwright and later by Travers in his *Explicatio* we see clearly what is special, original and durable in Hooker. We can see too why even if taken out of time and context the term 'liberal conservative' enables us to catch something of the essential Hooker. He has used the insights of Aquinas and Thomist commentators like Cajetan while rejecting their claim that final authority is in the papacy or the *magisterium*. He has used the biblical revival stemming from Erasmus. He is catholic with the learning of the Renaissance and the convictions of the Reformation, as when both in the *Discourse of Justification* and the Fifth Book he links justification, sanctification and the two sacraments, one of which is 'the beginning of new life' and the other the 'food. . . for continuance of life'.[43] He is a philosopher-theologian for whom reason cannot stand apart from grace and is therefore an aided reason. In faith there are 'two operations, *apprehension* and *assent*'[44] and the total Christian and human experience rejects radical biblicism 'as if the way to be ripe in faith were to be raw in wit and judgement; as if Reason were an enemy unto Religion'.[45]

V

DURING MY TIME as a divinity student, the fifth book of the *Polity* was part of the set course in theology. No doubt this was because therein is set out the rationale of the whole Anglican position from the nature of true religion down to the attire of ministers. (One remembers that Cartwright had claimed that 'one of the foulest spots in the surplice is the offence it giveth in occasioning the weak to fall' — which gives one the flavour of the contemporary radicalism). Possibly too the limitation of our Hooker studies to the fifth book was a tempering of the wind to the shorn academic lamb. *But it was a mistake* because the *Polity* as a whole is a splendid, cohesive and all-embracing explanation of the hierarchy of law upon which ecclesiastical polity depends for its ultimate authentication.

The fifth book is probably the first in-depth theological commentary on the Book of Common Prayer, a genre that would develop in a matter of decades with works such as those of Anthony Sparrow, Hamon L'Estrange and John Cosin. Of course, the *Companion* type of book had a far wider influence on the laity who read books like those of Thomas Comber, William Nicholls and Robert Nelson. Dr Johnson claimed that no book save the Bible had better sales than the latter's *Companion to the Festivals and Fasts of the Church of England*. Hooker's fifth book however is far more than a *rationale* of the Prayer Book. It is a profound theological exposition of why Anglicans believe, think and worship as they do. Church, ministry, sacraments, liturgical principles and practice, are all discussed and not in the merely 'parochial' setting but in the context of participation in the Life of the Incarnate Lord through the grace of the Word and Sacraments in the corporate fellowship of the Church.[46] 'Christ is whole with the whole Church and whole with every part of the Church, as touching his Person' and yet 'it pleaseth him in mercy to account himself incomplete and maimed without us.'[47] The heart and purpose of membership is participation in Christ which is 'partly by imputation' and 'partly by habitual and real infusion, as when grace is inwardly bestowed'.[48] We can only participate in a 'Christ who is present'[49] and 'in him we actually are by our actual incorporation into that society which hath Him for their Head, and doth make together with him one Body'.[50] 'Yea, by grace we are every one of us in Christ and in his Church, as by nature we are in those our first parents . . . and his Church he frameth out of the very flesh, the very wounded and bleeding side of the Son of man'.[51]

This great and biblical concept of the Church informs the whole of Book V: 'The Church of Christ which was from the beginning is and continueth unto the end'. But for Hooker the visible Church is neither infallible nor perfect and he adds 'of which Church all parts have not been always equally sincere and sound'.[52] So, whenever its proclamation and witness are defective, reform becomes a duty: 'We hope therefore that to reform ourselves if at any time we have done amiss, is not to sever ourselves from the Church we were of before. In the Church we were, and we are so still'.[53] Even heretics are 'a maimed part, yet a part of the visible Church'.[54] Hooker is aware all through his writings of the continuity and wholeness of the Church's tradition and seeks to present it in the context of his own day and disputes. For him, continuity is not a lineal thing, the establishing of a pedigree, so much as the transmission of certain living qualities of faith and order which link the present Church with the primitive Church, being at once the assurance and the norm of Catholicity.[55] Through the centuries, at the core of this participation in Christ are the sacraments of his grace: 'This is therefore the necessity of sacraments. That saving grace which Christ originally is or hath for the general good of his whole Church, by sacraments he severally deriveth into every member thereof'. Sacraments, says Hooker, are 'not physical but moral instruments of salvation', nor 'bare resemblances or memorials of things absent, neither for naked signs and testimonies assuring us of grace received before but (as they are indeed and in verity) for means effectual . . . of . . . that grace available unto eternal life'.[56] They are the sacraments of his risen Life in which the Christian participates: 'Life being therefore proposed unto all men as their end, they which by baptism have laid the foundation and attained the first beginning of a new life have here (i.e. in the eucharist) their nourishment and food prescribed for continuance of life in them'.[57] It is the heart of the fifth Book, in Hooker's own words 'that the strength of our life begun in Christ is Christ'.[58]

Resisting the temptation to course the many attractive hares which this exposition of the Anglican Way lets loose, I have stayed with what I believe to be its essential theme, the theme on which the rest of the book depends. And I do so because I detect that Hooker thought so too. In the third Book he notes that 'a Church, as now we are to understand it, is a Society . . . and of such properties common unto all societies Christian, it may not be denied that one of the very chiefest is Ecclesiastical *Polity* . . . which word I therefore rather use . . . because it containeth both government and also whatsoever besides belongeth to the ordering of the Church in public'.[59] That really explains the rationale of Book V.

I am deeply aware that I have presented a rough theological

sketch rather than a portrait of one who is a magnificent subject as a theologian.

> Others abide our question. Thou art free,
> We ask and ask: Thou smilest and art still,
> Out-topping knowledge.

What Anglicans owe to the humble Vicar of Bishopsbourne can hardly be reckoned. We think of him, dying at forty-six: '"Are my books and written papers safe? Then it matters not; for no other loss can trouble me". . . and then the doctor (his confessor, Saravia) gave him and some of those friends which were with him, the blessed Sacrament of the body and blood of our Jesus', — thus Izaak Walton describes the scene.[60]

As I reflect on Hooker's book, for like his friend Richard Field, he was a man of one great book, I feel that I shall have done Hooker a disservice if I do not end by underscoring the significance of that book's full title *Of the Laws of Ecclesiastical Polity* (1594, 1597 and posthumous). If an artist friend makes you a present of one of his canvases you may have noticed that a striking thing happens once you enclose the picture in a frame. Mysteriously, you are made aware of new definitions of depth, perspective and detail. In some undefinable way, more meaning, more clarity, are added to the picture. So it is with the *Polity*. Hooker encloses his threefold dialectic within a splendid framework which imparts light and enhancement of meaning to his whole theological synthesis, which some have even dared to call an Anglican *Summa Theologica*. That framework is Law.

VI

'ALL THINGS THAT ARE have some operation not violent or casual. . . That which doth assign unto each thing the kind, that which doth moderate the force and power, that which doth appoint the form and measure, of working, the same we term a Law'.[61] This is his introduction to a majestic, all-inclusive range of thought which sees law as the epiphany of God's wisdom and power in the universe: 'Of Law there can be no less acknowledged, than that her seat is the bosom of God, her voice the harmony of the world: all things in heaven and earth do her homage, the very least as feeling her care, and the greatest as not exempted from her power: both Angels and men and creatures of what condition soever, though each in different sort and manner, yet all with uniform consent, admiring her as the mother of their peace and joy'.[62] All I can do in this lecture is to offer some snap-shots which, taken together, may convey a fleeting impression of the landscape as a whole.[63] The influence here of Aquinas on Hooker (to which, needless to say, Travers objected) is very clear and particularly so in his moral theology where Hooker is treating of law and human acts. Nor is he alone in this for the Schoolmen had not vanished from the libraries of the Anglican divines. They continued to use the *Summa*, though frequently critically and in disagreement on various points. The capable theologian Bramhall, the moral theologians Taylor and Sanderson, even the poet Donne and many others, show their acquaintance with St Thomas, whom Hooker describes as 'the greatest amongst the school-divines'. One might be tempted to speak of 'the judicious borrowings of Mr Hooker' if it were not just triteness to do so. For in fact Hooker's mind is moving in the same swing and sweep as that of Aquinas. Both in their own settings were seeking a synthesis of faith and reason, a view of reality as a whole and both were defending the autonomy of a grace-enlightened reason.

The law which sustains the universe goes back to God, who is himself the law of his own operations: 'God therefore is a law both to himself, and to all other things besides'.[64] This is the first Eternal Law and, as it informs all the spheres of creation 'of nature, of angels and of men' it constitutes what we are accustomed to call the second law eternal 'to be kept by all his creatures, according to the several conditions wherewith he hath endued them'.[65] As it operates at these different levels it is variously named nature's law, the law of angels and the law of reason. Hooker analyses each of them and concludes that there is a law by which all things 'incline to something which they may be' because everything in creation is 'in possibility, which as yet they are not in act'.[66] At this point it is evident that for Hooker law is not so much a promulgation as an implanted directive by means of which all things tend towards their own proper perfection. The phrase is his own: 'which law directeth them in the means whereby they tend to their own perfection'.[67] The angels keep their ancient places and the tulip bulb becomes a tulip, not a daffodil. Jeremy Taylor puts it this way: our human condition and our liberty are both imperfect, 'it only sets us higher than a tulip and enlarges our border beyond the folds of sheep or the oxen's stall; but it keeps us in our just station, servants to God, inferior to angels, and in possibility of becoming saints'.[68] Man, too, says Hooker desires perfection as does the rest of the created order but for him this is goodness because he is capable of 'a more divine perfection' than the animal creation.[69] *How then can he attain it?* 'It resteth', he says 'that we search how man attaineth unto the knowledge of such things unsensible as are to be known that they may be done'.[70]

Here Hooker places his teaching on human acts firmly within the law of nature which he identifies simply with the law of reason: 'The natural measure whereby to judge our doings, is the sentence of reason, determining and setting down what is good to be done'.[71] In this his teaching is a mirror-image of Aquinas's, 'This participation of the eternal law in the rational creature is called the natural law'.[72] Just as he takes St Thomas's definition of a law as something pertaining to reason: 'A law is properly that which Reason in such sort defineth to be good that it must be done. And the law of Reason or human nature is that which men by discourse of natural reason have rightly found out themselves to be all for ever bound unto in their actions'.[73] Those actions, says Hooker, have 'two principal fountains . . . knowledge and will' which involves choice.[74] Human acts, however, are the acts of a nature that is marred and imperfect (as Taylor put it) so that although 'our sovereign good is desired naturally' the fulfilling of that desire by natural means is impossible. By God's grace the Law of Christ has been given 'to rectify nature's obliquity withal'.[75] This is the new Law of grace to teach man 'how that which is desired naturally must now be supernaturally attained'.[76] This Divine Law does not exclude but rather includes Natural Law and revelation does not override reason:[77] 'The benefit of nature's light be not thought excluded as unnecessary, because the necessity of a diviner light is magnified'.[78] Hooker concludes by depicting the setting as he sees it of human acts for the Christian: 'The law of reason doth somewhat direct men how to honour God as their Creator; but how to glorify God in such sort as is required, to the end that he may be an everlasting Saviour, this we are taught by divine law. . . . So that in moral actions divine law helpeth exceedingly the law of reason to guide man's life; but in supernatural it alone guideth'.[79]

This is the splendid, architectonic framework enclosing Hooker's response to the *Admonitions* controversy, a response which is not simply a reply but an epochal and seminal work of positive theology. This is how a great theologian, strongly conservative at times, vigorously liberal at others, *relates Scripture to the total human condition and to the ordering of the Church's life and witness in the world.* This is what Olivier Loyer was saying about the vital role in Hooker's thought of the categories of conjunction and participation. I close with A. M. Allchin's comment, 'So the disjunctions which in the course of sixteenth-century controversy had become sharpened and hardened, between Scripture and tradition, between grace and nature, between the inward and the outward elements in prayer and worship, and finally between faith and reason, are consistently rejected by Hooker. Always he seeks to unite the two'.[80] That is why he speaks to us today.

NOTES

1   See W. Speed Hill in W. Speed Hill ed. *Studies in Richard Hooker* (Cleveland and London, 1972), p. 329.

2   Georgina Battiscombe, *John Keble* (London, 1963), p. 138.

3   *Works*, Heber ed., 6, cccxlii, and see John E. Booty in *Studies in Richard Hooker* ed. W. Speed Hill (Cleveland and London, 1972), pp. 212, 235.

4   C. J. Sisson, *The Judicious Marriage of Mr Hooker and the Birth of 'The Laws of Ecclesiastical Polity'* (Cambridge, 1940), p. ix.

5   John S. Marshall, *Hooker and the Anglican Tradition* (London, 1963), p. v.

6   F. J. Shirley, *Richard Hooker and Contemporary Political Ideas* (London, 1949), p. 35–6.

7   *The Works of Francis Bacon* ed. Montagu (1825–1834), 3, 477.

8   Mandell Creighton, *Queen Elizabeth* (1923 edn.), p. 71.

9   J. E. Neale, *Elizabeth I and her Parliaments* (London, 1953/7), II, 198.

10   John E. Booty, *John Jewel as Apologist for the Church of England* (1963), p. 140.

11   ibid. p. 55; Strype, *Annals*, II, i, 148.

12   *E.P.*, II, vii, 5.

13   *An Admonition to the Parliament in Puritan Manifestoes* ed. W. H. Frere and C. E. Douglas (London, 1954), p. 16.

14   Hodges, loc. cit., p. 38.

15   *Studies in Richard Hooker* (Cleveland and London, 1972), p. 119.

16   Marshall, loc. cit., pp. 95–6.

17   See William Hamilton, *The Exemplary Life and Character of James Bonnell Esq. Late Accomptant General of Ireland* 3rd ed. (London, 1709).

18   *Life*, p. 242.

19   *Life*, pp. v–vii.

20   *Life*, p. 132.

21   *Life*, p. 242.

22   For 'liberal' and 'conservative', see John Habgood, *Confessions of a Conservative Liberal* (London, 1988), pp. 2–3.

23   Marshall, loc. cit. p. 66.

24   H. R. McAdoo, *The Spirit of Anglicanism* (London, 1965), p. 5.

25   *E.P.*, V, viii, 2.

26   *Studies in Richard Hooker*, p. 182.

27   F. Paget's *Introduction to the Fifth Book etc.* (Oxford, 1899); Michael Ramsey, *From Gore to Temple* (London, 1960), p. ix. and Dale Coleman ed., *The Anglican Spirit* (Cambridge, Mass., 1991).

28 H. R. McAdoo, *Anglican Heritage: Theology and Spirituality* (Norwich, 1991), p. 103.
29 *E.P.*, III, viii, 11.
30 Jaroslav Pelikan, *Luther the Expositor* (St Louis, 1958), p. 5.
31 *E.P.*, I, xiii, 3.
32 Marshall, loc. cit., pp. 171–2.
33 *E.P.*, II, viii, 5.
34 *Studies in Richard Hooker* (Cleveland and London, 1972), p. 191. The reference is to *E.P.*, I, xiv, 4.
35 *E.P.*, III, viii, 14.
36 *E.P.*, II, vii, 3.
37 *E.P.*, II, iv, 2.
38 *E.P.*, III, viii, 15.
39 *E.P.*, V, xx, 4.
40 *E.P.*, V, viii, 2.
41 William Laud, *A Relation of the Conference*, 3rd edn. (London, 1901), Preface.
42 *Continuity of Christian Doctrine* (1981), pp. 29, 77, 83.
43 *E.P.*, V, lxvii, 1.
44 *E.P.*, V, xxii, 8
45 *E.P.*, III, viii, 4.
46 cf., *E.P.*, V, lxviii, 6.
47 *E.P.*, V, lvi, 10.
48 *E.P.*, V, lvi, 11.
49 *E.P.*, V, lv, 1.
50 *E.P.*, V, lvi, 7.
51 ibid.
52 *E.P.*, III, i, 10.
53 ibid.
54 *E.P.*, III, i, 11.
55 Cf. H. R. McAdoo, *The Spirit of Anglicanism* (London, 1965), p. 335.
56 *E.P.*, V, lvii, 4–6.
57 *E.P.*, V, lxvii, 1.
58 ibid.
59 *E.P.*, III, i, 14.
60 Izaak Walton, *Life of Mr Richard Hooker* (1644)
61 *E.P.*, I, ii, 1.
62 *E.P.*, I, xvi, 8.
63 Here I draw on my book, *The Structure of Caroline Moral Theology* (London, 1949), C. II.
64 *E.P.*, I, ii, 3.
65 *E.P.*, I, iii, 1.
66 *E.P.*, I, v, 1.
67 *E.P.*, I, iii, 5.
68 Jeremy Taylor *Ductor Dubitantium* IV, C. I, Rule 1, 5.
69 *E.P.*, I, vii, 1.
70 *E.P.*, I, vii, 1.

71 *E.P.*, I, viii, 8.

72 S. T. Ia, IIae, 91, 2.

73 *E.P.*, I, viii, 8 and cf. 'Law rational therefore, which men commonly used to call the Law of Nature'.

74 *E.P.*, I, vii, 2.

75 *E.P.*, I, xi, 6.

76 *E.P.*, I, xii, 3.

77 *E.P.*, I, xii, 3.

78 *E.P.*, I, xiv, 4.

79 *E.P.*, I, xvi, 5.

80 *The Study of Anglicanism* ed. Stephen Sykes and John Booty (London, 1988), p. 319; Olivier Loyer, *L'Anglicanisme de Richard Hooker* (Lille/Paris, 1979).

ELIZABETH CLARKE

George Herbert's *The Temple*: The Genius of Anglicanism and the Inspiration for Poetry

A STRIKING CHARACTERISTIC of Anglican spirituality in the sixteenth and early seventeenth century seems to have been the ability to inspire written texts which were enduring in their influence and wide in their appeal. A brief consideration of other Reformation figures in this volume makes the point very clearly: Cranmer and his Prayer Book; Hooker's *Laws of Ecclesiastical Polity*; Andrewes' *Sermons and Devotions*. Incidentally, Herbert's *The Temple* shares with these works the distinction of having been Charles I's prison reading right up to his execution. Even Andrewes and Hooker, however, did not share in the ubiquitous nature of George Herbert's popularity in the seventeenth century. In the troubled period of the Civil War, Non-Conformists and sectarians alike joined with Royalists in praising the poetry of *The Temple*. The various factions were actually fighting one another over religious issues: yet they all found in the small book of this one poet a source of spiritual nourishment.

Royalists seem to have enjoyed, in the calm Anglican practice represented in *The Temple*, a nostalgic appreciation of the good old days of the 1620s and 1630s. Dudley, Lord North, admits in a poem of his own, that in praising George Herbert the Royalists were mourning their own loss:

> Thus living, sing we, (Swan-like singing dye)
> His Panegyrick, our own Elegie.

Moreover, the party victorious in the Civil War (however temporarily) seem to have gained both inspiration and ammunition from *The Temple*. Within a few years of Herbert's death, the radical Puritan, Samuel Ward, based one of his sermons on two lines from Herbert's poem *The Church Militant*. These particular two lines had given the licensers pause when the first edition of *The Temple* was being prepared.

> Religion stands on tip-toe in our land,
> Readie to passe to the American strand.[1]

The Vice-Chancellor of Cambridge University had finally allowed these lines to stand, remarking drily that although Herbert 'was a Divine Poet . . . I hope the World will not take him to be an Inspired Prophet'.[2] Later in the 1630s, in an England which was fast polarizing along a religious divide, no such fine distinctions were made. For taking Herbert to be an Inspired Prophet, and thus implying that England would soon be godless, Samuel Ward was arrested and died a lingering death in prison.

There has always been a tendency for readers of George Herbert to remake him in their own image. Many people's perceptions of the poet-priest are formed by Isaak Walton, the most famous biographer of George Herbert. However, in *The Compleat Angler*, Walton re-casts his hero as the perfect fisherman, which is an image rather more difficult to swallow. At the end of his discourse on fly-fishing, Piscator (the fisherman), quotes Herbert's *Vertue*: his auditor, Venator, is very appreciative, of the poetry as well as the advice.

> I thank you, good Master, for your good direction for fly-fishing, and for the sweet enjoyment of the pleasant day . . . and I thank you for the sweet close of your discourse with Mr Herbert's verses, which I have heard loved Angling; and I do rather believe it, because he had a spirit suitable to Anglers.[3]

This is a rather different picture of George Herbert, as a sort of seventeenth century J. R. Hartley, from that painted by the Puritans, as we shall see later. There also seem to have been differences in the literary critical practices of both factions. The Royalists appreciated the wit and rhetoric of the poetry in *The Temple*. Several important Royalist poets — Herrick, Crashaw, Vaughan — made explicit gestures towards *The Temple* in their own poetry. Joseph Poole's *English Parnassus* of 1657 used extracts from *The Temple* to teach would-be poets. *The Mirrour of Complements*, a handbook for courtiers first issued in the 1630s, included in the second edition of

1650 various extracts from *The Temple*, as illustrations of appropriately pious yet witty remarks. The 'Bishop of Nonconformity', however, Richard Baxter, dismissed Herbert's poetic achievements, valuing him below poets such as Abraham Cowley, and reading him entirely for his sincerity.

> I know that *Cooly* and others far excel Herbert in Wit and accurate composure. But . . . Herbert speaketh to God like one who really believeth a God, and whose business in the world is most *with God*. Heart-work and Heaven-work make up his book.

An adversary of Baxter, Cromwell's chaplain, Peter Sterry, recommended the poems of Herbert in a very desperate personal situation, presumably for their theme rather than their rhetoric. To his wayward son, he wrote

> How sad is it yt still your heart should bee as Tynder to every sparke of Temptation, burning up immediately into a fire of lust . . . when will you breake your league with hell and ye Devill? . . . The best advice I can give you is to pray constantly, meditate, reade the scriptures, Mr. Bolton, and Mr. Herbert, abstaine from evill company & fleshly delights.

This is a powerful recipe for reading. *The Temple* is set alongside not only the sermons of a Puritan divine, but the Holy Bible itself. It seems to have worked, for Sterry's son eventually returned to the fold.

Soon, more ministers of religion were using the works of Herbert to illustrate their theological points. Between Herbert's death and the Restoration of Charles II *The Temple* went through eight editions. The seventh of these contained *an Alphabeticall Table for ready finding out chief places*. This was a concordance, with the help of which a preacher of any persuasion could use the appropriate bit of Herbert's poetry to support his own position. Again, *The Temple* was being used in the same way as the Scriptures. References to Herbert proliferate in sermons and writings of various religious factions in this period. As is often the fate of the Bible, the literary quality of the spiritual texts was frequently ignored, and sometimes the poetry was completely destroyed in the mis-quoting. Thomas White, a Non-Conformist, undertook the unlikely task of constructing a children's alphabet out of improving sentiments from *The Temple*. His *Little Book for Little Children*, published in 1671, involves some distortion of the original poems, and it is doubtful whether the said 'little children' would have made much of the entry for Q:

> Quaint wits with words my Posie windows fill
> Less than these mercies is my Posie still.

Based on lines from *The Posie*, this makes no sense even with reference to the original poem. However, I feel that Herbert would have been less outraged by this abuse of his poetry than by a Restoration document entitled *The Way to be rich* which used the sentiments of *The Church-porch* to show how one of the richest men in London, Hugh Audley, the moneylender, accumulated his wealth.

This partisan practice of adopting Herbert to support any particular shade of religious opinion is not of course limited to the seventeenth century. Within the past thirty years critics have assigned Herbert to every religious and political category from revolutionary Puritan to enthusiastic Laudian. The most recent book on Herbert identifies an undercurrent of anti-authority sentiment in the rhetoric of *The Temple* and speculates that Herbert 'might have entertained the chance to trumpet the social frustration the monarch had come to represent'.[4] I shall resist the temptation to categorize Herbert here, but one thing I am sure of is that watching the various forces tear England apart in the Civil War would have deeply distressed him. This is made abundantly clear in the poem he wrote about religious divisions, *Church-rents and schismes*. Here his affection for the Church in England and his horror at her fate are expressed in equal proportions.

> Brave rose, (alas!) where art thou? in the chair
> Where thou didst lately so triumph and shine
> A worm doth sit.

Personally, I am glad for his sake that he died well before the outbreak of the Civil War. But the question remains: what is it about Herbert's poetry that makes it so readily accessible to any reading, whether politically motivated, theologically partisan, or simply the result of spiritual need?

Unfortunately for Herbert scholars there are very few surviving documents which can pin Herbert down to a particular theological position. Rumour in the shape of Aubrey's *Lives* has it that Mrs Herbert used her husband's Latin sermons as linings for pie dishes.[5] It does seem that there were other writings which his widow 'intended to make publick' but they were lost when her sec-

[130]

ond husband's home was burnt down in the Civil War.[6] There are other literary works by Herbert extant besides *The Temple* and *The Countrey Parson*, which is a handbook written for pastors in the same kind of parish as himself: but they are in Latin, or even Greek. The Latin works show a very different George Herbert from the simple, sincere minister of Bemerton portrayed in the English prose. The poetry is conventional, imitative, highly rhetorical: classical references abound, and there are frequent allusions to topical events and court politics. If the Latin poetry blurs one particular iconic image of Herbert, the Latin orations will shatter it entirely. Flattering in the extreme, they are highly artificial in sentiment and diction.

The traditional explanation for this split in Herbert's literary persona is to ascribe the Latin works to his early life as an ambitious scholar and courtier, and the lyrics of *The Temple* to the period spent at the tiny chapel of Bemerton, from which period *The Countrey Parson* certainly dates. However, the manuscript evidence simply will not bear this interpretation. The existence of the manuscript kept in Dr Williams's Library in London, containing both lyrics from *The Temple* and two cycles of Latin poems, reveals that he was working on both English and Latin poetry at the same time. The authoritative recent biography by Amy Charles dates the latest Latin poem as no earlier than 1623, the earliest English poem no later than 1619, and the whole manuscript as finished around the mid-1620s. Some of the finest lyrics of *The Temple* date from this period — *Love III*, beginning 'Love bade me enter' — and *The Pearl*.

> I know the wayes of Honour, what maintains
> The quick returns of courtesie and wit:
> In vies of favours whether partie gains,
> When glorie swells the heart, and moldeth it
> To all expressions both of hand and eye,
> Which on the world a true-love-knot may tie . . .
> Yet I love thee.

The only poetry actually published in Herbert's lifetime was written in Latin: a set of memorial poems for his mother, published together with John Donne's funeral sermon for her, in 1627. The *Memoriae Matris Sacrae*, Petrarchan in style and tone, must have been written at the same time or after the anti-Petrarchan poem *Jordan I*. Similarly, Herbert's grossly flattering elegy for Sir Francis Bacon, who died in 1626, must have been written after the rejection of 'courtesie' in *The Pearl*. It is simply not possible to trace spiritual development from the poems of *The Temple*, though many have tried to do so: one editor this century destroyed Herbert's careful ordering of the poems to show his conception of Herbert's spiritual biography, ending with the sadder poems in the volume to illustrate what he thought was the poet's final disillusionment.[7]

Herbert's earliest biographer, Barnabas Oley, has a straightforward explanation for the contradictions. In the Latin poetry

> he made his ink with water of Helicon, but these preparations propheticall (the English poems) were distilled from above. In those are the weake motions of Nature, in these Raptures of Grace.[8]

The inspiration for the Latin poems is secular, it seems, whilst the English poetry is inspired by the Holy Spirit. There are various features of *The Temple* which encouraged this view in the seventeenth century. The Latin poetry follows classical verse forms and metre: the English is highly innovative in metrical form. There is an abundance of classical reference in the Latin poetry, whereas the English lyrics eschew classical allusion altogether. The Latin poems are often concerned with contemporary politics and gossip: the English deal with the timeless issue of how an individual Christian can relate to his Creator. In fact, the Latin poetry is very much in the tradition of European academic composition, well-established in the Renaissance, whereas it is difficult to find anything resembling Herbert's religious lyrics, in form or content, within European literature. In other words, the poems of *The Temple* do not have an obvious literary source, and it is not surprising that many readers assumed they had sprung fully formed from some other creative power than Herbert's own. Thus *The Temple* was treated rather like Scripture, as we have seen: more particularly it was often described in the seventeenth century as a book of contemporary Psalms, with George Herbert as the Psalmist, 'that sweet singer of the Temple', as Barnabas Oley called him. The 'inspiration' theory is a tempting one where George Herbert is concerned, and it would help to explain why *The Temple* has given, and continues to give, spiritual help to Christians of all colours. Barnabas Oley's account of Herbert's life, published in 1652, and addressed to fellow ejected priests, practically constituted a political document. Complaining that his 'mouth is stopped' by the current regime, Oley's message of the inherent superiority of the Anglican Church is conveyed through the apparently objective reporting of Herbert's biography. In the 1671 edition, when he was free to make his opinions clearer, he represents George Herbert as the Anglican and Restoration ideal for the priesthood, and makes plain his loathing of the Non-Conformist religion of the Interregnum.[9] The second, and for centuries the received biography of Herbert, was Isaak Walton's. It has much in common with Oley's, indeed Walton admits his indebtedness to Oley's account: and like Oley, he relies to a great extent on the poems themselves for a source of biographical detail. Another resemblance is that Walton chooses to consider the life of Nicholas Ferrar of Little Gidding alongside his *Life of George Herbert*, as Oley had done. Walton's *Life* continues to be influential, if I may judge from reading the introductions to selections of Herbert's poetry by W. H. Auden and R. S. Thomas. Several investigations have recently appeared questioning the accuracy and bias of this biography, which reads far more like a hagiography.[10] However, as Nicholas Ferrar could be regarded as another example of the genius of Anglicanism, I think a brief examination of the relationship between Herbert and Ferrar is worthwhile.

Walton includes a short biography of Nicholas Ferrar within his life of George Herbert, and he does so not only because of their close friendship but because both lives seem to him to follow the same satisfying pattern. The two men met at Cambridge: both gained a reputation for prodigious learning, George Herbert becoming a lecturer in rhetoric and then University Orator, an extremely prestigious position. Later, in the troubled Parliament of 1624, both men served as MPs. The two friends seemed set for promising careers and possibly high office. Ferrar, however, took a deliberate decision to leave London and retire with his family to a manor house in Huntingdonshire to lead a life entirely devoted to God. What Herbert was doing in the mid-1620s is less well documented, but Walton imposes the same pattern on his life, reading in from some hints in the poetry a disillusionment with public life and a failure of court hopes which led the Orator of the University of Cambridge to renounce the world for the retired life of a country parson in the small parish of Bemerton. However, Herbert did not take up orders until 1630, and his ministry lasted less than three years, which is a painfully short time on which to found the myth of the holy pastor-poet which Walton develops at great length. It is also possible to exaggerate the retired nature of the post at Bemerton, which was only a couple of miles from Salisbury, and very close to Wilton House, the residence of the Earls of Pembroke, one of the greatest families in the country, to whom Herbert was both chaplain and distant relative.

Although I think parallels between Herbert and Ferrar's lives have been exaggerated, the extremely close relationship between

[133]

Herbert and Nicholas Ferrar is well documented, and can be summed up in John Ferrar's words in his account of his brother's life: 'as N. F. [Nicholas Ferrar] communicated his heart to him, [George Herbert] so he made him the Peruser, & desired the approbation of what he did'.[11] This extended to detailed spiritual advice in the running of the Ferrar household. Certain decisions are attributed specifically to Herbert, and some of them were to cause some controversy later into the 1630s: it was on his advice that Ferrar set up a night-long prayer vigil at Little Gidding, and at his suggestion a brass plaque was set up on the wall of the house, welcoming those who came to learn, and warning those who came to criticize. Both steps helped to earn Little Gidding the reputation of being a papist enclave in the hostile climate of the 1640s.

Perhaps the most lasting monument to the co-operation and closeness of the two men is the parish church at Leighton Bromswold. In 1626 Herbert had been made prebend of this church, which is about four miles from Little Gidding, although he resisted Nicholas Ferrar's invitation to move there. However, the fabric of the church was in a lamentable condition: and much of Herbert's surviving correspondence of 1631 relates to the enterprise of rebuilding it, which he undertook in close consultation with Nicholas Ferrar. Many noble acquaintances of the Herbert family and their patrons contributed toward this project: Sir Henry Herbert, who was Master of the King's Revels, seems to have been particularly useful in the fund-raising.[12] The result is a very handsome building, typical of the 1630s, which stands on a hill above the rolling cornfields of Huntingdon. It is the interior design of the church which has caused most comment. The position of the altar would have been particularly controversial in the early 1630s. This was an issue on which Archbishop Laud had recently given instructions, directing that the altar should be railed off at the east end. The 'altar' at Leighton Bromswold is not really an altar at all, but a communion table which could be moved down into the chancel amongst the communicants, as was Elizabethan church practice. The fact that Ferrar and Herbert could institute such a feature in spite of Laud's express directives shows an independence of mind perhaps not to be expected from Ferrar, at least, who had been ordained deacon by Laud himself. On entering the church one is also struck by what appear to be a pair of pulpits, one on each side of the aisle. In fact only one of these is a pulpit: the other is a reading-desk, for use during the prayers. The symbolism is obvious: Herbert and Ferrar wanted to show the equal status of prayer and preaching in the liturgy. Since the very practice of preaching was an issue which was beginning to polarize the church in the 1630s, with Archbishop Laud increasingly suspicious of preaching and the Puritans equally committed to its primacy, this design is in itself an indication of a particular doctrinal stance which is not a compromise between the two factions but a third position independent of them both.

Some clues to the position of the Little Gidding community (and therefore perhaps of George Herbert) within the English religious tradition are given in the Little Gidding Storybooks, a record of the proceedings of the 'Little Academy' which was formed by members of the Ferrar family, in which to tell each other improving tales. The stories are taken from the full range of Christian tradition, from biblical and patristic texts through to lives of saints and medieval Catholic kings. Only twenty-five per cent are drawn from Protestant sources, but perhaps that represents the *nouveau arrivé* status of the Reformed religion: there were simply not that many Protestant kings or martyrs. One telling passage recounts how both Elizabeth I and Charles V had been heard to utter the same religious sentiment, provoking this comment from the storyteller at Little Gidding, on Holy Innocents Day 1631:

> That Difference of religion may not derogate from this truth, God makes the greatest Opposites in this Age to agree therein. . . . Meethinks we may boldly conclude that what is thus jointly ratified by the Defender of the Faith, the Christian and Catholick kings, must needs bee an orthodox Christian, Catholick verity.[13]

Comments like these show why the present leader of the Little Gidding community, Robert van de Weyer, thinks that 'in the context of their time, (the Ferrar family) were an ecumenical community'.[14] It is hard to imagine what would constitute an ecumenical community at this period. One cannot help thinking that this is wishful thinking on the part of someone who is seeking to draw inspiration from the Ferrars for his own ecumenical vision, but one can see his point. It is very difficult to imagine any red-blooded Elizabethan Puritan finding her agreement with a Catholic king as anything short of heresy. An eighteenth-century biographer, Samuel Peckard, noted exactly this quality of tolerance and independence in the Ferrar household, and catalogued the consequences of such untimely broad-mindedness:

> No-one, who is acquainted with the spirit of those times, and considers to what a degree Religious Rancour had possessed the hearts of all men; how intolerant the Puritans were of the Papists,

and of the Church of England; what detestation the Papists had of
the Church of England, and of the Puritans; and what a shameful
persecution the governors of the established Church exercised,
often against the Papists, and always against the Protestant
dissenters; will wonder that a society of Devotees, who were
apprehended not to agree with any of them, should be persecuted
by them all.[15]

This persecution in the later 1630s took the form of slander, so
much so that Nicholas Ferrar's first biographer, Barnabas Oley, described it in terms of martyrdom:

> I have heard him say . . . that to fry a faggot, was not more martyr-
> dom than continual obloquy. He was torn asunder as with a mad
> horse, or crushed betwixt the upper & under millstone of con-
> trary reports: that he was a Papist, and that he was a Puritan.[16]

George Herbert was spared this type of persecution, and as we
have seen, gained rather the reputation of a saint. Nicholas Ferrar
himself died in 1638, not living to see the scandalous pamphlet
about his community, entitled *The Arminian Nunnery*, given out at
the doors of Parliament in 1641: nor to witness the sack of Little
Gidding by Roundhead troops in 1646. However, all the correspondence between George Herbert and Little Gidding indicates
that in matters of religious doctrine and practice they were in close
accord. Perhaps Herbert's virtue was to die at an opportune time,
before the propaganda war between Puritan, Laudian and Catholic
had really gained momentum.

Thanks to the efforts of John Ferrar and Isaak Walton, some of
the correspondence between Ferrar and Herbert survives, and is extremely revealing. It was not only letters which went back and forth
between them, but books. The vision of the family at Little Gidding
seems to have included the attempt to supply the lack of devotional
literature available to English Christians in the first part of the seventeenth century. Herbert assisted this publishing enterprise in the
role of translator and reviewer. He translated into English a small
work on fasting, a subject dear to the heart of both Ferrar and Herbert, by the Italian Luigi Cornaro. It was published by Nicholas Ferrar in 1634 as *A treatise of temperance and sobrietie*. Herbert in turn was
asked to approve for publication translations by Nicholas Ferrar of
Ludovicus Carbo's *Introductio ad Catechismum* and *The Hundred and
Ten Considerations* of Juan de Valdés. Ludovicus Carbo was an Italian theologian of the late fifteenth century. His work on catechism,

translated by Ferrar, deals with many issues of concern to Herbert: effective teaching, powerful prayer and the usefulness of human words. Carbo's conclusions are typical of Italian theology in this period, which has been called a *theologica rhetorica*. The preacher is recast as the divine orator: the sword, the image of powerful rhetoric, can be renamed as the sword of the Spirit. In other words, the techniques of classical rhetoric are effective in teaching and communicating the word of God. Along with the faith in human words demonstrated in the treatise, and presumably very attractive to a poet and trained rhetorician such as Herbert, there goes a faith in external ceremonies, and a long section on the importance of the sign of the Cross. It was probably these last elements, rather than the origin of the work in a Catholic context, which led to the book being denied publication by the licensers. The official line of the Elizabethan Church was that signs and ceremonies were 'things indifferent', a compromise position designed to accommodate the Puritans, and allowing freedom of conscience in these matters. The insistence of the *Introductio ad Catechismum* on the necessity of such external observances meant that it was simply too controversial to be published, despite Herbert's approval. Whatever Ferrar and Herbert were concerned with, it was not compromise.

Barnabas Oley notes with disgust the censors' refusal to publish this work, and Herbert's endorsement of it fits well with both Oley and Walton's portrait of Herbert as the model Restoration clergyman, with a concern for liturgy and ceremony. However, the image thus confirmed is undermined by a reading of another translation by Nicholas Ferrar sent to Herbert for approval. *The Hundred and Ten Considerations* was written by Juan de Valdés, or Valdesso as Ferrar and Herbert called him. He had fled from the Spanish Inquisition, who detected both Lutheran and illuminist tendencies in his writings, and settled in Naples in 1530, establishing there a circle of intellectuals and aristocrats which included some of the most influential names in European religious history. His teaching as represented in the *Considerations*, however, was too radical even for the Calvinist hierarchy, who attempted to suppress the work after it was published in French in 1550. Besides holding to an extreme predestinarianism, Valdesso is hostile to all external signs in religion of any kind. As well as liturgy, vestments and ceremonial, he is suspicious even of good works as the accurate sign of a Christian. Christ, he asserts, went out of his way not to appear holy.[17] It is very surprising that 'holy Mr Herbert' should approve a work which derogates traditional concepts of holiness, but Herbert did approve the work for publication, protesting only at Valdesso's attitude to scripture. The

[137]

dominant role which the Holy Spirit plays in the life of the true
believer means to Valdesso that he is led directly by the spirit of
God, and not through the reading of Scripture, which Valdesso
describes as a mere alphabet for Christians. As might be expected,
Herbert objects to this vociferously.

> The H. Scriptures . . . have not only an Elementary use, but a use
> of perfection, neither can they ever be exhausted.[18]

For the teaching of the Scriptures, Valdesso substitutes direct
inspiration of the Holy Spirit. The Christian is prompted by Him in
every situation, as long as his human nature is 'mortified' — one of
Herbert's favourite words. In Valdesso's scheme the Christian's humanity is to be utterly crucified so that God has the dominant role
in his life, and Herbert particularly applauds this 'observation of
Gods Kingdome within us'.[19] However, Valdesso makes a particular target of human knowledge and human words as being characteristic of the natural man and therefore to be 'mortified'.[20] Divine
language is silent, and consists of silent impulses to the human heart.
The most that the human author can do is to be faithful to these
inner impulses, which Valdesso calls 'inspiraziones e movimientos':
authorship becomes a kind of automatic writing, of the kind that the
Puritans assumed for the divine dictation of Scripture. The extrem-
ist element in Valdesso's thought is that he seems to envisage this
kind of inspiration as being accessible to all Christians.

This controversial work was published in 1638 through the
efforts of Nicholas Ferrar: ironically, George Herbert's reputation
had grown so much by this time that the very licensers who had
quibbled over publication of *The Temple* were happy to publish this
much more contentious work on his recommendation. Valdesso's
Considerations were condemned even by Puritans and welcomed
wholeheartedly by illuminist and spiritualist sects such as the Family of Love.[21] It is difficult to believe that Herbert foresaw either reaction. Some critics refuse to believe that Herbert read the work
properly before returning it to Ferrar with his approval. I prefer to
see his reaction to the *Considerations* as an example of an eclecticism
and open-mindedness. His comments, which were published with
the work, show an affirmation of everything that accords with
Scripture and his own experience. Direct inspiration he allows for,
but with this reservation:

> those that have inspirations must still use . . . God's Word: if we
> make another sence of that Text, wee shall overthrow all means,
> save catechizing, and set up Enthusiasmes.[22]

George Herbert, who appreciated the importance of reading and teaching in the Kingdom of God was not likely to be impressed by a theory of inspiration which bypassed all human intermediaries.

In continuing the search for a theory of inspiration which does justice both to Herbert's poetry and his theology I would like to consider Herbert's relationship to another famous figure in European religious history. Savonarola is a name to conjure with: the Dominican monk who ran Florence as a theocracy for a short period in the 1490s before he was tried and tortured by the Inquisition, and finally burnt at the stake. Our twentieth-century image of him is as a religious fanatic, an intolerant book-burner who had bonfires of classical writings in the squares of Florence before he perished in a bonfire of his own. A greater divergence of image between the fanatic dictator-priest and the gentle pastor-poet is hard to imagine, although both Ferrar and Herbert went in for book-burning in their own way. Ferrar made a bonfire of his secular literature at his death, and Herbert on his deathbed asked Ferrar to burn his poetry if he thought it was unedifying. In sixteenth-century England Savonarola was something of a hero. As early as 1500, England's fledgling printing industry was already publishing Savonarola's writings: out of less than 50 documents printed that year, one was a sermon by Savonarola, and it was followed by other works. For once, the English public were able to sample the writings of a European author as early as the peoples of other European countries. The very first prayer book in English, printed in the early 1530s, had appended to it two anonymous tracts, actually penned by Savonarola: meditations on the 51st and 31st Psalms.[23] These two particular works were reprinted several times and must have helped to form the English public's conception of devotional writing. In a Reformation as yet rather short of martyrs, Savonarola was seized on for inclusion in Foxe's *Actes and Monuments*, standard reading for every Elizabethan household from the 1560s onwards, and at the end of a hagiographic account of his life and death the meditation on the 31st Psalm, composed while Savonarola was awaiting execution, is specifically recommended.

Savonarola was one of Herbert's favourite authors, as a letter to Nicholas Ferrar from a mutual acquaintance tells us: 'Sauonorola in Latine he hath of the simplicity of Chr. Religion and is of great esteme with him.'[24] The work in question is *De Simplicitate Christianae Vitae*. Along with Savonarola's neoplatonic cosmology, this book expounds the principle of *simplicitas* which he believes is fundamental to all aspects of the Christian life. Contrary to what one might expect, Savonarola's *simplicitas* is not a harsh asceticism.

Rather, it is a God-given principle which is to be the source of all the Christian's actions, ensuring an integrity and consistency in his words and deeds. In many ways, the creative and harmonizing force which is *simplicitas* corresponds to the Protestant view of the Holy Spirit, and the attraction of such a formulation for the man who loved harmony and truth above all things is obvious. *Simplicitas* is fundamentally concerned with truth: all externals of a Christian's life, religious ceremony, moral behaviour, dress and rhetoric, are to testify accurately to his or her identity, which is internally and divinely determined. Surprisingly, the rich woman is not to wear wool, but silk; plain silk, perhaps, but nevertheless a fabric which testifies to her status. Anything less would constitute the ostentation of a false humility every bit as harmful as the ostentation of pride. This is a rich simplicity, a principle which unites internal reality with its external manifestations, which excludes display but insists on quality.

In the area of rhetoric, all mere flourishes must be excluded. Again, the standard is of accurate signification: the words must point to the inner, powerful truth they express. Herbert himself expressed this formulation of true rhetoric in one of the memorial poems to his mother, where he praises her use of language. He describes the relationship of rhetoric to meaning in terms of the shell and the kernel, an image very common in the Renaissance.

> Beautiful the shell, most beautiful the kernel,
> Thought and word exactly in accord.

Savonarola himself wrote poetry, and in his *Apologeticus de ratione poeticae artis*, which in many ways is an attack upon contemporary poetics, he argues for a poetry of things, not words, where it is the message of the poem which is all-important. The resonance of all this with the poet who wrote in the first *Jordan* poem 'Is there in truth no beautie?' is clear. The two poems entitled *Jordan* are Herbert's attempt to baptize poetry into the service of Christ, and the second articulates the suspicion, shared by both Savonarola and Valdesso, that language itself is a manifestation of the fallen humanity of the poet:

> When first my lines of heav'nly joyes made mention,
> Such was their lustre, they did so excell,
> That I sought out quaint words, and trim invention;
> My thoughts began to burnish, sprout, and swell,
> Curling with metaphors a plain intention,
> Decking the sense, as if it were to sell.

[140]

As flames do work and winde, when they ascend,
    So did I weave my self into the sense.

The solution that 'a friend', probably a divine friend, offers to Herbert at the end of the poem is one that would be acceptable to both Valdesso and Savonarola:

There is in love a sweetness readie penn'd:
    Copie out onely that, and save expense.

This is God's love, manifested both externally in the Scriptures and internally in the heart, and 'copying' is the accurate signification demanded by Savonarola. In many ways, to 'copy' rather than 'invent' spells death for the poet, certainly for one wanting to use the full resources of classical rhetoric to describe the greatness of God: 'Nothing could seem too rich to clothe the sun.' Mortification, however, is exactly what both Herbert and Valdesso require. The baptism in Jordan is a baptism into the death of Christ: the poetic gift too must be purified.

Throughout *De Simplicitate* Savonarola is keen to distinguish the spiritual sense of *simplicitas* from the more conventional uses of the word 'simplicity', and it is here, I think, that his distinctions are useful for Herbert's poetry. 'Simple' is a word that has often been used in connection with *The Temple*, but a cursory examination of the techniques and strategies employed there will show that the poetry is anything but 'simple' in the crude sense. Savonarola isolates four different states of *simplicitas*, from the 'simpleness' of mere stupidity through to the unity in complexity which sustains the universe and is the Christian principle of *simplicitas*. I hope that I have demonstrated that Herbert's 'simplicity' is of that nature. He did not suddenly withdraw from the controversies of public life, but throughout his life seems to have engaged with the complexity of the issues, both spiritual and rhetorical, which were vital in his period. He seems to have evolved a standard based on the twin touchstones of Scripture and his own experience of God, and to have used this to judge his own reading, writing and lifestyle.

If Herbert's manner of composition in *The Temple* is an inspired poetics, the form of inspiration is rather subtle. He does sometimes appear to attribute his poetry to divine agency, for instance in the Dedication:

Lord, my first fruits present themselves to thee;
Yet not mine neither: for from thee they came,
And must return.

[141]

Elsewhere he acknowledges that it is only through the grace of God that he can write at all. However, there is one of Herbert's lyrics that tries to establish the correct formula for the subtle mix of divine word and human words that is the Christian poet's — and preacher's — continual aim. The poem *The Windows*, a meditation on such stained-glass windows, perhaps, as illuminate Keble Chapel, poses the problem in the first two lines. How is the preacher-poet to let the light of revelation into the temple, which is both the church of God and the human heart?

> Lord, how can man preach thy eternall word?
> He is a brittle crazie glass.

The most immediate and obvious answer to this question is that the glass needs to be clear, whole and transparent so as to let the maximum amount of light through. However, Herbert rejects transparency of medium, and with it Valdesso's automatic writing, or the fundamentalist's dictation theory. Even if the human being were to be an absolutely clear channel for the revelation of God, the light coming through would be 'watrish, bleak and thin'. The alternative is to allow the light to shine through a stained-glass window, which for Herbert is a metaphor for the human being on whom God has worked to produce a unique story with its own colours.

> But when thou dost anneal in glasse thy storie,
> Making thy life to shine within
> The holy Preachers; then the light and glorie
> More rev'rend grows, & more doth win.

The successful, God-given formula is a combination of divine inspiration and human words: Scriptural doctrine worked out in a human life.

> Doctrine and life, colours and light, in one
> When they combine and mingle, bring
> A strong regard and awe.

Herbert's reference to 'colours' is a pun on rhetorical 'colours', which were the resources of classical rhetoric in which he was so well versed. The entire God-given identity of the Christian poet, including his holy life and his skill with words, is animated and activated by the inspiration of the Holy Spirit. The true Christian poet represents the place where that 'mingling' of divine and human can happen.

Herbert's achievement is to combine in one lifespan, and in one small volume of poetry, integrity in complexity, austerity and richness, life out of death, a rhetoric not divorced from significance, a simplicity not without learning. It is no wonder that *The Temple* was and continues to be a major text in the curio English religious tradition.

NOTES

1   *The Church Militant*, lines 235–6 in Hutchinson, ed., *The Works of George Herbert* (Oxford, 1941), p. 196.

2   From Walton's *Lives*, quoted in Hutchinson, op. cit., p. 547.

3   I am indebted to Professor Helen Wilcox who has kindly granted me permission to quote from her 1984 Oxford D. Phil thesis, *'Something Understood': The Reputation and Influence of George Herbert to 1715*. I have drawn freely from chapters III and V of this thesis for the argument and the quotations used in the first part of this chapter.

4   Michael C. Schoenfeldt, *Prayer and Power: George Herbert and Renaissance Courtship* (Chicago and London, 1991), p. 56.

5   Oliver Lawson Dick, ed., *Aubrey's Brief Lives* (Penguin, London, 1987), p. 218.

6   Hutchinson, op. cit., p. xxxviii.

7   George Herbert Palmer, *The English Works of George Herbert*, (London, 1905).

8   Barnabas Oley, *A Prefatory View of the Life and Virtues of the Authour and Excellencies of This Book*, p. N2 r. attached to George Herbert, *A Priest to the Temple* (London, 1671).

9   See *The Publisher to the Christian Reader*, prefaced to Oley's edition of *A Priest to the Temple* (1671).

10   See David Novarr, *The Making of Walton's 'Lives'* (Ithaca, 1958) for an account of the way Walton's ecclesiastical and political concerns shaped his approach to biography.

11   Hutchinson, op. cit., p. 564.

12   See the letter from George to Henry Herbert of 21 March 1631/32 in Hutchinson, op. cit., p. 377.

13   A. M. Williams, ed., *Conversations at Little Gidding* (Cambridge, 1970), p. lvii.

14   Robert van de Weyer, 'Nicholas Ferrar and Little Gidding: A Reappraisal' in R. Ollard, P. Tudor-Craig, eds., *For Veronica Wedgwood These Studies in Seventeenth Century History* (Glasgow, 1986), p. 171.

15   Samuel Peckard, *Memoirs of the Life of Mr. Nicholas Ferrar* (Cambridge, 1790), p. 235.

16   Barnabas Oley, op. cit., p. M2 r.

17   See Consideration 89 in Juan de Valdés, *The Hundred and Ten Considerations of Signior Iohn Valdesso. Written In Spanish, Brought out of Italy by Vergerius, and first set forth in Italian at Basil by Coelius Secundus Curio, Anno 1550. And now*

translated out of the Italian Copy into English, with notes. Oxford, printed by Leonard Lichfield, Printer to the Vniversity, 1638 tr. Nicholas Ferrar, (Oxford, 1638).

[18] Hutchison, op. cit., p. 309.

[19] ibid., p. 305.

[20] See Juan de Valdés, *The Hundred and Ten Considerations*, Consideration 88.

[21] See Samuel Rutherford, *A Survey of the Spiritual Antichrist, Opening the Secrets of Familisme and Antinomianisme in the Antichristian Doctrine of John Saltmarsh, and Will. Del, the Present Preachers of the Army now in England, and of Robert Town; Tob. Crisp, H. Denne, Eaton, and others. In Two Parts.* (Andrew Crooke, London, 1648), p. 164.

[22] Hutchinson, op. cit., p. 310.

[23] See the psalm-meditations appended to *A Prymer in Englyshe, with certayn prayers and godly meditations, very necessary for all people that understonde not the Latyne tongue* (London, 1534).

[24] Blackstone, ed., *The Ferrar Papers*, (Cambridge, 1938), p. 268.

A. M. ALLCHIN

Lancelot Andrewes

IN 1608, IN A TRACT later published under the title 'A Brief View of
the Church of England', Sir John Harington gave a remarkable
judgement on the abilities of Lancelot Andrewes, then Bishop of
Chichester and already renowned for the quality of his learning; 'to
conclude; I persuade myself, that whensoever it shall please God to
give the king means, with the consent of his confederate princes, to
make that great peace which his blessed word, *beati pacifici* seemeth
to promise, — I mean the ending of this great schism in the Church
of God, procured as much by ambition as superstition — this
reverend prelate will be found one of the ablest not of England
only, but of Europe to set the course for composing the
controversies . . .'[1]

It is a striking tribute to a man who had only been a bishop for
three years and was only now approaching the height of his renown
as a preacher at the court of King James I. It situates Andrewes at
once in a European and ecumenical context and it is in that way that
I shall look at him in this chapter. As we shall see Andrewes was in
many ways a man of his own time and place, firmly rooted in the
England of Elizabeth and James I. He lived through the defeat of the
Spanish Armada and the foiling of the Gunpowder Plot, and experienced both as divine interventions. So far as we know he never
travelled across the Channel to the continent of Europe. But there
was nothing narrowly parochial about his intentions and his aims.
His view of the Church was consistently catholic and inclusive, and
the Church itself he always saw as set within the context of the

[145]

whole human family. Indeed, in his *Preces Privatae* his concern goes out to the whole creation.

I

IN THIS CHAPTER I shall look at Andrewes as a man of prayer and a man of theology. With him those two things go closely together. I shall base myself not on his controversial writings, which seem to me to have a strictly limited interest, but on his sermons and prayers. It is there, as Nicholas Lossky maintains in his recent study, that the heart of Andrewes' thinking is to be found.[2]

Andrewes was born in 1555 during the reign of Mary Tudor. He was born and brought up in London. He came from a solid, indeed wealthy merchant family which had its roots in Suffolk. He attended the University of Cambridge and had a brilliant academic career becoming first a Fellow and then Master of Pembroke College. He was Bishop successively of Chichester, Ely, and Winchester, dying early in the reign of Charles I in 1626. His life was lived within an area which had London at its centre, Cambridge to its northeast, Winchester to its southwest. Already as a young man he combined the role of scholar and teacher in Cambridge with that of preacher and pastor in London. By the 1590s he was a prebendary of St Paul's and incumbent of St Giles' Cripplegate. A little before the death of Queen Elizabeth he was appointed Dean of Westminster, so that it was he who was involved with the arrangements for the coronation of King James I, an occasion which brought him into close personal contact with the King. James had a very high estimation both of his learning and his personal integrity. He was one of the few persons of whom the King stood somewhat in awe. So it was that in the next quarter of a century Andrewes came to occupy a special position at the centre of English life, a position which was expressed above all in his sermons preached before the royal court, not only at the great festivals of Christmas, Easter and Whitsun, but also at the two commemorations of events in the life of the King which were solemnly observed each year. Year by year it was Andrewes who mounted the pulpit on these occasions. Hence comes the corpus of the 96 sermons which form the centre and core of his work.

Thus Andrewes was a man constantly in the public eye at the court of King James. Judgements about the effectiveness of his interventions in the political life of his time have varied however. His latest biographer, Paul Welsby, is severely critical of the part Andrewes played in the Essex divorce case, judging that he yielded far too much to the pressures of the King in this tangled, unhappy matter. Others have assessed the question differently, giving a more favourable interpretation of Andrewes' actions, but no one can maintain that he was a great power in political affairs. As a diocesan bishop he seems to have been a thorough and conscientious administrator. He was liberal in his almsgiving. All office in the Church he regarded as a form of deaconing, 'on foot and through the dust, for so is the nature of the word', he declares. But it is significant that what was remembered of him was his skill as a confessor, as a counsellor in cases of conscience. He was a man with a profound knowledge of the meaning of repentance. Again there was the special quality of devotion which marked the services in his private chapel at Ely House; 'the souls of many, that *obiter* came thither in time of divine service, were very much elevated . . . Yea, some that had been there were so taken with it that they desired to end their days in the Bishop of Ely's chapel.'[3] Andrewes was a man of a scholarly contemplative cast of mind more than a man of action. It is the inward dimension of his life which will primarily claim our attention, for it is in this respect that he made his most lasting contribution to the English religious tradition and to the development of the genius of Anglicanism. It is here that he has most to give us four centuries after his own time.

The sermons preached before the court do not exhaust the content of Andrewes' preaching. There are other lesser collections extant, amongst them one which was not published until 1657, thirty years after the preacher's death.[4] This collection, published with the title *Apospasmatia Sacra*, was not included in the collected edition of Andrewes' works made in the middle of the nineteenth century in the Library of Anglo-Catholic Theology. For this reason it has been very little studied. These sermons were preached at St Giles' Cripplegate and St Paul's Cathedral in the last years of the sixteenth century. They make no pretence to be directly from Andrewes' own hand; the preface tells us that the text was reconstructed from notes made by those who were present at the sermons. Certainly their style is less highly wrought than in the case of the great sermons, and the patristic quotations are less numerous. But the substance of the doctrine is identical and it is interesting to see how positions characteristic of Andrewes' later teaching are here advanced in the last years of the sixteenth century and presented to a parochial congregation. I shall make some use of these sermons in this chapter since I can see no reason to doubt their substantial authenticity, and I am delighted to find that this was also Brightman's judgement of them.

Andrewes is not usually autobiographical in his preaching, but there are times when you can see a clear reflection of the society he lived in and the family from which he came in his handling of his text. As Nicholas Lossky remarks, he has a frequent tendency to make use of commercial metaphors and analogies. One particular passage in the St Giles' sermons seems to reflect the concerns of his London congregation in a striking way. In it he reflects on the situation of an island people, a people who need to be in constant traffic of exchange with others. He is preaching on the Genesis story of creation and to illustrate the nature of the sea he quotes the verse of Psalm 104 which says:

> There go the ships . . . that is God made it [the sea] a fit and good place for navigation, *non ad habitandum, sed ad navigandum et natandum,* by which passage of merchandise and sea-fairing men, we disburden ourselves of those superfluous commodities which our land affords and get thereby by exchange the commodities of other countries which we want . . . and by reason of this goodnesse and benefit of waters, God hath caused it, that the harvest of the seas and the treasures of the sands should be as great and greater than the harvest of the land, and that the wealth of merchants should goe beyond the wealth and treasure of the husbandmen. [Essay 23:3]

These words are simply a commentary on the growing wealth of the merchant class in this period in which his family was participating. Andrewes goes on,

> and this goodnesse of the seas especially concerneth us which are islanders, we best know it and feel here the singular and special goodnesse of the waters, and say as God doth, that we see that they are good; for were it not for this, we should be imprisoned in this little island and be without the knowledge of other countries, also we should cloyed with our commodities and be destitute of many others, which we want; but that which is most, we should have been without the knowledge of God's holy word; for how could that have come hither or how could we have gone beyond the seas for it, had it not been for the sea wherein goe the ships?[5]

To this consideration of the value of the sea for international trade and the exchange of knowledge, Andrewes adds another of the virtues which it has for an island people. In a passage which has some similarity to one of Shakespeare's most famous speeches, he says:

[148]

Another benefit of good which we receive by them [Nahum 3:14] is that they are made to us a ditch, fortresse, wall, or bulwark of strength of defense to the land. For in islands we are entrenched, as it were, round about with sands, with rocks, with ships and seas.[6]

It is striking that in this passage the sea is thought of only in defensive terms and not as a means whereby the islanders may set out on voyages of conquest. The building up of a British Empire, an aim which was being so assiduously canvassed by Dr John Dee and others at this time, does not seem to enter into the vision of Lancelot Andrewes. What we find is an appreciation of the sea as a medium linking one country with another, and allowing for the commerce of goods and ideas. This fits well with one of the traits for which Andrewes was best known by his contemporaries, his amazing knowledge of languages, ancient and modern. Thomas Fuller remarks, 'some conceive he might . . . have served as an Interpreter General at the confusion of tongues'.[7] Andrewes had gained this knowledge at least in part through his father's trading contacts. When coming home on vacation from Cambridge he would ask his father to find a visiting merchant or agent from whom he might learn a new language so that he should not be idle while at home. We see again how Andrewes' reputation even in his lifetime was that of an interpreter. 'He ought to have been at the Tower of Babel, he could have put them right.' Both as a linguist and as a theologian men thought of him as a go-between, one who might bring about the resolution of controversies.

In this connection we can hardly fail to mention his gift of friendship, a gift which brought him into personal contact with some of the most renowned scholars and thinkers of his day: Isaac Casaubon, the great French patristic scholar who retired to England in 1610 after the assassination of Henri IV, Francis Bacon at home, and in Andrewes' earlier days, Richard Hooker. Amongst his younger contemporaries he had a very special regard for the scholarship and theological judgement of George Herbert.

When we turn to the *Preces Privatæ*, those extraordinary pages which reveal to us Andrewes in his life of inner devotion, we begin to see more of how this might be. It is not only that he himself used them in Latin and Greek, and occasionally in Hebrew — the English editions are all translations — it is also that in his constant prayers his interest and concern go out to the whole creation, to the whole of humanity and in particular to the whole Church of God. Let us take as an example the prayers of intercession which occur on Mondays. 'Let us beseech the Lord for the whole creation; a supply of seasons, healthful, fruitful, peaceful.'[8] He goes on to pray for the whole human race, non-Christian as well as Christian, the departed as well as the living. And then again,

> For the Church Catholic, its confirmation and increase; Eastern, its deliverance and union; Western, its readjustment and pacification; British, the restoration of the things that are wanting, the strengthening of the things which remain.[9]

It is an all-inclusive petition yet it is precise and specific. He prays first for the whole Catholic Church, then for the Churches of the East, with which he can have had little direct contact, but which he knew not only through his reading but also through the merchants who travelled to Muscovy and the Levant. He prays for its deliverance from the oppression of the Turk, and also for its union, within itself and we may suppose with the Churches of the West. For those Western Churches he prays both for peace and readjustment. He looks here not only to Rome or only to the Reformation, but emphatically to both, both parts of one Western Church, with both of which, Rome and Geneva, he found himself at times in conflict. Then he comes nearer home, to the British Church, no longer England alone but England and Scotland united in the person of the King; he prays for the restoration of what is lacking and the strengthening of what remains. There is no kind of English or Anglican triumphalism here. His own Church is no less in need of the divine grace, which always heals what is wounded and makes up what is lacking, than any other. All the Churches of Christ stand in constant need of God's life-giving pardon and peace. And this petition is not an isolated one. It recurs day by day with slight variations; for the whole Church, Eastern, Western, our own.

Who is this man who prays so assiduously for the whole Catholic Church, for its union and increase? He is in the first place a man who is deeply concerned for the integrity of the Church of God not only in his own time, but through all the centuries of its existence. Even the most rapid reading of his sermons shows him to be a man of prodigious and highly organized learning. He knows the scriptures of the Old and New Testament and has pondered them at length in Hebrew and in Greek. He knows the Fathers of the Church, no less the Fathers of the Latin West than the Fathers of the Greek East. He is not unacquainted with the theologians of the Middle Ages, nor with those of more recent times, though they do not feature frequently in his preaching. All this knowledge is not

[150]

something external to him; he has made it his own to a quite remarkable degree. As Brightman remarks,

> His extraordinarily minute knowledge of the holy scriptures is plain to everybody . . . His wealth of reminiscence is such, and is so wrought into the texture of his mind, that he instinctively uses it to express anything he has to say. To one to whom knowledge is so large an element in life and is itself so living a thing; whose learning is so assimilated as to be identified with his spontaneous self, and has become as available as language itself, originality and reminiscence become in a measure identical; the new can be expressed by a combination of older elements.[10]

This is a very remarkable view of the nature of knowledge. Knowledge is not seen simply as something we possess and control, a certain quantity of information and expertise; it is so living a thing, so large an element in our life that it becomes part of ourselves. We know with the whole of ourselves, become people who are caught up into what we know and are changed by it. In such an understanding of the life of the mind, the academic study of theology is constantly verging on what the Middle Ages called *lectio divina*, and *lectio divina* itself is verging on prayer and adoration.

If we ask what it was that Andrewes was doing in those five hours which he reserved for study between seven and noon each day, we may be confident that it was something of this. It is evident that such a man in so immersing himself in tradition is not simply turning towards the past. He enters into its study not with the curiosity of an antiquarian but with the passionate interest of one who senses its contemporary significance. He may be, as Andrewes was, widely read in the current thought of his own time. As a personal friend of Francis Bacon, Andrewes was interested in the phenomena of nature no less than in the events of history. Such a man enters into the tradition and lives in it in such a way that the tradition itself enters into him and becomes living in him. Such a man may live the original vision which lies at the root of a tradition in such a way as to draw new life from it and to make it accessible and available to his contemporaries and successors. In him reminiscence and originality have become identical. He speaks from tradition; tradition speaks through him.

It was, I believe, this quality in Lancelot Andrewes which especially attracted T. S. Eliot to him, and made Andrewes of such importance in Eliot's own development both as a writer and as a man. It is true that he devotes only one quite brief essay to the work of

Lancelot Andrewes. But it is an essay which has a crucial place in Eliot's own story. It gives its title to the little book in which in 1928 he announced his adherence to the catholic Christian faith as professed by the Church of England. The encounter with Lancelot Andrewes had been of decisive importance in bringing him to the point of seeking baptism in the name of the Holy Trinity. For Eliot it was above all the work of Richard Hooker and Lancelot Andrewes which made the post-Reformation Church of England worthy of belief. He saw them as men of tradition, speaking 'with the old authority and the new culture', men of a tradition which was not uncriticized or impervious to criticism — they lived on this side of the Renaissance and the Reformation — but one in which the critical comment had not in the end obscured the original affirmation.[11]

Andrewes has not often received the attention which he demands and deserves in the twentieth century. Eliot was one who gave it to him. Here a great poet in verse pays tribute to a great poet in prose. Eliot begins with the sheer intellectual virtuosity of Andrewes' preaching.

> Reading Andrewes on such a theme [as the incarnation] is like listening to a great Hellenist expounding a text of the 'Posterior Analytics'; altering the punctuation, inserting or removing a comma or a semicolon to make an obscure passage suddenly luminous, dwelling on a single word, comparing its use in its nearer and in its most remote contexts, purifying a disturbed or cryptic lecture note into lucid profundity. To persons whose minds are habituated to feed on the vague jargon of our time, when we have a vocabulary for everything and exact ideas about nothing . . . Andrewes may seem pedantic and verbal. It is only when we have saturated ourselves with his prose, followed the movement of his thought, that we find his examination of words terminating in an ecstasy of assent. Andrewes takes a word and derives the world from it; squeezing and squeezing the word until it yields a full juice of meaning which we would never have supposed any word to possess.[12]

Certainly there can be few intellectual pleasures greater, few intellectual exercises more satisfying than that of listening to a man or woman who has given a significant part of their life to the study of one outstanding author or some one great work of the past, expounding the detail of that work, showing its coherence and its complexity, its spontaneity and its consistency, its unity in multiplicity, and multiplicity in unity. So it is with the preaching of Lancelot Andrewes.

> In this extraordinary prose which appears to repeat, to stand still, but is nevertheless proceeding in the most deliberate and orderly manner, there are often flashing phrases which never desert the memory. In an age of adventure and experiment in language, Andrewes is one of the most resourceful of authors, in his devices for seizing the attention and impressing the memory. Phrases such as 'Christ is no wild-cat. Why talk ye of twelve days?' or 'the Word within a word unable to speak a word' do not desert us, nor do the sentences in which before extracting all the spiritual meaning of a text, Andrewes forces a concrete presence on us.
>
> Of the wise men come from the East: 'It was no Summer progress. A cold coming they had of it at this time of the year, just the worst time of the year to take a journey, and especially a long journey. The ways deep, the weather sharp, the days short, the sun farthest off, *in solstitio brumali*, the very dead of Winter.' Of the Word made flesh, again, 'I add yet further; what flesh? The flesh of an infant. What *Verbum infans*, the Word an infant? The Word, and not able to speak a word. How evil agreeth this! This He put up. How born, how entertained? In a stately palace, a cradle of ivory, robes of estate? No: but a stable for His palace, a manger for His cradle, poor clouts for His array.'[13]

But here there is more than intellectual delight and intellectual appreciation, however precious these may be. In the earlier passage Eliot had spoken of Andrewes' rhetoric as leading us to an ecstasy of assent. And now he speaks with great lucidity of the meaning of that assent.

> When Andrewes begins his sermon, from beginning to end you are sure that he is wholly in his subject, unaware of anything else, that his emotion grows as he penetrates more deeply into his subject, that he is finally 'alone with the Alone', with the mystery which he is seeking to grasp more and more firmly. One is reminded of the words of Arnold about the preaching of Newman. Andrewes' emotion is purely contemplative; it is not personal, it is wholly evoked by the subject of contemplation to which it is adequate; his emotion is wholly contained in and explained by its object.[14]

Here Eliot speaks of a fusion of thought, precise analytical

[153]

thought, with an eventually overwhelming depth of emotion, a fusion in which mind and imagination, thinking and feeling become one, in which we are carried beyond ourselves into the object which we are considering, in this case nothing less than the nature of the triune God. This is a truly ecstatic movement of the heart and mind — a movement of assent which is also a movement of ascent. This movement is at the core and centre of Andrewes' thinking and praying. It is this which makes it appropriate to speak of his work in terms of a mystical theology, a theology of the communion and union of divine and human, 'not by conversion of the Godhead into flesh, but by taking the manhood into God'.

If we are to take the full force of such affirmations we shall need to turn from Eliot to the one writer from our own century who has fully devoted himself to the work of Lancelot Andrewes, the Russian Orthodox scholar, Nicolas Lossky. Here for the first time we have a study of a major representative of the Anglican tradition from the pen of an Eastern Christian scholar. From the heart of the tradition which comes from Constantinople to the Slavonic lands, from a writer who comes from a distinguished Russian academic family, we have a detailed penetrating study which examines and in the end embraces the teaching of the merchant's son from Barking, the scholar at Merchant Taylors' School in London.

Lossky's study of Lancelot Andrewes was first published in Paris in 1986; the English translation was published in Oxford in 1991. It is primarily a theological work. Those who wish to see something of its literary quality should turn to the original and ponder the excellence of the French translation of Andrewes' dense and idiosyncratic prose. It is a work which, whether we look at it from a literary or a theological viewpoint, is evidently not one which has been taken in hand unadvisedly or lightly. It has in it a weight of knowledge and a sureness of judgement which do justice to the matter in hand. For Lossky there can be no question but that Andrewes is an authentic witness to the apostolic faith of the one Catholic Apostolic Church, one who in his own place in time is a Father of the Church. I quote,

> For Andrewes, an authentic witness of the apostolic faith is not simply someone who is content to think more or less correctly. It is someone who, like him, has made deeply his own the experience of the Church. It is someone for whom theology is not a system of thought, an intellectual construction, but a progress in the experience of the mystery, the way of union with God in the communion of the Church . . . Theology then is for the service

of the entire man on his way towards union with the personal God, the way of deification. It is this most profound experience of the Church that the theologian expresses in the Church and for the Church.[15]

Such an evaluation of a teacher of the English Church by a scholar of the Russian Church is not only an unprecedented event but a highly creative one. It creates a new bond of mutual recognition and communion between two parts of the one Church which have been too long estranged from one another. It does not of itself, of course, bring that estrangement to an end but it does mitigate its harshness to a remarkable extent.

II

WE HAVE BEEN looking at the work of Lancelot Andrewes and the impact it has had on two writers of our own century, one whose origin was American, the other whose family background was Russian. We have seen that the heart of the teaching of Andrewes is to be found in the teaching that human persons are made for union with the divine, in the faith that God became man in order that man might become God. The patristic doctrine of deification, which many think to be absent from Western Christianity, is seen to be vital to one of the greatest representatives of the Anglican tradition. In what remains of this chapter I want to examine this theology again briefly and to let Andrewes speak in his own terms. I intend to do this not by quoting from the great and already well-known sermons, nor yet from the *Preces Privatæ*, but from the 'posthumous and orphan' lectures given at St Giles' and at St Paul's in the last years of the sixteenth century. In them Andrewes expresses many of the essential positions which he was to elaborate in greater detail in the sermons of the next twenty-five years. We shall be hearing his voice as it is relayed to us by his hearers, hearers who I believe have nearly always captured his meaning even if at times they have lost something of his style.

Let us come directly to the heart of the matter, to the teaching about our call to become partakers of the divine nature. I quote from a sermon on the text in the second epistle of St Peter where alone in the New Testament this precise formula is used.

As Christ took part of our nature, so he makes us partakers of his. It is the Christian only that believes this; and therefore he is capable of this so pretious promise; for albeit Christ were man, yet it pleased God, that the fullnesse of the Godhead should dwell in him bodily [Col 2:9], and as he is in us by his humanity, so we are in him in respect of his divinity. God partakes with Christ because of his divine nature, and man partakes in Christ inasmuch as he hath assumed our humane nature. He is partaker of our humane nature for he is flesh of our flesh and bone of our bone [Eph 5], and we by his Spirit are partakers of his divine nature; for as St. Paul saith, 'he that cleaveth to the Lord is one Spirit [I Cor 6]': 'hereby we know that we dwell in him, and he in us, by the Spirit which he hath given us [I John 4:13]'.[16]

It is very typical of Andrewes that he supports his teaching out of the two great mystical theologians of the New Testament, St Paul and St John. He wants to show that this doctrine is firmly rooted in Scripture.

But how do we become partakers of this nature? For Andrewes there are two ways, first by our participation in the sacraments, secondly by our active growth into the life of grace and virtue. To take the sacraments first,

By regeneration in baptism, for except ye be born again of water and of the Holy Ghost . . . and by eating and drinking in the sacrament: in which respect the apostle saith that we must *bibere Spiritum* [I Cor 12:13]. In this life we must seek for God's grace and glory; and he hath promised to give both [Ps 84] and then we shall *intrare in gaudium domini* [Mt 25]; and we shall be alwaies with him [I Thess 4]; and see him as he is [I Jn 3], that is, be partakers of the divine nature; and which goes beyond all, he shall not be glory in one and joy in another and immortality in a third, but he shall be *omnia in omnibus* [I Cor 15:28].[17]

The promise is for all. There is nothing esoteric or elitist in the great and precious promises of the Gospel. They are offered to all with undistinguishing regard.

Andrewes insists much in his sermons on the importance of the sacraments. The Fathers, he says, teach us that they are necessary for us, 'in regard of ourselves, which consist of body and soul, and therefore have need of bodily and ghostly meanes', but also in regard of Christ himself.

As in the hypostasis of the sun [sic] there is both the humane and divine nature, so the sacrament is of an heavenly and earthly

nature. As he hath taken our body to himself, so he honoureth bodily things, that by them we should have our sins taken away . . .[18]

It is evident in these sermons no less than in those of the subsequent decades, that Andrewes' knowledge of the liturgies of the
early Church, and particularly the Eastern liturgies, had a decisive
influence on his understanding of the nature of Christian life and
worship. So in a sermon where he speaks of the prophet Isaiah's vision of the divine glory and of the seraph who comes to touch the
prophet's lips with a live coal from the altar, he says,

> In the liturgy of the ancient Church, these words are found ap-
> plyed to the Blessed Sacrament of Christ's body and blood; for it
> is reported by Basill, that at the celebration thereof, after the
> sacrament was ministered to the people, the priest stood up and
> said as the seraphim doth here, 'behold this hath touched your
> lips, your iniquities shall be taken away, and your sins purged'.
> The whole fruit of religion is 'the taking away of sin [Is 27:9]', and
> the special way to take it away is the religious use of this sacra-
> ment; which as Christ saith is nothing else 'but a seal and signe of
> his blood that was shed for many for the remission of sins [Mt
> 26:28]' . . .[19]

It is noteworthy that here as in other places, Andrewes insists
on our partaking of the blood of Christ through drinking from the
chalice. This was of course an issue of burning controversy in this
period between Rome and the churches of the Reformation. But
his concern in the sermons is much more than controversial. He
seeks to express the fullness of the eucharistic mystery and particularly to underline the role of the Holy Spirit in the celebration of the
sacrament. Participation in the Eucharist does not only make us
members of the body of Christ, it makes us sharers in the one Spirit.
As Lossky points out, all prayer for Andrewes has a eucharistic
character.

> Expounding the verse of the psalm — 'I will receive the cup of
> salvation and call on the name of the Lord [Ps 116:12]' — he
> demonstrates that in this prayer *par excellence* the voice of the com-
> municant is mingled with and sustained by the voice of the blood
> shed by Christ for the remission of sins, thus for our salvation. In
> it, there is encounter, communion, and exchange; the pouring
> out of the Spirit of God on all flesh, and, through the eucharist,

the giving of thanks, the pouring out, on our part, of gratitude to God for the sending of the Spirit.[20]

But while Andrewes underlines the importance of the sacraments as ways by which we may be incorporated into Christ, he also stresses the importance of the virtues as ways by which we can partake in him. It is not one virtue alone, no not faith itself, which can build us up into the life of God. It requires all of them together, beginning with faith, concluding with love, and bringing in all the intermediary stages. 'The apostle's mind is to show that the life of the Christian is no single thing but a Quire or Dance, and the beginning of the train is faith.' But faith alone is not enough.

> It must not be *totum integrale*, or alpha and omega, but like a quire, wherein are diverse parts, faith is but a part, and the eighth part of Christianity. This company is not added *ad ornatum*, but for necessity; therefore he exhorts, give all diligence, and he that hath not these is blind.[21]

So in the same sermon Andrewes says,

> As they that are partakers of the divine nature are a body compact of many joynts and sinnews; so the divine Spirit is not one alone, but as the ancient fathers define, the eleventh verse of Isaiah 7 and the fourth chapter of the Apocalypse,

a reference to the seven lamps before the throne of God which are the seven spirits of God. So the Spirit is manifold in his gifts and activities and even in his being. But Andrewes affirms:

> This is not *promiscue*, confusedly; but orderly as in a quire, one begins, another follows; this multitude of virtues is *acies ordinata* [Cant 6], like the marching of soldiers; for it comes from God, who is the God of order and not of confusion . . . All at once do not break out, but there is a successive bringing in, one after the other.[22]

The gifts of God given to us in the sacraments are then many and varied, and they call on us to respond actively and to co-operate in a variety of ways with the grace which is given. Not surprisingly, Andrewes uses images of growth to express this gradual progress into the life of God, images which he applies to the sacramental gift itself and to our subsequent life of obedience to the divine commands.

> In this sacrament the tree of the life of grace is sown in us, that is a measure of grace wrought in our hearts by the power of God's Spirit, by which we shall attain to eat of that tree which shall convey unto us the life of glory. As there are two trees of life, so we must have a double paradise: we must have liberty to be of the paradise on earth, that is the Church Militant, which is called *hortus conclusus* [Cant 2] before we can be received into the heavenly paradise, that is, the Church Triumphant. The kernel of grace is planted in us by the participation of the body and blood of Christ; of which kernel cometh a tree, which bringeth forth the fruits of holiness and righteousness, which God will in due time reward with the crown of life and glory in the world to come.[23]

If on the one side Andrewes is keen to avoid any sort of mechanical attitude towards the use of the sacraments, or any setting them apart from the other means of grace, on the other side he insists time and again on their centrality and necessity. We may come to Christ in many ways, but this way is at the centre of them all.

> There are diverse sorts of coming: first, we are said to come to Christ in baptism [Mk 10] . . . Secondly in prayer, for as Augustine saith, *precibus non passibus itur ad Deum*. Thirdly in the hearing of the word. Fourthly by repentance . . . but Christ receiveth none of these but that we come to him as he is *panis vitæ*; when we come to Christ as he offers himself in the sacrament to be the lively food of our souls; when we come to the same and do it in remembrance of his death . . .[24]

It would take us far beyond the scope of this chapter to consider in detail the long sequence of sermons on the first four chapters of Genesis which make up a large part of this collection. One point, however, demands attention, and that concerns Andrewes' interpretation of the name 'Eve', and growing from it his attitude towards women. Nicolas Lossky remarks on the emphasis which Andrewes gives to the role of the women at the sepulchre on the morning of the Resurrection. Here in the story of creation he makes much of the name 'Eve', life, and of the fact that it is given to woman after the Fall. He understands it as involving a promise not only of the continuation of physical life in this world, but also as a pointer to eternal life in the world to come.

[159]

> The mystery of this name compared with the former sentence is great; she is called here *Hevah*, she hath no name of dejection and despair but of life and comfort: hereby is to be gathered that notwithstanding the sin committed and the sentence pronounced, yet there was in Adam some matter of hope . . .[25]

This name Andrewes sees as a token of God's love for his fallen children.

> So out of this name there is a work of charity to comfort us and Eve herself, that was dejected and miserably plunged in sorrow . . . making her by her new name partaker of God's love and charity; this charity is not conteined in Eve alone, but continued in her posteritie unto the end of the world . . .[26]

In these passages on the role of Eve it is striking that there is no use made of the comparison and contrast between Eve and Mary which was so loved by the Fathers. It is true of Andrewes' preaching as a whole that he does not say much about the mother of Christ, but what he says about her always carries weight. So in these sermons he makes an instructive comparison between Hannah's song of thanksgiving and Mary's Magnificat, and just as he sees God's promise to Eve as extended to all her descendants, so he sees Mary as speaking on behalf of all creation.

> Hannah prayed alone; but as for Mary's prayer it was accompanied by the desire and prayer of all creatures, as both prophets and apostles do show . . . The virgin's key of prayer, accompanied with the prayer of all God's people in all ages, opened the heaven of heavens, so as they *dropped down righteousness*.[27]

If in these passages Andrewes sees Mary as praying and giving thanks on behalf of all creation, that is, sees the world and humanity as feminine in its response to God, in another place where he speaks of God's blessing resting on his creation he clearly affirms that there is something feminine in the heart of God.

> The world *barak* is applyed to knee, and signifieth as it were mother's tenderness to the babe sitting upon her knee . . . When the babes are upon their mother's knee, they kiss them, they wish [them] well, they cherish them: so doth God setting us on his knee, so that *blanda est in Deo matrum affectio*.[28]

This taking up of feminine themes in Andrewes, even if it is not a very frequent feature of his writing, is, as Lossky remarks, sufficiently surprising, particularly in view of the age in which he lived.

> Everything would lead one to expect on the part of this celibate bishop — in his ascetic life altogether comparable with the strictest monks — an attitude which many tend to qualify as 'monastic' in relation to women: woman is above all an object of temptation, the cause of the sin of Adam. But there is nothing of this at all.[29]

III

WE BEGAN THIS chapter with an affirmation of the ecumenical and international significance of the theology of Lancelot Andrewes. It is to the same point that we return in our conclusion. In his vision of the Christian faith and of its coherent and theological articulation, the central and controlling point for Andrewes was to be found where it was found in the life of the Church of East and West alike in the first millennium of Christian history, in that simple yet complex knot of teaching which we refer to as the doctrines of the Trinity, Incarnation and theosis. In this vision, God comes out of himself in his love for creation. The Father gives himself in the Son and the Spirit. In the union of human and divine in the person of Jesus, and in his triumph over death through death, all humanity is lifted up to God. In the coming of the Spirit at Pentecost, in the subsequent communion of human and divine which is the very heart of the Church, and through the distribution of the Spirit's many gifts, human persons are incorporated in Christ and made to share in the divine nature. The central controlling point of the Christian faith is not to be found in speculation about divine predestination as in the schools of Geneva. On these matters Andrewes remained purposefully and consistently silent and agnostic. Nor is it to be found in a more and more systematic elaboration of the doctrine of justification by faith alone as in the schools of Wittenberg. Here too there were dogmatic assertions which Andrewes were not willing to make. These questions to him were not necessarily unimportant but they were secondary and derived, and needed always to be seen in relation to the central mystery of Trinity, Incarnation and theosis.

The same would be true of many other points of theology

which were in dispute then, some of which are still in dispute now; questions about the nature and efficacy of the sacraments, about the shape and significance of the ordained ministry, about the location of primacy and the nature of primatial authority within the body of the Church. To say that such questions are derived and secondary is not to say that they are unimportant or matters of indifference. It is simply to refer them back always to the Church's central affirmation of faith in the mystery of God's creative, redemptive, transfiguring love. Seen in this light, however important the question of the Roman primacy may be, it cannot be of final and ultimate significance. There are matters of greater weight than that.

It is difficult to assess the extent of Andrewes' influence in the subsequent history of Anglicanism. He founded no school and had no immediate followers. But it cannot be denied that his influence in the seventeenth century was great and that the spirit of his teaching recurs in Anglican history in a variety of forms. It underlies the eclectic catholicity of approach to matters of faith and life which we find in John Wesley, his consistent and lively Trinitarianism, his stress on the doctrine of the Holy Spirit, his longing for the way of Christian perfection. Andrewes' vision came to life again in the days of the Oxford Movement when the great collected edition of his writings was made, and when John Henry Newman made a new translation of the *Preces Privatæ*, a book which he kept on his prayer desk in the Oratory at Birmingham throughout his life. It lies behind the ecumenical vision and the ecumenical method worked out by F. D. Maurice, perhaps the most creative of Anglican theologians in the nineteenth century. It appears again in a public form in the heroic efforts for Christian unity of a William Temple or a Michael Ramsey in our own time. At the present moment an echo of it is to be heard far beyond the Anglican world in the massive attempt being made by the Faith and Order Commission of the World Council of Churches to elicit from all the Churches a reaffirmation, a re-reception of the apostolic faith as it was defined and articulated in the first four centuries of our era. That faith is still shared, at least in principle, by East and West alike, by Rome and the Reformation. Can the Churches reaffirm it together in such a way as to reveal the underlying bedrock of their unity in faith? Can the teaching of Lancelot Andrewes be of some significant service in helping towards this universal aim?

It is the considered judgement of Nicolas Lossky, who has been one of the leading representatives of the Orthodox tradition in the Faith and Order discussion of the last decades, that the answer to this question must be 'yes'.

It would then, it seems to me, be right for Christians in dialogue with one another in the twentieth century to develop an interest in the work of Lancelot Andrewes the preacher. In fact, in more than one area, this theologian, who lived at the heart of a period of crisis in Western Christianity, anticipated in his sermons several lines of theological reflection that are developing more and more in ecumenical contexts. More than one of his theological intuitions could be brought to shed light on the ecumenical quest ...In particular, his conception of theology itself understood as an *élan* concerned with human beings in their entirety, that reminds them of their responsibility to transfigure the universe that surrounds them.[30]

Citing the judgement of John Harington, with which this chapter began, Lossky concludes that perhaps the time has come for the realization of its prophecy of a reconciliation of those estranged from one another, not on a European scale alone, but on a worldwide level.

English and Anglican Andrewes certainly was. But by God's gift the limitations inherent in our creaturely status need not become things which imprison us and cut us off from others. The very specificity of our gifts may become not barriers between ourselves and others but points of contact, ways by which communion in love and knowledge may grow. In a time of violent conflicts by which he was certainly not untouched, the scholar, the pastor and the man of prayer had wished to put his life at the service of God and at the service of his fellow men and women. More than the monarch whom he served, the motto 'blessed are the peacemakers' was appropriate for him. It seems as if that gift of making peace might be exercised still at the end of the twentieth century.

NOTES

1   Lancelot Andrewes, *Two Answers to Cardinal Perron and Other Miscellaneous Works*, L.A.C.T., (Oxford, 1854), pp. xxxvii–xxxviii.
2   Nicolas Lossky *Lancelot Andrewes The Preacher (1555–1626)* (Oxford, 1991).
3   *Two Answers*, p. xiii.
4   Lancelot Andrewes *Apospasmatia Sacra, or A Collection of Posthumous and Orphan Lectures* (London, 1657).
5   ibid., pp. 62–3.
6   ibid., p. 63.
7   See Lossky, p. 12.
8   *The Preces Privatæ of Lancelot Andrewes, Bishop of Winchester, translated with an Introduction and Notes* by F.E. Brightman, (London, 1903), p. 59.

[163]

[9] ibid., p. 60.
[10] ibid., p. xxix.
[11] T.S. Eliot *For Lancelot Andrewes: Essays on Style and Order* (London, 1928), p.18.
[12] ibid., pp. 23–5.
[13] ibid., pp. 27–8.
[14] ibid., pp. 29–30.
[15] Lossky, p. 345.
[16] *Apospasmatia*, p. 622.
[17] ibid., p. 622.
[18] ibid., p. 519.
[19] ibid., p. 515.
[20] Lossky, pp. 284–5.
[21] *Apospasmatia*, p. 628.
[22] ibid., p. 626. The O.T. reference is evidently in error here. It should presumably read Isaiah 11, not Isaiah 7. Cf. the passage in the Second Whitsun sermon quoted in Lossky, p. 277.
[23] ibid., pp. 577–8.
[24] ibid., p. 597.
[25] ibid., p.327.
[26] ibid., pp. 329–30.
[27] ibid., pp. 567–8. It is possible that the original texts may have contained Marian references which the editors in 1657 thought it wiser to omit.
[28] ibid., p. 90.
[29] Lossky, p. 201.
[30] ibid., p. 352.

GORDON WAKEFIELD

John and Charles Wesley:
A Tale of Two Brothers

LIKE SOME OTHERS, the brothers Wesley need to be saved from their friends, for whom their lives, families, devotional verses and ecclesiological system constitute, as John Knox said of Calvin's Geneva, 'the maist perfyt schooole of Chryst that ever was in the eryth since the dayis of the Apostylls'. But their story, even when seen in the crepuscular light of historical scepticism refracted by the social sciences, has some remarkable features, while for the Church historian it is a question whether in the whole of the Christian era the lives of two brothers have been so curiously intertwined in Christian experience and the service of the Gospel, apart from the Sons of Zebedee about whom far less is known.[1]

They were children of Epworth Rectory, John born on 17 June 1703, Charles in 1707, the date not precisely known — he was not sure of it himself. John was probably the fourteenth child of the Rector, Samuel Wesley and his wife Susanna, but no one knows for sure. At least one girl and five boys died in infancy and John was the third child to be so named. Three sons and seven daughters finally survived.

Samuel and Susanna were both children of ministers who had been ejected from Church of England livings because they could not conform to the Book of Common Prayer and the Anglican settlement after the Restoration of Charles II. They returned to the Church in their young adulthood, for the Age of Reason was replacing the passionate conflicts of the previous century and orthodox dissent was drifting into Unitarianism. They were both vehement believers in the Christian doctrine of God as Trinity. Susanna was sympathetic to the 'non-jurors', those Anglicans who felt that they could not renounce the solemn oath of loyalty which they had sworn to James II and were therefore deprived of their offices and their livings after 1689. Samuel was pledged to William III and once absented himself from home for a whole year because Susanna would not say 'Amen' to the State prayer for him as King. It was an agonizing conflict and not easily resolved. Samuel had called down the Divine vengeance upon himself and his posterity, if he so much as touched her again or went to bed with her until she had begged God's pardon and his. When Samuel was persuaded to return, the result was the conception of John Wesley. Such matters apart, Samuel was an old-fashioned High-Churchman, non-Roman, non-ritualistic, stiff for the Prayer Book, harsh against dissent, strict about prayer and fasting.

Both parents shared what in some ways was an ecumenical spirituality. Samuel was passionately interested in the early Church and the French school both in a somewhat peripheral representative of the Counter- or Catholic Reformation, such as Gaston Jean-Baptiste de Renty (1611-49), a Parisian nobleman, who seems to have learned a holy detachment from both his wealth and his wife and who, amid many works of philanthropy, organized branches of a Company of the Blessed Sacrament; and Bossuet and Pascal. Susanna was an intellectual, 'all reason and piety', with a temptation to scepticism, which Pascal's *Pensées* helped her to overcome, so that she was able to balance reason and faith. But she once wrote in a letter to John:

> I still continue to pay my respects to an unknown God. I cannot know him. I dare not say I love him — only this, I have chosen him for my only happiness, my all, my only God. . . .And when I sound my will, I feel it adheres to its choice, though not so faithfully as it ought.

Susanna administered a strict regime, not without something of Puritanism as well as the Prayer Book, contending for the souls of her children, convinced that their rebellious infant wills must be broken, insisting that they cried quietly and addressed one another as 'Brother Jackie', 'Sister Hetty' and the rest. Samuel has been described as a kind of cross between Patrick Brontë. and Mr Barrett of Wimpole Street. He had literary ambitions to lift his gaze above the barbarous and melancholy fens and his surly parishioners, but also at times to distract him from his family. His was a philological and textual learning — Susanna was the practical theologian — and it was accompanied by a constant struggle to make ends meet and he was gaoled for debt. His large Latin treatise on Job was published posthumously and had few readers. Fortunately, he had friends in high places, such as Archbishop Sharp.

The girls were given the same parental education as the boys and were just as intelligent; they read and wrote much. But social convention and their father's lack of sympathy kept them at home and destined them to unsatisfactory marriages. Mehetabel (Hetty), the most brilliant and beautiful, was condemned to a wretched life and a tragic end with a callous and brutal Axholme plumber.

John Wesley was dramatically rescued from a fire which destroyed Epworth Rectory in 1709. He was known to refer to himself as a 'brand plucked from the burning'; but he also denied that he had any sense of a special Providence and destiny during his childhood and youth and maintained that, as a young man, his one expectation was to spend all his days as an Oxford don. But his recollections are often inconsistent, depending both on an inexact memory and his mood at the time. He certainly owed much to his mother and as a grown man far from home would crave for the Thursday nights which she had devoted to his instruction and counselling — she allocated one night a week to each of her children. Susanna wrote down a resolve in 1711, some time after the fire, 'I do intend to be more particularly careful of the soul of this child that thou hast so mercifully provided for than ever I have been'.

It may well be that it was from his close relation to his mother that there arose in John Wesley his life-long susceptibility to women and his need for their companionship and affection. He unburdened himself most easily to women. He always wanted to impart to those to whom he was attracted knowledge of the latest book he had been reading, (and he was always in danger of being bowled over by the latest book). To some of them he must have seemed a quaint lover, 'primitive Christianity' a Cotswold girl called him, forever seeking theological improvement. It may have been mother-love which prevented him from being an unequivocal suitor, though High-Church notions about clerical celibacy may have been mixed up with it. The strictness of maternal rule may have made him constantly defensive and always anxious to justify himself. This is characteristic of the scolded boy in whom has been implanted high standards of goodness. When reproved he is always concerned to show that he is really in the right. John Wesley was like his mother in his own notions of child psychology, notions which have been deplored for many years. Children should above all be serious ('he who plays as a boy will play as a man') and should be early encouraged in the ways of godliness and the experiential knowledge of Christ. He also resembled Susanna in the fluctuations of his religious experience. In spite of his insistence at the beginning of his mission on assurance, he never attained the calm, unruffled certainty and conviction that he thought were essential gifts of the Spirit. In a letter of 27 June 1766, he wrote to his brother, partly in shorthand:

> I do not love God. I never did. Therefore I never believed in the Christian sense of the word. Therefore I am only an honest heathen. . .And yet to be so employed of God; and so hedged in that I can neither go forward nor backward! Surely there never was such an instance from the beginning of the world! If I ever have had *that faith* it would not be so strange. But I never had other. . .'awareness' of the eternal or invisible world than I have now; and this is none at all, unless such as fairly shines from reason's glimmering ray. I have no direct witness I do not say that I am a child of God but of anything invisible or eternal.
>
> And yet I dare not preach otherwise than I do, either concerning faith, or love, or justification, or perfection . . . I am . . . so swept along I know not how that I can't stand still. I want the whole world to come to . . .'what I do not know myself'. Neither am I impelled to this by fear of any kind. I have no more fear than love. Or if I have any fear, it is not of falling into hell, but of falling into nothing.[2]

Charles Wesley was born prematurely and 'appeared dead rather than alive when he was born', says his first biographer. 'He did not cry nor open his eyes, and was kept wrapt up in soft wool until the time when he should have been born according to the usual course of nature, when he opened his eyes and cried'. He was undersized and frail and late in learning to talk — something for which he made up later on! But he went to Westminster School, where his elder brother, Samuel, was an usher — John was at Charterhouse — and was said to be good with his fists. He became head boy. He was invited by a distant relative to go over to Ireland as his heir. His father left him to make up his own mind. He decided to stay in England. Another relative took his place and became Earl of Mornington, whose third son was Arthur Wesley or Wellesley, the Duke of Wellington.

Charles was in many ways the son of his father, as John was of his mother. The two brothers were not alike in temperament. 'I have much constitutional enthusiasm' said John, 'but you have much more'. Charles was the more emotional, exuberant, mercurial, depressive. He was even more Tory and patriotic and something of a snob. He cruelly lampooned his brother over John's ordinations. He could use extreme and affectionate language, which John deplored and censored as 'nambi-pambical'. There are traces of absorption in mysticism and John would not have 'Take away our power of sinning' in the hymn 'Love Divine'. Yet, in the hymns, there are evaluations of Methodist doctrine, more subtle, more guarded and more consistent, than in some of John's statements. And he was the more realistic. John saw in the paroxysms and hysteria which attended the preaching, signs of the Kingdom. Charles kept a bucket of cold water handy!

Most of the Wesleys wrote verse and John, whose hymns are not always easily distinguished from Charles's, was a fine translator. But Charles seems to have thought in rhyme and could turn almost anything into verse. Gordon Rupp used to say that he would have had a go with Bradshaw's railway timetable. There is a story of him in later life arriving at the City Road Chapel on his old grey nag and leaping from it into the house with the cry 'Pen and ink! Pen and ink!' No conversation was possible until he was delivered of the hymn with which he had become big on the journey. If Eliot's dictum be allowed, 'lesser poets borrow, great poets steal', then Charles Wesley qualifies for the latter, since his hymns are full of allusions and direct quotations from the Bible, from early liturgies, from Shakespeare and Milton and a host of others.[3] Donald Davie has applauded Martha Winburn England's work in regarding him as no sectarian versifier but one with a place among English poets. In *Hymns Unbidden*, she most fascinatingly compares and contrasts him with William Blake.[4] It has been estimated that he wrote 7,300 hymns in all, of which 3,000 remained in manuscript. Much is bound to be doggerel which has deservedly perished. Some, no longer in use, is of profound spirituality.

The Shared Crisis

JOHN WESLEY entered Christ Church, Oxford and in 1725 he decided to take orders and become a serious Christian. He had been reading a book well-known to his parents, the medieval Thomas à Kempis's *The Imitation of Christ*, influential in the conversion of Ignatius Loyola, founder of the Jesuits, two hundred years before; and a notable book from the Church of England in the previous

[169]

century: Jeremy Taylor's *Rules and Exercises of Holy Living and Dying*. 'Instantly', he wrote, 'I resolved to dedicate all my life to God, all my thoughts and words and actions, being thoroughly convinced that there was no medium but that *every* part of my life (not some only) must be a sacrifice either to God or to myself: that is, in effect, to the devil'.

From then on his Oxford life was an interesting combination of seriousness and society. He became a Fellow of Lincoln College in 1726 through family influence and to his father's delight — 'My Jacky is a Fellow of Lincoln'. He was undoubtedly a good and conscientious teacher, though later he may have used his tutorials to try and convert his pupils. He kept a diary in Puritan fashion, a means of rigorous self-questioning and examination, not just a record of events. He kept a strict rule based on Jeremy Taylor and sought to live by the standards of primitive Christianity, interpreted by the early Fathers of the Greek and Latin Church of the first five centuries. He looked upon them with something of the rationalist superiority of his time, yet believed that they had a unique understanding of what it meant to be a Christian. His rule was severe; but for him cheerfulness was always breaking in. He was of sanguine temperament, an optimist at heart. He reacted to some extent against Taylor in his belief that 'Holiness is happiness'. But holiness was his quest from first to last and it is this which binds the days of his life together and gives him a consistency which the varieties of his experience and his later change of course and his differing accounts and interpretations might seem to belie.

At this time also, John Wesley discovered William Law's *Christian Perfection* and *A Serious Call to a Devout and Holy Life*, which was published in 1729. The latter was destined to have great influence on John Keble and the Oxford Movement. Law was a non-juring clergyman, very much in the tradition of Jeremy Taylor and the seventeenth century but with the literary style of the contemporary first novelists. He was later influenced by the mystical teaching of Jacob Boehme. He was a great enemy of formal religion and of Samuel Wesley's style of scholarship. For him, Christianity made inexorable demands.

This reinforced Wesley's resolve to be an 'altogether Christian', 'all-devoted to God'. Law also taught him not only to read but to study the Bible and apply it to himself, to make it his 'frame of reference' for all events, circumstances and decisions of his life. He also accepted Law's doctrine of Providence: 'Every man is to consider himself as a particular object of God's Providence; under the same care and protection of God as if the world had been made for him alone. It is not by chance that a man is born at such a time, of such parents and in such a place and condition'. And very much of what Wesley wrote in after years about charity and the 'Catholic spirit' may be paralleled in William Law, who wrote of 'a communion of saints in the love of God and all goodness, which no one can learn from what is called orthodoxy in particular churches, but is only to be had by a total dying to all worldly views, by a pure love of God and by such unction from above, as delivers the mind from all self-ishness and makes it love truth and goodness with an equality of affection in every man, whether he be Christian, Jew or Gentile'. Law goes on to say that 'we must enter into a Catholic affection for all' and 'love the spirit of the Gospel wherever we see it, not work ourselves up into an abhorrence of a George Fox or an Ignatius Loyola, but be equally glad of the light of the Gospel wherever it shines. . . .'[5]

For some years all this was not incompatible with a social life which included delightful female company and close and affection-ate relationships bordering on the improper, which in his inno-cence he did not regard as such, though his mother and sisters saw through it all. But from 1730 he became even more serious and tended to withdraw from worldly pastimes such as cards, chess and dancing. He had spent some time as his father's curate at Wroote, the parish held in plurality with Epworth, but this had convinced him that he was not cut out for the life of a parish priest. In any case, he was needed for teaching duties in Oxford.

Meanwhile Charles had gone up to Christ Church about the time John left it for Lincoln. He was a lively and popular under-graduate, engaged in 'harmless diversion', fond of the theatre, but not dissolute. When John spoke to him about religion, he rejoined, 'What, would you have me to be a saint all at once?' But while John was away at Wroote, he became more diligent and more serious. 'I went to the weekly Sacrament and persuaded two or three young students to accompany me and to observe the method of study pre-scribed by the University. This gained me the harmless name of Methodist'. This was the beginning of what was nicknamed 'the Holy Club'. Notice that it had an academic component. The group was by no means as tightly knit as some have thought, but they eventually combined High-Church disciplines of sacrament, prayer, office, Bible study and fasting, with social work, especially prison visiting. (The poverty-stricken sisters at Epworth wished that some of the philanthropy had been directed to them). John, on his return, became unofficial leader. The group was accident prone. One of them, William Morgan, died, apparently insane. Malicious gossip attributed this to the Club's austerities; and it is true that a servitor at Pembroke College, son of the landlord of the Bell Inn at Gloucester, named George Whitefield, suffered a nervous break-down through his extravagance in keeping its rules. Charles Wesley helped him to recover by lending him Henry Scougal's, *The Life of God in the Soul of Man*. He sought ordination and became the great-est popular preacher in both England and the American colonies since Hugh Latimer. It was he and not the Wesleys who may be said to have begun the Evangelical Revival in 1737.

John Wesley published his first work, *A Form of Prayers*, in 1733. This is by no means original, mostly drawn from non-jurors such as Nathaniel Spinckes. He was reading widely in theology, mystics, medieval as well as later Catholic writers, Scougal and Scupoli's *Spiritual Combat*.

He preached a University Sermon on 1 January 1733, which encapsulates the doctrine of his whole life. It was on 'The Circum-cision of the Heart' (Romans 2:29). Outward forms and obser-vances are not the marks of the true followers of Christ but rather 'a right state of soul, a mind and spirit renewed after the image of him that created it'. This is attained by humility, by faith in God, by joy-ful assurance, but also by 'a constant and continued course of gen-eral self-denial', and above all by love, 'cutting off both the lust of the flesh, the lust of the eye and the pride of life', engaging the whole person in the ardent pursuit of God. 'Let your soul be filled with so entire a love of him that you may love nothing but for his sake'. This teaching does not divide faith and works. The inspira-tion of both is God and the love of God.

Wesley changed this not one iota for the rest of his long life. But in these Oxford days, which he sometimes, years later, craved for — 'Let me again be an Oxford Methodist' — there was deep dissatisfaction, which Charles experienced too. It was as though the wood was assembled on the altar but awaited kindling, or in the Scriptural metaphor Wesley used, he had the faith of a servant but not of a son.

After their father's death in 1735, his dying words counselling them not to forget 'the inward witness', John and Charles set sail for Georgia. They hoped that through converting the Indians and planting primitive Christianity in virgin soil, they might attain the assurance which they lacked of being right with God.

On the face of it the mission was an abject failure. Charles was soon home after some monumental tactlessness. John had few en-counters with the Indians and offended the colonists with his High-Church impositions such as triple immersion of infants, opposition to private baptism and insistence that Lutherans and Calvinists must be rebaptized. He had a disastrous love affair with a young woman named Sophia (Sophy) Hopkey. In outline, he, deeply in love and by no means undemonstrative, could not bring himself to make his intentions crystal clear. She, probably feeling out of her depth, married another suitor in circumstances which both smacked of infidelity and breached his clerical jurisdiction. He, most inadvisedly, sought to continue his ministrations after marriage, but when it seemed that Sophy was not observing the necessary church disciplines, he, after due warning, excommunicated her. It appeared to be 'a phrenzy of disappointed love' and was the end of his effective ministry in Georgia. Everything was complicated by disputes and corruption among the colonists themselves. The Board of Trustees in London, before whom he appeared on his return, revoked his commission, thinking him a strange, eccentric and perhaps hypocritical little parson and 'an incendiary of the people against the magistrates', which was inconceivable. His reputation suffered for many years.

Georgia was not a total disaster. When he visited the colony, George Whitefield found many who spoke well of John Wesley. And the mission made possible an encounter with the Moravians which was crucial in his spiritual pilgrimage. They had their origins in Central Europe and were spiritual descendants of the late medieval Bohemian Brethren, who survived persecution and, after the Reformation, found affinities with the Lutherans. They retained their separate existence, produced at least one outstanding leader in the educationalist, John Amos Comenius (1592-1670), and were revived by Count Nicholas Ludwig von Zinzendorf (1700-60), who made a home on his estates for their refugees from Catholic persecution in Austria and received their consecration as a Bishop. They believed that they were in the Apostolic Succession. Some of them were crossing the Atlantic in the ship which took the Wesleys to Georgia in 1735 and John felt his own fears rebuked when they remained calmly singing a hymn during a storm in which he was terrified. They preached a personal faith of tender and childlike simplicity within a disciplined liturgical order. They seemed to have the faith which Wesley lacked, the knowledge of God in the bottom of the heart, not simply in the top of the mind. When he was in London again he made contact with them and one of them, Peter Böhler, gave him some famous advice, 'Preach faith till you have it; and then when you have it you will preach faith'.

It was in Georgia that John Wesley had his principal encounter with German Pietism, that movement of personal religion and

mystical spirituality, influenced by English Puritanism. He translated many of their hymns at this period as well as some by Zinzendorf. He would be one of the few Englishmen to know German in
spite of the Hanoverian succession. Here is an example from Johann
Andreas Rothe (1688-1758):

> O Love, thou bottomless abyss
> My sins are swallowed up in thee!
> Covered is my unrighteousness,
> Nor spot of guilt remains on me,
> While Jesu's blood through earth and skies
> Mercy, free, boundless mercy! cries.

And one from Paulus Gerhardt (1607-76), whose hymns were
among Dietrich Bonhoeffer's spiritual helps in Nazi prison:

> O grant that nothing in my soul
> May dwell but thy pure love alone;
> O may thy love possess me whole,
> My joy, my treasure, and my crown;
> Strange flames far from my heart remove;
> My every act, word, thought, be love.

There are also hymns of Johann Scheffler, better known as
Angelus Silesius. One, now almost disappeared, based on the
'Anima Christi'; another with reminiscences of Augustine's *Confes-
sions*, 'Too late have I loved thee', and the prayer:

> Give to mine eyes refreshing tears,
> Give to my heart, chaste, hallowed fires,
> Give to my soul with filial fears,
> The love that all heaven's host inspires;
> That all my powers with all their might,
> In thy sole glory may unite.

Charles, back for some months, was undoubtedly undergoing
a nervous breakdown, which manifested itself in a series of petty
quarrels with his friends. He was intermittently distraught for two
years with no one, it seemed, able to help. William Law declared,
'Nothing I can either speak or write will do you any good', and
Moravian exhortations to seek justifying faith seemed little more
than futile nagging. He found no comfort in the ordinances. 'I received the Sacrament but not Christ'. He had, however, though not

as yet under Moravian influence, in 1737, talked to his sisters about 'the inward change' and the 'new creature'; and on 17 May 1738, he encountered Luther on Galatians, just like Bunyan in the previous century.

On 21 May 1738, Whit Sunday, he lay almost at the point of death with pleurisy, in the house of a mechanic, Mr Bray, in Little Britain, the sort of domicile he might have despised. He heard a voice, which was in fact that of Mr Bray's sister, but which seemed to come from out of this world, telling him, 'In the name of Jesus of Nazareth arise and believe and thou shalt be healed of all thine infirmities'. (The sister said that the words were inspired by a dream, but that 'the words were Christ's'). Charles was convinced that this was supernatural intervention and with Isaiah 40: 1 in front of him — 'Comfort ye, my people' — found the peace he had hitherto been denied and was rejoicing in the hope of Christ.

John Wesley had soon found pulpits closed to him on his return to England. His preaching had mysteriously changed in ethos if not in content. Three days after Charles had found peace, on 24 May 1738, John opened his Bible at five in the morning at II Peter 1:4, 'There are given unto us exceeding great and precious promises, even that ye should be partakers of the divine nature' and, later, on the words, 'Thou art not far from the kingdom of God'. In the afternoon, at St Paul's Cathedral, the anthem was 'Out of the deep have I called unto thee O Lord; Lord hear my voice. . .' In the evening he went 'very unwillingly' to a society in Aldersgate Street, heard a reading from Luther's preface to the *Epistle to the Romans* and at a quarter to nine felt his heart 'strangely warmed'. This made him feel that he trusted in Christ, Christ alone, for salvation and gave him the assurance of forgiveness. Immediately he began to pray 'for those who had in a more especial manner despitefully used (him) and persecuted (him)'. He testified openly as to what he felt in his heart and the evening ended when he was brought in triumph by a troop of friends to Charles's lodgings. They sang 'the hymn' which Charles had written the night before with some hesitation because of the fear of pride. Mr Bray had encouraged him to complete it.

> Where shall my wond'ring soul begin?
> How shall I all to heaven aspire?
> A slave redeemed from death and sin,
> A brand plucked from eternal fire,
> How shall I equal triumphs raise,
> Or sing my great Deliverer's praise?

[175]

Its conviction is that the experience of God's love must be shared. It is steeped in St Luke's Gospel and speaks of Jesus as the 'friend of publicans and sinners'.

> Outcasts of men, to you I call,
> Harlots and publicans and thieves!
> He spreads his arms t'embrace you all
> Sinners alone his grace receives:
> No need of him the righteous have;
> He came the lost to seek and save.

The Wesleys, devout, dedicated, donnish, ordained, did not regard themselves as superior to the 'vilest offenders'. They were as much in need of grace as the most debauched, the worst criminals.

Too much must not be made of 24 May 1738 in John Wesley's spiritual journey. He never calls it his 'conversion' and never looks back to it except by implication that at that period, he saw that justification, which he defines as the forgiveness of sins, and which was granted by the free grace of God to penitent sinners, was 'the porch of religion'. Faith was 'the door', Holiness 'religion itself'. He did, however, publish, possibly as early as 1738, abridged extracts from the Homilies of the Church of England, the work of Cranmer, which proclaim that salvation is by faith. And in October the same year, while walking from London to Oxford, he had read of the Great Awakening in North Hampton, New England and was overwhelmed by it, so that it became in some sense his model and his prayer for his own mission; yet he still felt that he himself lacked joy and the full assurance of faith and was not in 'in the full sense of the word, "in Christ, a new creature"'.

While still in Aldersgate Street, he had been slightly disturbed by the absence of joy in his emotions. And after a short time of evangelical priggishness, his mood fluctuated. He visited the Moravian headquarters at Herrnhut in Saxony that autumn, a mixed experience in which he did not feel entirely at home and indeed was not made to feel so. He would soon break with the Moravians and suspend his interest in German spirituality, due to their belief in 'stillness'. This resulted from the notion that faith is attained by a total cessation of works, such as prayer, searching the scriptures, receiving the Sacrament. Even the charity of believers must result from the inward feeling that they are 'free' to act in this way. This was anathema to Wesley. We are not saved by our own efforts but by our trust in Divine grace, yet the goal of the Christian life is love of God and of our neighbour and to attain this we must make full use of those channels or 'means' by which the love of God flows into our lives that it may flow through us, 'the poor, the helpless to relieve/My life, my all for them to give'.

In January 1739, John Wesley completed a ruthless self-analysis in which he concluded that he did not *feel* the love of God and the fruits of the Spirit and therefore did not possess them. 'I am not a Christian'. He may still have been disturbed by his susceptibilities to women. But his attention may have been turned away from himself and his own state by his activity as a recruiting agent for Religious Societies in London and Bristol and his opportunity to address meetings of several hundred people. There were revivalist scenes and charismatic outbursts. It seemed like the Acts of the Apostles all over again. He began to speak of an 'awakening'. He was being led beyond the bounds of Church order and was charged with irregularities such as preaching in a parish without the incumbent's consent. He argued that he had this right as a Fellow of Lincoln, but the contention led to one of his most famous sayings in a letter of March 1739.

> I look upon all the world as my parish; thus far, I mean that in whatever part of it I am, I judge it meet and right and my bounden duty to declare unto all that are willing to hear the glad tidings of salvation.

About this time, George Whitefield invited John Wesley to share in the field preaching to colliers in Bristol. Wesley trembled. Apart from the hazards, preaching in the open air offended his notions of good order. 'I should have thought the saving of souls a sin if it had not been done in Church'. But he remembered the Sermon on the Mount, 'one pretty remarkable precedent of field preaching', and on 2 April:

> At four in the afternoon I submitted to be more vile and proclaimed in the highways the glad tidings of salvation speaking from a little eminence adjoining the city to about 3,000 people. The Scripture on which I spoke was this (is it possible that anyone should be ignorant that it is fulfilled in every true minister of Christ?), 'The Spirit of the Lord is upon me because he hath anointed me to preach the Gospel to the poor'.

This may be seen as the completion of a very long process, perhaps lifelong, of which 24 May 1738 is a vital incident. Was John

Wesley saved, not by works apart from a deep religious desire and longing for the love of God, but by the activities, the responsibilities, the controversies into which he was now plunged as he sought to offer to all and sundry, particularly the unchurched, that which he never attained with unshakeable certainty himself? This may have saved him from undue self-absorption and provided a substitute for the love of women.

Partners in Mission and Methodism

CHARLES DOES NOT seem to have subjected himself to such rigorous examination, but he was always prone to 'ups and downs'. He remained in London, preaching a good deal in Church pulpits, including Westminster Abbey and caring for the newly-formed Societies. He worked particularly among condemned criminals. On the anniversary of his 'conversion', he wrote the hymn, which now begins with its second stanza, 'O for a thousand tongues to sing/My dear Redeemer's praise', altered in some versions, possibly by John, to 'my great Redeemer's praise'. And he says in his Journal:

> I now found myself at peace with God and rejoiced in hope of loving Christ. . .I saw that by faith I stood; by the continual support of faith which kept me from falling, though of myself I am ever sinking into sin. I went to bed still sensible of my own weakness (I humbly hope to be more and more so) yet confident of Christ's protection.
>
> Under this protection I waked next morning and rejoiced in reading the 107th Psalm, so nobly describing what God had done for my soul. . .
>
> > Then they cried unto the Lord in their trouble,
> > And he saved them out of their distresses.
> > He brought them out of darkness and the shadow of death,
> > And brake their bands in sunder

For 12 July 1739, there is this entry:

> I preached at Newgate to the condemned felons and visited one of them in his cell, sick of a fever, a poor black that had robbed his master. I told him of One who came down from heaven to save lost sinners and him in particular; described the sufferings of the Son of God, His sorrows, agony and death. He listened with all

the signs of eager astonishment; the tears trickled down his cheeks while he cried, What! was it for me? Did God suffer all this for so poor a creature as me?

A week later, Charles wrote of his being present on the cart going to Tyburn for an execution, which included young children. And how they died convinced that like the criminal on the Cross they would be with their Lord in Paradise. They did not struggle, but meekly gave up their spirits. 'I returned full of peace and confidence in our friends' happiness. . .The hour under the gallows was the most blessed hour of my life'.

It was from experiences such as these that the hymn was written, so beloved among evangelicals and Methodists:

> And can it be that I should gain
> An interest in the Saviour's blood?
> Died he for me who caused his pain?
> For me who him to death pursued?

All this provokes many questions. The social background of capital punishment gives an entry to the evangelist denied today. The hopelessness of the lot of so many in this England makes heaven their only possible hope and death, so cruel, so barbarous, a blessed release, while the thought of the suffering Son of God is no unhealthy masochism, but the experience of Divine compassion which brings strength and hope. Charles Wesley beneath the gallows thought only of another gallows become a rood, and like Methodist soldiers a very few years later, maimed and bleeding amid the carnage of the battlefield, was happier than on a summer morning of nature's peace.

The two brothers were at one at this stage, equally facing violent, intoxicated mobs and bearing the opprobrium of clerics and magistrates, though Charles was apt to discover that prosecutors had been contemporaries at the House. John Wesley was thought to be the young Pretender in disguise and some lines of Charles's 'O bid thy banished ones rejoice' could be construed as treasonable. . . There were some frightening moments, worse for the ordinary Methodists than their leaders. The answer to the mob was to try and sing above the noise — does this account in part for hearty, if not sometimes raucous Methodist singing which makes Anglican singing so tame? The hymn 'Ye servants of God your Master proclaim', often sung decorously to a fine tune by Sir Hubert Parry, was

[179]

to be sung 'in a tumult'. Its original second and third stanzas are these:

> The Waves of the Sea Have lift up their voice
> Sore troubled that we in Jesus rejoice;
> The Floods they are roaring, But Jesus is here,
> While we are adoring, He always is near.

> Men, Devils engage, The billows arise,
> And horribly rage and threaten the Skies;
> Their fury shall never our steadfastness shock
> The weakest believer is built on a Rock.

The Wesleys and Whitefield were guilty of some extreme and unbalanced statements against the Churchmen of their day and some of the scenes which attended the preaching could have aroused fears of corporate insanity. There are some interesting and not unmoving controversies between John Wesley and Bishops Gibson, Lavington and Warmington and the pseudonymous 'John Smith'. But apart from the Moravians and 'Stillness', the disagreement which, in the words of W. F. Lofthouse threatened to 'kill Methodism in its cradle', was with the Calvinists over predestination. This led to the separation of Whitefield in the early 1740s, though it was even more vehement thirty years later. But it was in 1741 that Charles's *Hymns on God's Everlasting Love* proclaimed with awesome emphasis the Evangelical Arminianism which was the Wesleys' creed.

> The *world* he suffered to redeem
> For *all* he hath the atonement made
> *For those that will not come to him*
> The ransom of his life was paid.

Methodism spread to all parts of the country and involved constant itinerary for its leaders, not only as evangelists but as pastors of its new, strange flock. In the end, Charles turned from the strain and excitement to a love match and most happy marriage with Sarah Gwynne, half his age, whom he had met at her home at Garth in wild central Wales. John approved, made a financial settlement which enabled Charles to keep a wife, and on the wedding day, 8 April 1749, 'seemed the happiest person among us'. There was still to be much travelling, often dangerous, and much separation until they settled first in Bristol and then in more stable home life in London. Charles governed his sex life better than John and reared a happy family, though not without those anxieties inseparable from parenthood. It has been said that 'it was Charles's household that rang night and morning with music, some of it highly sophisticated'.[6]

Six months later Charles behaved rather like his father might have done when he heard that John, without consulting him according to an agreement which Charles himself had kept, was about to marry the attractive housekeeper of the Newcastle Orphan House, who had nursed him through an illness. She was a seaman's widow and Charles may have felt that John was going to marry beneath him. Like Sophy Hopkey, she had another suitor, the itinerant preacher John Bennet, whom she had also nursed and with whom she had 'an understanding'. But twice she pledged herself to John Wesley before witnesses when parts of the marriage service were read.

Charles dashed to the north, declared that Grace Murray had broken *his* heart — he did fear for the revival — and ensured that she married John Bennet before John could be aware. One is bound to think that she may have been in love with Bennet but flattered by Wesley's attentions and the way in which he shared his life and learning with the woman dear to him. Technically, Grace was in breach of promise, but legal action would have been complex, long-drawn out and damaging. John, heart-broken, acquiesced, but soon after, again without consultation, married Mrs Mary (Molly) Vazeille, a wealthy widow, who had also looked after him in an illness. Charles, possibly penitent, and Sarah welcomed her, but she never concealed her dislike of them. The marriage had its smooth passages, but was almost wholly calamitous. It is customary to blame Mrs Vazeille, who was jealous, prying and ill-tempered. She once tore out some of Wesley's hair in her rage and threw him to the floor, a position hardly commensurate with the veneration he has received from his followers, or his place in English Church history. There is something to be said in her defence. She was a good business woman and kept the books. She made attempts to share his ministry and his journeys, but did not appreciate the rigours and deprivations, nor the rather uncouth hospitality. His obsession with punctuality could be irritating, while there were always other women in the societies, some predatory, some with whom Wesley had intimate spiritual relationships. There were rumours and 'dirty tricks'. His wife was paranoid with suspicion and Wesley's belief that reason could solve everything and his attempts to excuse himself in response infuriated her the more. She left him several times and after twenty years departed never to return. She died in Newcastle in October 1781, but John was not told for some days; by which time she was buried.

Charles became increasingly concerned that the Societies into which they had gathered the converts might become separate from the Church of England. By the mid-1750s, some of the preachers were demanding this and also the right to administer the sacraments. Charles was alarmed and found support in the Reverend William Grimshaw of Haworth, a clergyman who was sympathetic to the Methodists. He wrote some strange sentences in his Journal about the double blessing when a service is held in Church rather than in the open fields. He propounded an impossible solution that those preachers who did not want to separate should be ordained by bishops, and the others become Dissenting ministers. Mercifully the crisis blew over and those preachers who had taken it upon themselves to administer the sacraments, refrained.

The matter, however, could only be postponed. John Wesley was a moderate episcopalian. He preferred government by bishops either to Presbyterianism or Independency, though he came to have no truck with Apostolic Succession; in these things as in much else, he was a pragmatist. But he became persuaded of a view that in at least one part of the early Church, there had been no distinction between bishops and presbyters.

He did not himself visit America after his ignominious return from Georgia, but some of his followers, notably Francis Asbury, established Methodist Societies there. The situation became extremely delicate because of the War of Independence, in which High Tory Wesley, after early sympathy with the colonists, took the British side, like Dr Johnson, whom he plagiarized.

The colonists' victory left the Church of England in a difficult position; Church of the defeated imperial power, with some devout and conscientious clergy but others whom Thomas Coke described as 'the parasites and bottle companions of the rich and the great'. The Methodists had been there for eighteen years, Asbury for thirteen. There was a great desire for the sacraments and one American Conference had decided on a scheme of ordination which Asbury persuaded them to abandon. Armed with his theory about presbyter-bishops, Wesley took it upon himself in 1784, to 'set apart' Thomas Coke by the imposition of hands as Superintendent for the Church in America. Coke was already a Presbyter of the Church of England. Wesley also ordained two of his preachers for the American work. It was done in great secrecy. Charles was furious. Convinced that Coke, of whom he was undoubtedly jealous, was the evil genius who had perverted his eighty-year old brother, he wrote these lines:

> So easily are Bishops made
> By man or woman's whim?
> W... his hands on C... hath laid,
> But who laid hands on him?

> Hands on himself he laid, and took
> An apostolic chair
> And then ordained his creature C...
> His heir and successor.

Nevertheless in spite of these disagreements and Charles's impetuous interventions, there was a tie between the two brothers which could not be severed. A fortnight after Charles's death in 1788, just over two years before his own, John, preaching at Bolton tried to give out his brother's hymn, 'Wrestling Jacob' and broke down at the words:

> My company before is gone
> And I am left alone with thee.

John himself mellowed and became ever more tolerant as he grew older and acknowledged former excesses in his opinions with 'ingenuous frankness'. Though he was 'Pope John' in his connexion, he became a nationally venerated figure, whom people would travel far to see and hear. And he preached ever of the Divine love for all humanity and of infinite hospitality for sinners in the house of God.

The Dual Contribution

IT IS TRITE BUT TRUE to say that John was the organizer, Charles the poet of Methodism. The importance of hymns in the movement and as a Methodist contribution to Christian spirituality cannot be exaggerated. Not only was excessive enthusiasm contained by the singing; the hymns implanted sound doctrine in the minds of men and women converted from vicious habits and helped colliers and the exploited and downcast victims of the new industries to aspire to the heights and raptures of perfect love. John Wesley, like Dietrich Bonhoeffer in his illegal seminary at Finkelwald, regarded singing as a spiritual exercise and laid down strict rules — sing exactly, sing all, sing lustily, sing modestly ('do not bawl'), do not sing too slow, sing spiritually, so that the heart is not carried away by the sound, but offered to God continually. The 1780 Collection, which gathers up some previous publications, has a remarkable contents table, its sections exhorting and beseeching to return to God, describing the pleasantness of religion, the goodness of God, but also the four last things. Formal and inward religion are described and there are prayers for repentance, hymns for mourners convinced of sin, for those brought to birth, for backsliders and those recovered. And then for believers, rejoicing, fighting, praying, watching, working, suffering, groaning for full redemption, brought to birth, saved, interceding for the world. And finally for the Society. No wonder in the Methodist tradition, the hymn book has been the prayer book also, as influential in private prayer as in groups or congregations. The hymns on the great doctrines of the creeds are not found in the Collection, nor those on the sacraments. When it was published, Wesley still hoped that the parish churches would welcome Methodists to the Liturgy.[7]

But good order was necessary if Methodism was to survive and if its members were to grow in grace. Wesley gathered his converts into Societies in each place and these, as early as Christmas 1738, into Bands and later into classes. In this he was probably following the model of the religious societies for the deepening of the spiritual life which had been a feature of English and European Christianity for some time. Discipline and direction were matters for a small body gathered from the membership, sexually segregated, meeting regularly and rigorous in mutual examination, testimony and confession. These were the 'Bands'. Faults must be confessed and told 'plain and home'. There must be no disguise and no reserve. There was attempt at casuistry.

The Bands were for the especially dedicated members, but when a financial levy became necessary, a Methodist in Bristol thought that this was best collected by a weekly meeting of the Society divided into groups for convenience. Wesley agreed and saw the spiritual possibilities. So every member was henceforth under obligation to meet in class, twelve being the maximum number in each. The principle was the same as that of the Bands and the discipline only a little less rigid.

On 25 December 1744, Wesley supplemented the 1738 Rules with a series of 'Directions Given to the Band Societies'. These are a more exacting version of 'The Nature, Design, and General Rules of the United Societies, in London, Bristol, Kingswood, Newcastle upon Tyne, etc.' of 1 May 1743. Members are to abstain from doing evil and 'zealously to maintain good works'. Under the former they must not buy or sell anything on the Lord's Day, taste no spirituous liquor, unless prescribed by a Physician, pawn nothing, 'no, not to save a life', not mention anyone's fault behind his back and 'stop short those who do', wear no needless ornaments, 'such as rings, ear-rings, necklaces, lace, ruffles', use no needless self-indulgence like snuff or tobacco. Good works include almsgiving, rebuke of sin, frugality. Thirdly there must be constant attendance upon what Wesley called 'the ordinances of God'. These included five particular duties:

1. To be at church and at the Lord's table every week, and at every public meeting of the Bands.
2. To attend the ministry of the word every morning, unless distance, business, or sickness prevent.

This refers to the preaching at 5 a.m. which became an unrealistic demand, though Wesley said that its cessation would mean the end of Methodism. What we should note is that *preaching* was one of Wesley's means of spiritual direction as in the Anglican and Puritan tradition of the seventeenth century.

3. To use private prayer every day; and family prayer, if you are head of a family.

In 1745, Wesley issued *A Collection of Prayers for Families*, much reprinted; and in 1772, *Prayers for Children*. The Oxford Collection of 1733, mentioned above, was reissued many times.

4. To read the Scriptures and meditate therein, at every vacant hour.
5. To observe, as days of fasting or abstinence, all Fridays in the year.

Wesley saw fasting as an act of love for God. He made short shrift of the argument that it is better to abstain from 'pride and vanity, from foolish and hurtful desires, from peevishness and anger, and discontent than from food'. 'Without question it is is'; but abstinence from food is a means to the greater end. 'We refrain from the one, that, being endued with power from on high, we may be able to refrain from the other... For if we ought to abstain from evil tempers and desires, then we ought to abstain from food; since these little instances of self-denial are the ways God hath chose, wherein to bestow that great salvation.'[8]

There were those who saw in Wesley's Methodism covert Popery and the Roman Catholic confessional closeted in the class-meeting. If so, they were likely to be disabused by Bishop Challoner's vehement *A Caveat Against the Methodists* (1760) in which the Methodist preachers and leaders are castigated as 'ministers of Satan', 'false prophets', 'wolves in sheep's clothing'. This roused Wesley's Protestant ire and he replied in terms very different from those of his remarkably eirenical 'Letter to a Roman Catholic' written in Ireland in 1749.

The strictness of Wesley's Rules is understood if we remember that he was not founding a Church but an Order of Societies bound to him and to each other in a nation-wide 'Connexion', but not in rivalry with the established Church. He contemplated, though did not introduce, the 'communism' of the primitive Church as described in the *Acts of the Apostles* and a distinctive dress for Methodists. He was concerned with an *élite corps* particularly in the Rules for the Bands. This presupposed the Church, with its liturgy and sacraments, the hinterland of the pilgrims' progress to perfection.

The revolutionary aspect of Wesley's system of spiritual direction is not only that it is social, a matter of fellowship, but that it is lay. Christians of suitable gifts, graces and dedication, but otherwise ordinary people of no particular education or social cachet, have the power to be spiritual guides and to exercise the priestly office of the remission and retention of sins. Of course, Wesley expected that they would learn from reading and experience. But, in principle, the Methodist laity are not only to be consulted in matters of doctrine, they are to be pastors of the flock. The minister, itinerant, is the *pastor pastorum*, responsible for their training in priesthood. Of course, it does not often work out like that today. Human nature is inveterately hierarchical and a large Church will require a clerical caste for purposes of order and administration.

This system, however, demanded a central authority. While he lived this was Wesley himself in the Chair of an annual Conference of his travelling preachers. In his later years, he was nicknamed 'Pope John'. He often encountered opposition. There were difficulties between those preachers who were ordained clergymen and those who were not, while some Societies sought independence from the 'Connexion', which Wesley, who was no Congregationalist, much less nonconformist, resisted strongly. When Conference became 'the living Wesley' after his death, its autocracy helped to cause many nineteenth-century divisions, grievously bitter in communities which preached perfect love. They are now mostly healed, through democratization, though Conference is still supreme, the heart of *episcope*.

There is no doubt that the system was too severe, too intense. And it confined people's lives too much to a narrow and perhaps self-absorbed piety, even though there were fruits of social good. Some think that subsequent Methodism has become too activist, lacking the contemplative element in spirituality, ignoring Wesley's questions.

Be that as it may, there is no doubt that the class-meeting could be culturally deficient and that as Methodism became a Church there was demand for concerts too. Wesley himself as a young man at Oxford combined a liberal social life with his strict Anglican rule, though he may always have been preternaturally serious. Yet he possessed a copy of Shakespeare, which he had copiously annotated. One of his preachers destroyed it after his death. Martin Thornton's is an intriguing suggestion: 'The Methodist class meeting, in part reviving the English empirical tradition, would have been still more creative had Parson Woodforde presided'. (The clericalism is a serious misunderstanding. The Parson should not preside.)[9]

Criticisms may stand. Yet one cannot endorse the conclusions of an undergraduate essay of a few years ago, clearly influenced by E. P. Thompson, that Methodist doctrines 'perverted all that was healthy in men's emotions, its creed was cruel and grim, its view of life bleak and joyless'. At the heart of spiritual direction was Fellowship, rather in the sense of the Prayer Book Marriage service, 'the mutual society, help and comfort, that the one ought to have of the other, both in prosperity and adversity'. This did happen and there was joy, in sins forgiven and in the friendship of Christ mediated by his people. One of Charles's hymns, abbreviated these days, is specifically for the class-meeting:

> Try us, O God, and search the ground
> Of every sinful heart:
> Whate'er of sin in us is found,
> O bid it all depart!
>
> When to the right or left we stray,
> Leave us not comfortless!
> But guide our feet into the way
> Of everlasting peace.
>
> Help us to help each other, Lord,
> Each other's cross to bear
> Let each his friendly aid afford,
> And feel his brother's care.

[187]

Help us to build each other up,
Our little stock improve;
Increase our faith, confirm our hope,
And perfect us in love.

Up into thee our living Head,
Let us in all things grow,
Till thou hast made us free indeed,
And spotless here below.

Then, when the mighty work is wrought,
Receive they ready Bride;
Give us in heav'n a happy lot
With all the sanctified.

It is impossible not to mention the eucharistic teaching of the Wesleys, especially that contained in the best-selling *Hymns on the Lord's Supper* of 1745, written to be sung at the crowded communions of sometimes well over a thousand people throughout the Wesleys' lives. It is nearly all Charles, but has John's imprimatur. The Eucharist was for the Wesleys the supreme means of grace and 'constant communion' was a duty in obedience to Christ's irrefragable command, as they believed it, 'Do this in remembrance of me'. 'If Jesus bids me lick the dust, I bow to his command'. Wesley also maintains that the Lord's Supper was a 'converting' as well as a 'confirming' ordinance, on the precedent of the Apostles at the Last Supper and his own Mother, who, in old age, found peace at the table of the Lord. The Hymns are a paraphrase of a treatise, which would be otherwise forgotten by a Caroline Dean of Lincoln, Daniel Brevint, called *The Christian Sacrament and Sacrifice*.

The heart of this eucharistic theology is Anamnesis, Memorial, the conveyance of God's grace, though there is Anglican agnosticism as to how bread and wine become its channels, the anticipation and pledge of heaven, and Sacrifice. The once for all Sacrifice of Christ on the Cross, offered in the temple which is the world, releases the Divine life, like the smoke of a burnt offering, or the blood of an animal sprinkled on the people and the altar to expiate sin and reconcile God and humankind in a perpetual covenant. This Sacrifice is re-presented in the Supper, so that Christ and all his benefits are made real and we are able to offer the Sacrifice of ourselves through union with him in his death. We share the fellowship of his sufferings and continue what he began, so that while he went to the altar of his Cross alone, to do for us what we cannot do for ourselves, he is now no longer alone. All the things which happen to us as his disciples, our own sufferings, and our mean gifts, intentions and oblations of good are joined to his great Sacrifice.

> Would the Saviour of mankind
> Without his people die
> No, to him we all are join'd
> As more than standers by.

This is high doctrine, though it does not venture beyond the Anglicanism of the Caroline Divines. It cannot be pretended that the Methodist people as a whole have either understood it or made it their own. In the 1780 Collection, seven of the 166 *Hymns on the Lord's Supper* were dispersed among the sections and few realized their source. There is a certain ambivalence in Charles Wesley himself in his devotion to the Sacrament and his relentless preaching of justification by faith. He never really integrated the two. As W. F. Lofthouse wrote in the finest study of Charles Wesley this century: 'His passion and jealousy for the Lord's Supper were lifelong. If he thought that it, or the Church that administered it, were threatened, he took up arms in its defence as if it were the very citadel of the Christian life. But if he were dealing with the great evangelical doctrine of justification by faith, the Sacrament might be unmentioned'.[10]

The spirituality of the Wesleys was defined by an American author, George Croft Cell in 1935 as 'a necessary synthesis of the Protestant ethic of grace with the Catholic ethic of holiness'. That is misleading as a summary of the argument of Cell's book and it needs some qualification if it implies that Protestantism has no concern with holiness and also if it ignores the affinities with Orthodox spirituality, which Canon Allchin has shown in various writings. But it may be claimed that the Wesleys' spirituality was a synthesis of religion and morality, grace and law, faith and reason, scripture, tradition and experience and inward and outward religion.[11]

There are three keys to it. One, the belief that, as Canon Allchin put it in drawing a parallel with the eleventh-century Byzantine saint, Symeon the New Theologian, 'Christians in every age are to expect to know and to feel all that the first Christians knew and felt, that there is no dimunition in the action of the Spirit throughout the ages'. Two, that there is an immediacy about salvation. This can be dangerous doctrine, especially when it becomes a belief that one may attain the 'second blessing' and become perfect 'at a clap'. Salvation is a process as John Wesley in particular knew and the grace of God works 'imperceptibly' in an adverb Charles used:

> Happy the man, who poor and low,
> Less goodness in himself conceives
> Than Christ doth of his servant know;
> Who saved from self-reflection lives,
> Unconscious of the grace bestowed
> Simply resigned and lost in God.

Yet there should be an impatience in the Christian life. We should not be content for the Kingdom and the life of perfect love to be postponed to the Greek calends. The ancient Christian cry .was *Maranatha*, the drowning nun in Hopkins's *The Wreck of the Deutschland* prayed 'O Christ come quickly'. And so Charles Wesley, longing for the vision of God:

> Haste, my Lord, no more delay,
> Come, my Saviour, come away.

And in a very different hymn, about Christ's heavenly inter-cession, 'This instant now I may receive/The answer of his power-ful prayer'. Some of the cures of Jesus in the Gospels were instantaneous, though some gradual, and it is not beyond the power of Divine grace to complete his work in the soul in a moment, as perhaps in a sudden death. But we must not rest anywhere short of heaven, nor believe that Christ wills to leave his work half done. We must desire God with 'nothing between'. This teaching has been interpreted by Dr Newton Flew in terms of de Caussade's 'Sacra-ment of the Present Moment'. We should live the 'moment-by-moment' life of Matthew 6:25ff. Salvation is not simply a matter of future longing, nor should it wait for death. Each moment should be of expectancy and of life in the Kingdom.[12]

The third key is Love. This rather than Faith is the transcen-dent virtue. Here is John Wesley:

It were well you should be thoroughly sensible of this: the heaven of heavens is love. There is nothing higher in religion; there is in effect nothing else. If you look for anything but *more love*, you are looking wide of the mark, you are getting out of the royal way. And when you are asking others, 'Have *you* received this or that blessing?, if you mean anything but *more love* you are leading them out of the way, and putting them upon a false scent. Settle it then in your heart, that from the moment God has saved you from all sin, you are to aim at nothing more, but more of that love described in the thirteenth of Corinthians.[13]

God knows, love is an ambiguous term and the whole relation of sexuality to spirituality cannot be evaded, especially in a study of the Wesleys. John, in the Minutes of Conference of 1745, in answer to the question whether an entirely sanctified man would be capable of marriage, replies, 'We cannot well judge. But supposing he were not, the number of those in that state is so small, that it would produce no inconvenience'. A puzzled and curious answer indeed!

We may sometimes have cause to think so, but it is not true that sexual love is all evil, or that the sexual impulse is in itself the barrier that separates us from God. It may be selfish, destructive, fickle. And yet in the desire for perfect union, for total self-giving, it points to the love of God. What we must never forget is that perfect love is ethical, in some sense disinterested, not just feeling, arousal, excitement. It is deed.

Love is inseparable from mysticism in religion because it longs for union. Wesley, after much reading in some mystics — though not alas! the great Carmelites — in the 1730s, became critical through the 'stillness' controversy. He felt also that mysticism led to melancholy through quietism and solitude. 'The Gospel of Christ knows of no religion but social; no holiness but social holiness'. One may lose oneself in God, but never one's neighbour. Charles's finest hymns redress the balance, though he was always in danger of being carried away on the wings of poesy. But his greatest in this genre, 'Thou Shepherd of Israel and mine', never goes beyond New Testament spirituality even though it is based on the Song of Songs 1:23. It is of a shared beatitude with 'the lambs of thy flock' and shows his devotion to Christ crucified and the historic passion.

Wesley's teaching on perfection was confused, divisive, provoked scandals, errors, mania and the very evils of pride, malice and all uncharitableness it was intended to obliterate forever, and rested on an inadequate concept of sin. But it may be redeemed from its dangers if there is perceived a link with the Orthodox spirituality of the fourth-century Cappadocian Father, Gregory of Nyssa. He seems to have been an influence on Wesley through the Homilies of the so-called 'Macarius the Egyptian', who was in fact a Syrian monk. He taught that perfection is not a state, but progress. 'This', said Gregory, 'truly is the vision of God, never to be satisfied in the desire to see him. But one must always by looking at what he can see, rekindle his desire to see more. . ... Thus no limit would interrupt growth in the ascent to God, since no limit to the good can be found, nor is the increase of desire for the Good brought to an end because it is satisfied'. In some sense, as W. F. Lofthouse said in a review of Newton Flew's book in the *Journal of Theological Studies*, attainment and non-attainment imply each other as every lover knows.

All in all, there is an amazing optimism in the Wesleys' spirituality, an optimism found rarely today in the best theologians, if one excepts the liberationists. The slogan 'Holiness is happiness' rests on more solid foundations than 'I am H-A-P-P-Y' or 'Smile, Jesus loves you'; but it is in some contrast to Newman's 'Holiness rather than peace'. The Wesleys could be too exuberant, not least in the face of natural disasters such as earthquakes, yet there is a lyrical strain in Christianity and in theistic religion found sometimes among the most oppressed, like the Jews in the death trains to Auschwitz who sang of the day when they would feast upon Leviathan.

Keble found much of Methodism distasteful, not least its lack of reserve and of reverence. Did it not coarsen the Gospel and make it cheap, selling it at every street corner? There is a great difference in style between Methodism and the Oxford Movement and we have reluctantly to admit with Marshall McCluhan that 'the medium is the message', or often seems to be. Yet Keble, quiet, shy, afraid of undue excitement and emotion, thinking that for most of the time the practice of religion should be dull duty for God's glory, not our delectation, was not without his concern for the poor as the foundation of this College bears witness. He was Professor of Poetry and was thought to be in peril of being deemed a Methodist in composing the lyrics of that once popular book, *The Christian Year*. He taught the spirituality of the 'moment-by-moment life' and Charles Wesley and he could have sung together that prayer of his evening hymn, which even modern editors dare not eschew, that we journey through this world with its vicissitudes and its backslidings, in the presence of the Christ:

Till in the ocean of thy love
We lose ourselves in heaven above.

NOTES

[1] Substantial paragraphs about John Wesley, particularly his early life, are reproduced from my *John Wesley* (Foundry Press, 1990) by kind permission of the publishers.

[192]

The latest and definitive biography of John Wesley is Henry D. Rack *Reasonable Enthusiast* (Epworth Press, 1989). His works, first published by the Clarendon Press, Oxford, are being reissued at Nashville, Tennessee. The most relevant are Vols 18, 19, 20, *Journals and Diaries (1735–51)* ed. W. R. Ward, and Vols 25, 26, *Letters (1721–55)* ed. F. Baker.

See also Isabel Rivers, *Reason, Grace and Sentiment I Whichcote to Wesley* (Cambridge, 1991). Ernest Gordon Rupp, *Religion in England 1688–1791* (Clarendon Press, Oxford, 1986) has studies of both brothers. Charles Wesley's *Life* and *Journals* were edited by Thomas Jackson in the 1840s. *The Poetical Works* were published in 1872. The 1780 *Collection* ed. F. Hildebrandt and O. A. Beckerlegge is in the *Works* (Oxford, 1983). J. E. Rattenbury, *The Eucharistic Hymns of John and Charles Wesley* (Epworth, 1948) is important.

2   *Letters* ed. J. Telford (London, 1931) V, 15–17.
3   See Henry Bett, *The Hymns of Methodism in their Literary Relations* (London, 1913 and subsequent editions).
4   Donald Davie, *A Gathered Church* (Routledge and Kegan Paul, London, 1978), p. 49f.
5   *Works* ed. G. Moreton, (London, 1893), VI 183–4, 188.
6   Donald Davie, ibid.
7   See Franz Hildebrandt and Oliver A. Beckerlegge eds., *A Collection of Hymns for the Use of the People called Methodists* (Clarendon Press, Oxford, 1983), passim.
8   *Sermons* ed. E. H. Sugden, (London, 1921) I 451ff.
9   Martin Thornton, *English Spirituality* (SPCK, London, 1963), 285.
10 Davies and Rupp eds., *A History of the Methodist Church in Great Britain* (London, 1965) 123f.
11 Cf. G. C. Cell, *The Rediscovery of John Wesley* (New York, 1935), 360–1.
12 Cf. R. Newton Flew, *The Idea of Perfection in Christian Theology* (Oxford, 1934), 405–8.
13 *A Plain Account of Christian Perfection* 25 Q. 33.
14 Gregory of Nyssa, *The Life of Moses* ed. A. J. Malherbe and E. Ferguson (New York, 1978), 116.

STEPHEN PRICKETT

Church and University in the Life of John Keble

I WANT TO BEGIN with a passage from one of the Victorian Church's most sincere friends and admirers, Anthony Trollope. It concerns the Reverend Francis Arabin, fellow of Lazarus, late Professor of Poetry at Oxford, and . . . vicar of St Ewold, in the diocese of Barchester.

> '. . . the favoured disciple of the great Dr. Gwynne, a high churchman at all points; so high, indeed, that at one period of his career he had all but toppled over into the cesspool of Rome; a poet and also a polemical writer, a great pet in the common rooms at Oxford, an eloquent clergyman, and a droll, odd, humorous, energetic, conscientious man, and, as the archdeacon had boasted of him, a thorough gentleman.'[1]

No, this is clearly not *quite* John Keble, but as clergyman, poet, Oxford don, and even Professor of Poetry there is clearly more than a passing resemblance between the fictional saviour of Barchester, future husband of Eleanor Bold, and the real man whom we commemorate in these essays — and it is also true, I believe, that in the creation of the many-sided Mr Arabin Trollope has seen and captured one particular quality about John Keble that very few of his other contemporaries had noticed; that is the way in which this many-sidedness relates to, and centres on, the University of Oxford. This may seem, at first sight, like a monstrous cliché : *of course* Keble was an Oxford man; *of course* we associate his name with this ancient University — if not from the cradle to the grave, at least from the astonishingly early age of fourteen, when he first came into residence at Corpus Christi. What I am referring to is something different: the fact that both the Church of England and this University are subtly different kinds of places because of the way in which Keble himself associated them.

Regina Schwartz has shrewdly observed in her introduction to a recent collection of essays on biblical interpretation,[2] that just as the Reformation tells us not merely about arguments between translators, but also about the realities of political power in the sixteenth century, so too the shift of theological and biblical studies from the Church to the University in the nineteenth and twentieth centuries tells us not merely about the growth of academic scholarship in the last hundred and fifty years, but also about another, no less profound shift in the balance of political power between Church and University. Since this was to happen, in various ways, in Germany and in the USA as well as in Britain, we can reasonably infer that this shift was part of a general pattern of cultural change — at least in the advanced Protestant economies — but it will be my contention that John Keble was a crucial figure in the particular way in which this happened in England.

Let us return for a moment to Trollope, that acute observer of the Victorian ecclesiastical scene. It has often been commented upon, inevitably as a criticism, that the clergy of Barchester are everything except clergy; that is, that they have no spiritual life, just as Trollope's engaging politicians in his Palliser novels, are everything except politicians — that is, that they never engage in debate over what we know from the history books to be the great political issues of the day. But that is with hindsight and the often spurious clarity of focus that we dignify with the title of historical interpretation. What Trollope portrays with such uncompromising clarity in his massive sequence of political novels is that for the vast majority of the Members of Parliament in the mid-years of the nineteenth century, drawn as they were from essentially the same class and with a similar education and culture, there *were* no such divisive political issues. Politics was less about policy than the division of the spoils of office. So too with Trollope's venal and politicking clergy. It is only with hindsight, with a knowledge of the doctrinal differences that lay behind the Gorham case, or the controversy over *Tract Ninety*, that we think we see the great theological issues of the day. As Mark Pattison's *Memoirs* make clear, Oxford of the 1830s and 1840s, with its sinecures, its indifferent scholarship, and endless petty feuding, was much more like the world Trollope portrays than that of godliness and good learning so often seemingly presented by the Tractarians.[3] For the working diocesan clergy of Barchester, and a dozen other dioceses like it, their reality, like that of the politicians, *was* the division of spoils: who was to be vicar of Eiderdown and Stoppingum, not to mention St Ewold's; who was to be Archdeacon; who was to be the new Bishop? Even the great doctrinal differences were perceived largely in terms of personalities. Nowhere, as I recall, is the odious Mr Slope described, as the histories would have him, as Low-Church or Evangelical; only once is it even mentioned that Mr Arabin is a Tractarian. What we *are* told at some length is how he sat at the feet of the great Newman — and that it was only after the most profound spiritual wrestling that the young Arabin was prevented from following him to Rome.

> It was from the curate of a small Cornish parish that he learnt to know that the highest laws for the governance of a Christian's duty must act from within and not from without; that no man can become a serviceable servant solely by obedience to written edicts; and that the safety which he was about to seek within the gates of Rome was no other than the selfish freedom from personal danger which the bad soldier attempts to gain who counterfeits illness on the eve of battle.
>
> Mr Arabin returned to Oxford a humbler but a better and a happier man; and from that time forth he put his shoulder to the wheel, as a clergyman of the Church for which he had been educated.[4]

What is interesting about this passage is not so much what Trollope thinks he is saying about the difference, as it were, between Newman and Keble, important as that is, but what he takes absolutely for granted: that the young Arabin, having come through this spiritual crisis under the guidance of a saintly but nameless West Country curate, *returned to Oxford*. So closely interconnected are the images of University and Anglican Church in his mind that it does not even apparently occur to Trollope that his hero might have 'put his shoulder to the wheel' at some other, perhaps slightly muddier, point on the ecclesiastical vehicle.

Moreover, we are left in no doubt what this returning means in his life. Trollope's irony may not be obtrusive, but in conjunction with the following paragraph its thrust is unmistakable. Despite its superficial suggestion of getting one's hands dirty, 'putting his shoulder to the wheel' does not turn out to be a matter of self-mortification and hardship. Quite the contrary: we are told a couple of paragraphs later, he became 'the pet of the college.' We are also told in some detail of what that role of pet consisted. Quitting his discipleship of Newman, he becomes instead a follower and ally of the head of his college, Dr Gwynne. The new, purged and spiritually mature Arabin

> . . .was great in sermons, great on platforms, great at after dinner conversations, and always pleasant as well as great. He took delight in elections, served on committees, opposed tooth and nail all projects of university reform, and talked jovially over his glass of port of the ruin to be anticipated by the Church, and of the sacrilege daily committed by the Whigs. The ordeal through which he had gone, in resisting the blandishments of the lady of Rome, had certainly done much towards the strengthening of his character. Although in small and outward matters he was self-confident enough, nevertheless in things affecting the inner man he aimed at a humility of spirit which would never have been attractive to him but for that visit to the coast of Cornwall. This visit he now repeated every year.[5]

It is easy enough to dismiss this shift in tone as harmless satire — an attempt, perhaps, to avoid making our future hero too much of a good thing. Yet that may be too easy a way out. Arabin's good-living knee-jerk conservatism *is* uncomfortably close to the behaviour of many of the later Tractarians — and there is not much evidence that, in spite of the explicit contrast between the poverty of the Cornish curate and the opulence of Oxford, Trollope necessarily disapproved of the latter. My point again, however, is not what is being said, but what is being taken for granted: that ' . . . Mr Arabin returned to Oxford.'

In other words, by 1857 it could confidently be taken for granted that the real powerhouse of the Church of England — the place where its policies were debated, its theologies formulated, its biblical criticism practised — was not within the structure of the church itself, but in the semi-autonomous world of a university. Now clearly this is an assertion that needs unpacking with some care. Though Trollope explicitly sets his novel in his own time, the world of the 1850s, there is a case to be made that Arabin's Oxford still belongs to the unreformed world of the 1840s, when all fellows of colleges had still to be in holy orders and when disputes over ecclesiastical minutiae ruled the day. Such an Oxford was, in effect, little more than the Church of England at its books. Yet, as I have indicated, Trollope was an acute observer of his contemporary scene, and would have known about the 1851 Royal Commission into the University of Oxford, its findings and recommendations, not to mention the flood of reforms that actually preceded it. 'If any Oxford man had gone to sleep in 1846', wrote Pattison, 'and had woke up again in 1850, he would have found himself in a totally new world.'[6] Pattison himself, of course, was by this time one of the leaders of reform, and the Lazarus set would have seen what was going on very differently. But Trollope's dating is unusually precise over Arabin's career, and there is an equally strong case to be made that Arabin does indeed belong to that new, reformed Oxford, and that what he represents is therefore something much more disturbingly schizophrenic. Certainly the ritual denunciation of the Whigs and of university reform in general belongs very much to the rear guard of the 1850s, when Oxford was in such a period of continuing change. If, with the disappearance of Newman and the secularization of the university, spirituality has been marginalized to the coast of Cornwall, ecclesio-political power and influence had been centralized, as perhaps never before in Oxford.

As we have said, Keble is not Arabin. If anything, he more closely resembles the anonymous Cornish curate. He had, after all, resigned his fellowship at Oriel and left Oxford in 1823; even his Professorship of Poetry from 1832–41 did not require residence. In the years immediately after Newman's departure scores of earnest young Oxford men did indeed make pilgrimages to the modest and retiring Vicar of Hursley to receive tacit rather than verbal reassurance that their place was still with the Church for which they had been educated. But we are, I think, justified in seeing in the curious and complex relationship between Oxford and Barchester that Trollope so vividly portrays a changing world that was, more than either he or it would have acknowledged, influenced by Keble. Nor is this influence solely that symbolized by the Cornish curate on the one hand, or that of the 'port-and-grumbling kind' of either the Oriel (or the Lazarus) common room on the other. To understand the background to Keble's attachment to Oxford we must turn back to that tradition of English Romanticism that was in so many ways the mainspring of the Tractarians — and in particular to two influences, one fully acknowledged, the other less so: those of Wordsworth and Coleridge respectively.[7]

Keble's admiration for Wordsworth is well-documented. It is stylistically evident throughout *The Christian Year*, and was made fully explicit when, as Professor of Poetry, he published his lectures with a fulsome dedication to the elder poet. Yet the real influence of Wordsworth was, I believe, far deeper than even Keble himself could recognize. Though, as the yet unpublished poem, *The Prelude*, makes clear, Wordsworth had been disparaging about the quality of his actual Cambridge education, he nevertheless also came to display a veneration for the tradition and ethos of his old university that almost rivals that of Keble. In so doing he offers a solution to a problem that was in its own way as important to Keble as it was to himself: what to do with the palpable dead weight of past tradition in a time of profound social, economic, and spiritual change. On first coming down from Cambridge Wordsworth, as we all know, had become an ardent supporter of the French Revolution: a faith that even being a witness to the first wave of massacres in September 1793 was insufficient to shake. His revulsion, when it did eventually come, was the more complete for its slowness in arriving. Society, he came to believe, must accommodate to change not by clean breaks and revolutionary violence, but by appropriating and revitalizing its own sense of the past. This was at once both a social and a critical maxim; as much a profound shift in sensibility as it was a change of ideas. Romanticism was the first literary movement to be self-consciously historical. But with Wordsworth and the English Romantics, as with Schleiermacher in Germany it was never historicist. In the sense which Schleiermacher was to give to the word, it was 'hermeneutical', seeking not to distance or relativize the past, but to understand it in its own terms, and to allow it to speak to the contemporary condition. Thus though, like all literary movements it was quick to repudiate the critical theory of its immediate predecessors, significantly it did not include in that condemnation the works of the past, though it introduced its own criteria for re-evaluating them. This is the period when the idea of a literary canon that extended beyond classical times takes hold for the first time. Whereas Dryden and the other early Augustans could dismiss the metaphysicals and admire Shakespeare as a primitive to be purged of his more obvious barbarities of diction and construction, the Romantics turned back to him as the archetype of sublimity. The cult of Shakespeare pre-dates Wordsworth and Coleridge by a few years, but reaches with them, and with their German counterparts, Goethe, Tieck, Schiller, and the Schlegels, a pre-eminence which it has still largely retained. It is a remarkable fact that Coleridge's *Biographia Literaria* tells the story of his own literary development not through an account of his own works, but by examining the importance of Shakespeare and Wordsworth and the literary tradition that links them. The Romantics looked to the past not for models to be followed as patterns of correctness, but for sources of inspiration that could be appropriated, revitalized, and used in essentially new ways. Wordsworth's *White Doe of Rylstone* or his *Ecclesiastical Sonnets* are in this of a piece with his attacks on poverty and the abuse of privilege in the *Lyrical Ballads*. What so often takes the form of autobiography at an individual level, at a communal level becomes historiography. The Gothic revival, the Tractarians' *Lives of the Saints*, and Keble's rediscovery of the unity of the Church and the Vincentian canon are all aspects of the same fundamental shift in sensibility.

By contrast the influence of Coleridge was less in terms of sensibility than of ideas — but it is a framework of ideas that is grounded in that new sensibility, and would in many ways be incomprehensible without it. Georgina Battiscombe has pointed out that Keble was in fact one of the very first Anglican clergy to recognize that the Church, even in its ideal conception, was not coextensive with the State, and that they might operate 'as separate and even opposing forces'.[8] Though she does not say so, in this conception of a balance or dialectic of forces, Keble is drawing heavily on Coleridge's *Church and State* (1830), written in response to the original proposal to enfranchise Catholics — the success of which had led to the crisis of 1833.[9] Similarly he also preserves Coleridge's more subtle idea of the relationship between what he calls the 'National Church' and the 'Church of Christ'. Thus in his Assize Sermon of 1833, Keble's vision is of the Anglican Church as the representative in England of the whole Church, Catholic and Apostolic, which is 'built upon the Apostles and prophets, Jesus Christ himself being the chief corner-stone.' This Apostolic Church is a much greater thing than the Church of England, although the latter is emphatically a true part of it, and it is to this metaphysical — but to Keble sacramental and therefore entirely concrete — entity that the Christian's loyalty is ultimately due. If the present generation were to fail her, it might be said by those coming after 'There was once a glorious Church here but it was betrayed into the hands of libertines for the real or affected love of a little temporary peace and good order.' But if the Church of England were to vanish, as the Churches of Byzantium and Ephesus had vanished, still the Catholic and Apostolic Church would survive, and the gates of Hell could not prevail against it. The Churchman is, therefore, possessed of an infallible and certain hope: 'He is calmly, soberly, demonstrably sure that, sooner or later, his will be the winning side, and that the victory will be complete, universal, eternal.'[10] In the meantime, there was the Church of England, not to mention the National Church, that was entrusted to the movement of 1833 and must be defended.

[201]

This Coleridgean distinction between the National Church and the Church of Christ is, I believe, crucial to understand Keble's thinking about Oxford. Central to Coleridge's idea of the National Church is that it represents the highest ideals and spiritual aspirations of any particular actual community. Thus it need not necessarily be Christian at all; Coleridge illustrates this with some rather unconvincing references to the role of the druids among the ancient Britons, and to the Levites in Old Testament Israel, and a rather better analogy from viticulture.

> As the olive tree is said in its growth to fertilize the surrounding soil, to invigorate the roots of the vines in its immediate neighbourhood, and to improve the strength and flavour of the wines; such is the relationship of the Christian and the National Church. But as the olive is not the same plant with the vine . . . even so is Christianity . . . no essential part of the being of the National Church, however conducive or even indispensable it may be to its well being. And even so a National Church might exist, and has existed, without . . . the Christian Church.[11]

It is, however, a 'blessed accident' that the National Church of England, in the nineteenth century, *should* be Christian — in other words that it should also represent, for Keble at least, the true Catholic and Apostolic faith. But, for Coleridge, the English National Church was much more than simply the Anglican Communion. In its role as guardian and preserver of what one might call the fundamental national values, his National Church includes not merely the clergy, but also the universities and what he calls 'the great schools.' These three 'estates' of the realm together make up the 'Clerisy' whose function and task it is to educate and guide the nation, intellectually, morally, and no less spiritually. In coining, or rather, appropriating this word for his purposes Coleridge had deliberately chosen a term that seemed to have ecclesiastical and religious undertones, and it appears to have been precisely these conservative and undenominationally religious connotations that most appealed to those fellow-Victorians most moved by Coleridge's vision, including the Arnolds, Carlyle, Mill, Maurice, Sterling and their fellow members of the Cambridge debating society later to be known as 'The Apostles'.[12] In Mill's own submission to the 1851 Royal Commission on the University of Oxford he speaks of the national need to create an 'educated clerisy' for the maintenance of its values and culture.

It is, I believe, in Coleridge's idea of the Clerisy that we are most likely to discover the origins of Keble's idea of the university. But that suggestion immediately requires two important caveats. The first is that, as we have already seen, his attitude towards the university was not primarily a matter of ideas, but of emotions. This is not just a matter of a former student's sense of loyalty to his Alma Mater — especially when that student had gone up university at the impressionable age of fourteen, and been elected to a fellowship at nineteen; an age when most modern students are still in their first year. Nor is it simply a matter of that general Wordsworthian shift of sensibility referred to earlier. It is also an attachment to an ideal less of behaviour or way of thinking than of a particular quality. Again, Trollope hits the mark when he has Archdeacon Grantly insist that Mr Arabin is, above all, a gentleman. Keble had himself coined a new word from Greek etymology to convey something of this very quality of mind and manners. That word is 'ethos'. His first biographer, J. T. Coleridge describes it thus:

> With Keble it imported certainly no intellectual quality, scarcely even any distinct moral one, but an habitual toning, or colouring diffused over all a man's moral qualities, giving the exercise of them a peculiar gentleness and grace; it was not that the Oxford lad was more dutiful, more brave, more truthful, more punctual in his religious duties than any other, but that these qualities were habitually exercised by him with more deference, and reverence towards his elders, more gentleness and loving-kindness to all.[13]

And that definition leads us to my second caveat: that the idea of a university in the abstract was for Keble inseparable from the concrete and particular: the University of Oxford. Indeed, it may well be that it was because Keble had resigned his fellowship at Oriel comparatively early in his career, just after he was thirty, that he was able to hold so consistently an idealized vision of an institution which, as we have seen, in other eyes smelt more of corruption and cynicism than of sanctity.

What Wordsworth and Coleridge offered Keble, therefore, was not so much a new concept of the university, but a new sensibility and a structure by which his existing reflexes of love and loyalty towards Oxford might be brought into his total theological scheme of things. As an expression of the National Church, the University of Oxford could itself be seen to mirror the qualities that distinguished the Anglican Church. Moreover Wordsworth's maxim, 'We murder to dissect', was for Keble as equally applicable to the University as to the Church . One of his duties as Professor of

Poetry was in 1839 to deliver the Crewian Oration, and it is significant that he chose this occasion of the conferring of an honorary degree on William Wordsworth, to give us his fullest account of this deeply-felt analogy between Church and University. Though J. T. Coleridge gives us a lengthy and glowing account of what was evidently a deeply moving ceremony, it is striking that the original text of Keble's speech was never published, and all subsequent accounts of it have been from that one secondary source. All that has survived of the original are Keble's scrawled and abbreviated Latin notes in the Keble College library. Only with the recent painstakingly established text by Mr Paul Jeffreys-Powell, and his English translation from it, can the full course of Keble's argument — and its astonishing radicalism — be appreciated now for the first time. The outlines are nevertheless familiar enough to anyone who has followed the argument so far:

> ... one thing above all joins the Academy and the Church with a single bond, that their realm lives in the memory of our ancestors and is yet present among us ... But if I am to tell the truth as it is, I find a doubt arising: does this grateful, this honourable similitude limp a little on one side? For there are three names especially with which the Church is wont to be honoured: she is called Holy, Catholic, and Apostolic: now surely the shadow of the Church, the Academy, does not lack her own sanctity; she does not lack her own admirable succession, by which her life and being have been propagated these near thousand years; but this I fear, that she does not at every point achieve that third attribute, which is called Catholic. For by the mere judgement of the eyes, this Athens of ours belongs not so much to the poor, as to those who were born to some position in the world.[14]

This is perhaps Keble's most explicit statement of his view of the University. If the Church was inalienably Holy, Catholic, and Apostolic, so too should be what he calls this secular 'shadow' of it. For Keble the 'holiness' of the Church lay not merely in its capacity to change the hearts and minds of its adherents — the Nonconformists believed as much — but also in its mysterious and hidden capacity to work through an entire sacramental community. Keble's notion of 'ethos' is, in effect, very much a secularized version of this theological principle, and it goes a long way to explain why Trollope was right in making the Arabins of this world, with their deep spiritual sense of the sacramental community of the Church, also those most adamantly opposed to the secularization of the University and the most elementary reforms of the curriculum.

The Church was Apostolic not merely in the sense of having an unbroken organic and historic continuity with the first Christians, but also, through that living stream of Grace, by partaking of the immensely rich and complex organic wholeness of its tradition. The Vincentian formula of *quod ubique, quod semper, quod ab omnibus*,[15] pointed towards the University in the etymological sense that the word was popularly given as 'universal' in its scope[16]: its very ethos, as Newman saw, demanding that all knowledge be ultimately related to all other knowledge, and studied with that sense of its corporate wholeness. What mattered was the health and balance of that organic whole. To elevate the authority of the Church over scripture, as the Romans did, was as much to endanger this balance of health as to elevate scripture over the interpretative tradition of the Church, as evangelicals and Nonconformists were wont to do. Similarly the University was not merely an organic whole, but it was also the heir to a long and complex tradition, as much cultural as intellectual. It was not simply concerned with instruction, but also with the needs of the growing person in all his aspects. Such an ideal was still just possible in the early nineteenth century. Keble's own double First had been in Classics and Mathematics; Newman, the year after his own spectacular crash in Schools had turned to the study of mineralogy, chemistry, and music.[17] Classics, at this period, embraced almost the whole learning of the ancient world, including not merely its language and literature, but its philosophy and even the little there was of archeology. Even later in the century, Gladstone, when Leader of the Opposition, could fill in his spare time by writing a two-volume study of Homer — and seemed secretly convinced that the study of Greek politics was a great deal more rewarding and educative than British politics. But the lack of Catholicity, in its most fundamental sense, could not be ignored, and here Keble springs a real surprise on us. The Crewian Oration embodies so passionate a belief in the values of the past, that even to question their use is seen as fundamentally 'unnatural' and a breach of faith:

> Nature herself somehow protests, when such Epicurean doctrines are proclaimed, as that antiquity is to be ignored; that utility is the measure of all things; that even the ancient rites should be held of no account, unless they seem to bring some immediate advantage.[18]

How could such a quintessential conservative argue for the kind of reforms that would lead to the opening up of Oxford to every obscure Jude that might turn up at the gates? The answer is breathtakingly simple. Oxford, like the Church, was originally founded not for the wealthy and illustrious, but for the poor. What qualified a man for Oxford was not a desire for advancement but a thirst for knowledge. In medieval times poverty and scholarship went hand-in-hand: the poor clerk of Oxenford was less a stock figure than he was a historical reality. And that historical reality had also included the creation of a real and functioning clerisy:

> . . . I pray you, recall and re-imagine what was the shape and figure of academic things, at the time when we began to enjoy a firm succession of records. There were more than thirty thousand clerks: some attending to learning here, some wandered all over England, in such a condition of life, for the most part, that the phrase became proverbial: Oxford means poor; while meantime aristocratic youths despised and detested all pursuits except soldiering.[19]

If Coleridge, in *Church and State*, had performed the near-impossible by inventing a past to change the future, Keble has here out-run his master. Not merely was the Church in danger from the so-called 'reforms' of a basely utilitarian nineteenth century, so was the University as well. Keble is, in effect, calling not merely for Oxford to be opened up, but for scholarships to support poor grammar-school boys on the grounds that this was a return to the medieval purity of the pre-Reformation University. He continues:

> . . . let the Academy join itself more closely with the views of those who, at this very moment, have by divine inspiration (for I shall speak boldly) formed the plan of propagating in each town not only elementary schools or places to learn a profitable trade, let alone the studios of a wordy and empty philosophy, but those schools which nurture servants and children worthy of Holy Church.[20]

Mr Arabin, one imagines, cannot have been present at this extraordinary scene; no doubt he had already departed for his summer vacation in Cornwall.

Just as the Tractarians had, in effect, re-invented the idea of the Church, so Keble, here and elsewhere, is now re-inventing the idea of the university. Though there are many strands of influence in this, ranging from Coleridge to local campaigns for Parish Schools, it is not a mere synthesis of others' ideas. Nor has the scope of this remarkable achievement, I believe, been fully appreciated. Keble's work has been overshadowed by that of Newman, but we need to remember the degree to which Newman's own thinking on this topic was shaped over many years by his close contact with Keble and his admiration for him. We need to remember, too, that Newman was utterly unsuccessful in attempting to persuade the Irish bishops to follow his prescriptions — and the bishops may well have been wise after their own generation. As later experience has shown with the founding of other new universities, the idealized ethos of collegiate Oxford is not a particularly transplantable quality. Other traditional models, most notably those of Scotland and Germany, have always prevailed. What is noticeable about both these models, however, is that they involved what were, in effect new institutions. Though the Universities of Glasgow and Edinburgh were founded in the fifteenth and sixteenth centuries respectively, they were in Keble's time very largely new universities in the sense that they were the products of that amazing cultural flowering that we now call the Scottish Enlightenment. Norman Stone has commented that modern Europe was invented in the lecture theatres of Glasgow University in the last quarter of the eighteenth century — not even its worst enemies would, I think, ever make that claim for Oxford. The relative standing of the Scottish and English universities in Keble's time was well illustrated by the education of the young Viscount Palmerston, who was sent to Edinburgh for three years to gain an education, and to Cambridge for one, to meet the right people. Similarly, the re-vitalizing of the German universities in many cases involved their total re-foundation, as in the case of Humboldt's new University of Berlin. With it came fresh ideas from a brilliant new wave of Romantic educationalists and humanists: among them Fichte, Schiller, Schelling, Schleiermacher, and Steffens. When later in the nineteenth century the Americans set about creating the greatest mass-system of higher education the world has ever known, it was by and large the German and Scottish models that prevailed. How, then, is it possible to argue that Keble has a significant and permanent place in this process?

A cynically-minded historian might observe that Keble's famous Assize Sermon of 1833, from which the Tractarian Movement was to grow, was less an assertion of the weakness of the Church, and the danger in which it then found itself, than of the power of the University. While he, and his supporters may have believed that, by following Coleridge in his redefinition of the National Church to include the universities, they were defending the Church of England from the threat posed by Catholic Emancipation, what they were in fact doing was allowing the univerities to appropriate the interpretative power traditionally vested in the Church. What was at stake here, so the argument would run, was a question of hermeneutics. Who had the right to interpret the basic texts, legal and religious, that defined the Church of England? The complexity of this question can be measured by the fact that the Assize Sermon is in effect the symbolic point where the religious, legal, and university establishments meet. The preacher, on this occasion, was an ordained clergyman of the established Church, a former university teacher and currently Professor of Poetry, speaking from the pulpit of the University Church to a congregation composed of members of the judiciary, the university, and the clergy. The answer, as it emerged, was that the prerogative of interpretation was *de facto* vested in the university — a fact interestingly symbolized by Newman's notorious *Tract Ninety*, which claimed to demonstrate that it was possible to subscribe to the Thirty Nine Articles as a Roman Catholic. It was the signal for Newman to leave both Church and University, but it was also a demonstration that the debate about the nature of the Church was essentially from thenceforward a *university* debate.

Keble's vision of the university as a 'shadow ' or 'reflection' of the church is in some ways a bolder one even than Newman's. It depends not merely on a concept of the National Church with its clerisy free from class distinctions; it also depends on a concept of the Christian Church which is truly national in the sense of having no bounds within the state. It is only not schizoid because Keble sees such poles as being like those of a magnet, where it is impossible to think of one without the other. The existence of the Church implies also the existence of the Academy: while different, each supports and nurtures the other. There is no Church without interpretation; there is no interpretation without the Church. Church and Academy are not the same, but, properly understood, they are mutually interdependent. Like Maurice's *Kingdom of Christ*, published only the year before the Crewian Oration, which sees the Church only as spiritual because universal, and only universal because it is spiritual,[21] Keble's vision is one of a shared community potentially, at least, open to all. It is rooted in that enormous theological confidence of eventual victory we saw displayed in the 1833 Assize Sermon; a confidence that can embrace a reverence for the past with a visionary ability to contemplate change; a confidence, one might add, totally at odds with the private bearing of the shy and even diffident Vicar of Hursley.

As we have seen, the passing of interpretative power from Church to University was part of a trend right across the Western world; to that extent it would almost certainly have happened anyway in Oxford. In that sense I have to agree with the essence of the historicist argument I have just outlined. But I think it must be understood in hermeneutic rather than historicist terms. Keble played a crucial and largely unrecognized role in this reinterpretation of texts; in effect, he ensured was that it was to happen *his* way: on the Church's terms and not on the university's terms. It is possible to see the Tractarians, or as the popular phrase revealingly has it, the *Oxford* Movement, as being an interpretative theory that allowed for the peaceful and uncontested transition of power from one institution to another. In this sense Keble's 1844 Lectures on Poetry, *De Poeticae Vi Medica*, can be understood as the conclusion to a process begun almost exactly a hundred years earlier with his predecessor Robert Lowth's epoch-making Lectures on Poetry. Nor was his vision of the university as the prime engine of the National Church to be entirely lost. We only have to compare the close, even controversial connection between learning and moral and spiritual values in England with that assumed in the German, and even the Scottish system to see something of the difference. It is true that this distinctive difference has a much older and more complex history than simply the arguments of John Keble and the Tractarian Movement, but that is not to invalidate Keble's part in it. The reverence for such a long and complex history is of the very essence of what he stood for: in his appeal to open the university to all, regardless of privilege, wealth, or status, he invokes not the future of the university, but its past. He defended and even strengthened that tradition at a time when its values were being questioned from all sides, and that it survived in the form in which it has is, I believe, probably more due to John Keble than to any other single individual.

NOTES

[1] Anthony Trollope, *Barchester Towers* (Everyman, London, 1906). Ch. XIV, p. 107.
[2] *The Book and the Text: The Bible and Literary Theory*, ed. Regina M. Schwartz, (Basil Blackwell, Oxford, 1990). p. 12.
[3] Mark Pattison, *Memoirs* (Macmillan, London, 1885). e.g. pp. 164–70.
[4] op. cit. p. 160.
[5] ibid. p. 161.
[6] Pattison, p. 244.

7   See Stephen Prickett, *Romanticism and Religion: The Tradition of Coleridge and Wordsworth in the Victorian Church* (Cambridge University Press, Cambridge, 1976).

8   Georgina Battiscombe, *John Keble: A Study in Limitations* (Constable, London, 1963). p. 155.

9   See *Romanticism and Religion*, Ch. 4.

10 Battiscombe. pp. 15–16.

11 *Church and State*, 2nd. edn. ed. H. N. Coleridge (London, 1839), p. 60.

12 See Stephen Prickett, 'Coleridge and the idea of the Clerisy', in *Reading Coleridge: Approaches and Appreciations*, ed. Walter B. Crawford (Cornell University Press, Ithaca, 1979); Ben Knights, *The Idea of the Clerisy in the Nineteenth Century* (Cambridge University Press, Cambridge, 1978); and P. L. Allen, *The Cambridge Apostles* (Cambridge University Press, Cambridge, 1978).

13 J. T. Coleridge, *Memoir of the Rev. John Keble*, (Oxford and London, 1869), pp. 384–5.

14 Original unpublished translation by Paul Jeffreys-Powell. f. 1.

15 'what [has been believed] everywhere, always, and by all. . .'

16 The word 'university' originally meant something more like 'corporation', but the notion of universality greatly influenced the word's later usage. See O.E.D. and Geoffrey Faber, *Oxford Apostles* (Faber, London, 1933), p. 61.

17 *Oxford Apostles*, p. 61.

18 op. cit. f. 1.

19 ibid. ff. 2–3.

20 ibid. f. 6.

21 F. D. Maurice, *The Kingdom of Christ* (London, 1838); see also Prickett, *Romanticism and Religion*, Ch. 5.

ADRIAN HASTINGS

William Temple

A man so broad, to some he seem'd to be
Not one but all Mankind in Effigy:
Who, brisk in Term, a Whirlwind in the Long,
Did everything by turns, and nothing wrong,
Bill'd at each Lecture-Hall from Thames to Tyne
As Thinker, Usher, Statesman, or Divine.

RONALD KNOX's well-known lines describing Temple in his satiric poem of 1912, *Absolute and Abitofhell*[1] the Chaplain of Trinity's response to *Foundations: A Statement of Christian Belief in terms of Modern Thought*, by Seven Oxford Men, have all the brilliance of Oxford disputation at its best, mingling the profound, the personal and the comic. Temple was just thirty at the time but, thirty-five years later, would it have been less appropriate to speak of him as 'all Mankind in Effigy who . . . did everything by turns and nothing wrong'? The friendly sarcasm of the Chaplain of Trinity had become, or remained, a strangely apt account of the man whom, when he became Archbishop of Canterbury, Bernard Shaw could describe as 'a realized impossibility'.

Who was this prodigy? Born in 1881 in the episcopal palace of Exeter, he moved as a child from there to Fulham Palace and then, once more, to Lambeth Palace when his father, Frederick Temple, became Archbishop of Canterbury in 1897. By then William was at school at Rugby, where his father had long been headmaster in pre-episcopal days, and where his godfather, John Percival, was headmaster when he began his schooling. Frederick was sixty when William was born and an autocrat. 'Father says so' was the decisive rule of his childhood but it seems not to have been a rule which bound him in any way he found irksome. Both his father and his very aristocratic mother greatly loved him and he responded with the profoundest *pietas* which, indeed, he kept extending to other father-figures in his life — to Percival, whose biography he eventually wrote, rather boringly, to Randall Davidson, once he succeeded his father at Lambeth, to Bishop Gore, whom he described as the one 'from whom I have learnt more than any other now living of the spirit of Christianity'[2] and to Edward Caird, Master of Balliol when William arrived there. Caird succeeded Jowett and Frederick Temple had been at Balliol with Jowett. It was all of a piece. William was quintessentially the perfect heir of late-Victorian ecclesiastical and academic education at its most perfect, and the totally grateful heir. He never had an unkind word to say about it or about the great patriarchal figures who had towered over his youth, whom he venerated unstintingly but who seem never in the slightest to have intimidated him. Benign *pietas* was coupled in youth with an equally benign — almost conceited, it seems so confident — exploration of the mystery of all things, philosophical, religious, historical. Asked by his tutor at Rugby to write an essay on Ghosts, and told that it was too theological, he reports back to his father 'I asked Cole how one could discuss "Ghosts" without being theological and he only said it was not what he wanted. He also said some people would object to my discussing St Paul's vision and a banshee under one head, but I made him confess that that was because they do not think'.[3] 'As regards Berlioz' *Faust*, I think you would understand it', he could write patronizingly to his mother at sixteen.[4] Fat, everlastingly good-humoured, with a passion for strawberry jam and strawberry ices, this very superior know-all might appear a quite insufferable schoolboy but, of course, as he enjoyed at Rugby the most distinguished teaching and only left school when aged over eighteen and a half, he had by then acquired an intellectual sophistication far beyond the average undergraduate of today.

At Oxford he experienced for a little while a mildly rebellious mood. His early intentions to be ordained came slightly under question and he could write, as he hoped sounding rather radical, to a friend that:

the doctrine of the Incarnation, permanently present in its true purity to Browning, is hopelessly mauled by nearly every clergyman who touches it . . . the Christ men believe in and worship is to a great extent a myth and an idol — very different from Him who lived and died 'to bear witness to the truth', and whose Spirit lived and spoke in Socrates and Buddha and Mahomet as it did also in Hosea and Luther and Browning.[5]

By 1905 he had been President of the Oxford Union, had published an essay on Browning, become a Fellow and Lecturer — principally on Plato's *Republic* — at Queen's College and joined the Workers' Educational Association, of which he would soon be President. His theologically radical days were nearly over. Late that year he could already write:

To be at one with the Church in fundamentals is vital. On the other hand . . . it is not quite easy to see what are fundamentals . . . It is the great wisdom of our church that it was not founded to support any particular doctrines, as the Protestant bodies were . . . freedom in doctrine is the life-breath of the Church of England . . . What I have been taught to regard as the fundamentals do seem to me strictly continuous with my philosophy.[6]

He still hesitated about Virgin Birth and Bodily Resurrection, but not very greatly nor for long, and in 1908 he was ordained a deacon in Canterbury Cathedral by Randall Davidson, acting very clearly as Archbishop and as successor to Frederick Temple.

Temple read omnivorously but one wonders how much formal theology he bothered with. He claimed when still quite young to have read St Thomas's *Summa Theologiae* through from beginning to end. I confess it is the only thing he said about himself which I have found quite hard to believe, but it may, I think, explain why in later life his almost intuitive convictions about war, property or natural theology came to have such a Thomist look to them. Nevertheless the creative minds whose thoughts most stimulated him and to which he kept recurring throughout life were, apart from the New Testament, Plato, Shakespeare, Browning, not the Fathers, not the Scholastics, not the Continental Reformers of the sixteenth century, not even the great Anglican divines of the seventeenth, not finally the biblical critics of his own age for whom he had very little time. He was, perhaps, characteristic of the modern Anglican theological temper, in being so much more shaped by literature and music than by theology. Music was very important. It had been so at school and remained so. He was fortunate in having a splendid singing, as well as speaking, voice, a voice for liturgy, for preaching, for lectures, for the conversation with everyone which was so central an activity of life and which was so frequently intermixed with his extraordinary laugh.

There can be no question that for many people Temple's laugh remained the most precisely memorable thing about him. Already at school he was remembered for 'that queer high laugh that went on so long and never left him'[7] and which would be referred to sometimes with irritation, more often with delight, throughout his life. He once laughed so loudly and continuously at a performance of *John Bull's Other Island* that Tawney, who was with him, began to wonder if they would be asked to leave the theatre. A human being, it may be said, is actually definable as an animal that can laugh — at least qu. 16, a. 5 of the III Pars of the *Summa* rather suggests that. It is Temple's humanity in all its subtlety which revealed itself in the sheer range and quality of his laughing, but it could certainly be concentrated with particular delight upon certain subjects. When he got away for a few days' holiday with his wife just as the Second World War was about to begin, he was reading her *Alice through the Looking-Glass*. Limericks were especially favoured and he once compared Bishop Gore's taste in limericks with his own. Gore, it seems, enjoyed something fairly simple, like this:

> There was an old man of Calcutta
> Who had a most terrible stutter;
>   'G-g-give me', he said
>   'Some b-b-b-bread
> And b-b-b-b-b-b-butter'.

Temple felt that this achieved the absurdity which a good limerick is meant to express at the cost of being, linguistically I suppose, not 'quite fair'. Temple, on the other hand, greatly admired the following against which Gore, he tells us, 'vigorously protested':

> There once was a gourmet of Crediton
> Who ate pâté de fois gras; he spread it on
>   A chocolate biscuit
>   And said, 'I'll just risk it'
> His tomb gave the date that he said it on.[8]

What seems to have tickled Temple here was not only the complicated rhythm but an altogether more subtly absurd story line clinched by its terrible denouement.

The laughter was just a natural part of someone on the surface

always extraordinarily relaxed, friendly, 'simple' in manners, wholly
unpretentious, never 'rattled', never confrontational, never angry.
He became an archbishop who liked to stand in bus queues and
open his own front door, to chat with anyone he encountered and
at a level of profound equality and openness. He really did lay all his
cards on the table. When praised by a speaker in a vote of thanks for
being the greatest and simplest of Archbishops of York, he could not
help but burst forth 'God, who made me simple, make me simpler
yet'. When students at Leeds greeted him with 'Where have you
been all the day, Billy boy?', he could not resist responding at once
'Well, if you must be so personal, I spent most of the morning with
an archdeacon, and before that I did my letters with my secretary'.
When Gore and Temple once walked away from a meeting at
Church House, which had had to be adjourned because Gore had
lost his temper, Temple was as usual his genial, smiling self and Gore
remarked bitterly 'I have a vile temper. It is a terrible thing to have
a bad temper'. But then, looking at his companion's smile, he added
'But it is not so bad as having a good temper'.[9]

Behind all this lay a photographic memory, an outstanding
fluency with the English language, an unruffled life of prayer, an
often pretty ruffled flow of enthusiasms, and a quite unflagging
sense of personal vocation as teacher and priest. 'William propounds
the wildest plans at breakfast', remarked his mother when they were
living together, 'but he has generally forgotten them by lunch
time'.[10] That quotation presents us with a useful hinge for advancing now a step or two in a new direction. Very perfect and equable
characters tend to be rather dull. If Temple unquestionably avoided
dullness through his extraordinary sense of enthusiasm and interest
in every side of life, how far could that enthusiasm get without turning confrontational? Gore had had the enthusiasms but was confrontational, Davidson avoided the enthusiasms and held the
Church together, but was very dull. Temple's problem always
would be how to carry enthusiasms through to achievement without, meanwhile, breaking any eggs.

Any adequate evaluation of Temple is up against a number of
considerable hurdles. The first is the effusively laudatory character
of almost everything written about him. There was an undiscrimi-
nating degree of praise on the part of his numberless ecclesiastical
followers which does not help one to sift the grain from the chaff.
On some accounts it would seem a belittling and unfair disparage-
ment to suggest that there could be any chaff around at all. This
is not helped by the inadequacy of the one official biography.
Nothing, perhaps, is needed more for the religious history of Britain

in the twentieth century than a really major new biography of Temple. It would certainly not be easy to write but, without it, there are large holes in the canvas. It would need to consider very subtly such matters as a lack of sustained sense of direction despite his quite frenetic activities until he was forty or more, the depth of his grappling in the 1930s with Fascism and Nazism, his relationships with Bell and Tawney. I feel an underlying worry as to whether Temple was ever critical enough of his own image, or whether in a way he came to be dangerously bamboozled by the more superficial side of his own extraordinary successes.

Michael Ramsey, a great admirer of Temple, once remarked of his predecessors as judges of character: 'Cosmo was flawless; Temple was hopeless; Fisher was superb; I am erratic'.[11] If Temple's judgement about people was poor, it seems probable that the same was true in regard to situations. One feels that all his geese were swans, especially but by no means exclusively all the important people he continually met in Church and State. One feels that he was somehow disarmed by the sheer goodness and affability of his own heart. Hence while he could proclaim a crusade before he had really approached a situation, once he was in it, he tended to be very over-conciliatory. Take the example of his brief period as Headmaster of Repton. When elected by the School Governors in 1910, he had written what has been termed a 'revolutionary' letter about the way the public schools still seemed to 'reproduce our class-divisions in accentuated form'[12] and what he hoped to do if they actually wanted him. 'If they take me, knowing this, I come', he wrote, threateningly enough, to Ford, his predecessor. They took him. He went and rumours were aroused: 'What form would the revolution take and what would be the first moves?' But nothing much happened, other than a change of music master, and Iremonger revealingly comments: 'As term followed term with no rocking of the foundations, it began to be suspected that there was to be no revolution after all. The suspicion proved to be well founded, the revolution never came; Temple's experience had led him to change his mind'. As a member of the Repton staff, D. C. Somervell, explained:

> I remember Temple telling me, near the end of his last term, that when he wrote the revolutionary letter, his ideas of public school policy were of the vaguest: a mixture of boyhood recollections and WEA Utopianism. As he said to me on that occasion — 'If there is one thing my time has taught me, it is that institutions must be run on their own lines or else scrapped'.[13]

I believe the Repton episode is far more of a parable for Temple's whole career than is usually admitted. I suspect that when he helped mount the 'Life and Liberty' campaign with such ringing, revolutionary words, he had little more idea as to how the Church of England worked than in 1910 he had had about public schools. I also doubt whether he had any real sense of the plight of the industrial poor or what they were up against when he called COPEC or endeavoured to negotiate in the later stages of the Miners' Strike, and I doubt whether he had any very sharp sense as to what was going on in Germany in the 1930s or, say, the British wartime policy of obliteration bombing. Perhaps his later pleasure in opening his own front door derived secretly from the absence of any of the normal experiences of a common man, unswathed in palaces, public schools and Oxford colleges. When he went to Canterbury, an admiring journalist, Sidney Dark, admitted that Temple preferred 'to inspire the revolutionaries rather than to lead the fighting at the barricades'.[14] That was kindly put and Dark may not be saying anything so very different from William's mother's remark that his 'wildest plans at breakfast' had generally been forgotten by lunch. That was Temple and it would be quite mistaken to argue otherwise, to prove him an effective reformer, a man who could administer revolutionary change or whatever. He wasn't, being someone open to rather easy conviction that 'institutions must be run on their own lines', and it is only when we clearly recognize he wasn't that we may begin to recognize too what he really was.

Better than anything else he was a teacher. His huge flow of schoolboy letters to his parents constituted the first great expression of his irresistible urge to explain, to pass on to others lucidly, imaginatively and agreeably the knowledge and insights he had himself just attained. At Queen's lecturing on Plato, at Repton in his readings of Lear and Hamlet or in his sermons, in writing *Mens Creatrix* and *Christus Veritas*, in his radio talks or the famed university missions he gave, we see always the same: not so much a scholar, a theologian, or even primarily a leader, but a mind committed to communicating a vision with infectious enthusiasm — 'the magic fascination of the love of Christ' as he called it to the boys of Repton. That was what he wanted Repton to instil, what he always and everywhere wanted to instil. There was exceptionally little difference, I think, between Temple the lecturer and Temple the preacher. His lectures always led to a more obvious religious and moral conclusion than we quite care for these days, while his sermons tended to range over things and sources well beyond what preachers were expected to do — the urge to link together St Paul and the banshee never left him.

It was a vision of wholeness. To a quite exceptional extent what Temple was always concerned with, both in his major writings and in his addresses of all sorts, was a coherent account of total experience, a dialectical account which worked through tension and contrast to expose the central meaning of things in the Incarnation. It was always moral, always philosophical, always Christ-centred. Here was a man, highly conscious of the secularizing, the disintegrating but also very much the pessimistic tendencies within society and culture around him. He could not yield to them. It was almost a weakness of his spirit to remain so cheerfully optimistic, so determined to harmonize the philosophy of dialectical idealism, the socialism he saw advancing across the world, the literature, art and music of Europe he had so profoundly imbibed, in a vast incarnational synthesis. The Incarnation for Temple as for Scotus did not derive its meaning from the need for redemption, it was rather the inevitable and perfect crowning in grace of the whole order of things in created nature. More and more as the years passed the central purpose of Temple appears as this one: a theological teacher rather than a theologian, certainly not a theological scholar. As such he had no peer. No Archbishop of Canterbury since Anselm could conceivably be compared with him in this regard, no bishop of his own age. Despite the lack of time he had in which to write the principal books of his later years, one suspects that they do not suffer greatly as a result. He would not have improved them through a larger availability of scholarly space because he never had been that sort of scholar. It was always as a teacher, at the interface of his faith and other people, that he shone, but this very incarnational dimension of his own work — the hereness and nowness of his teaching — makes it inevitably less satisfactory for anyone of a later age, unable to share the spell of Temple's unique here and now: of that moment, to give just one instance, at the end of the great Oxford mission of 1931, when in a crammed St Mary's he stopped the singing of 'When I survey the wondrous Cross' before the last verse and asked the students present to read the words first and then 'if you mean them with all your heart, sing them as loud as you can. If you don't mean them at all, keep silent. If you mean them even a little, and want them to mean more, sing them very softly'. Suddenly two thousand voices whispered together:

> Were the whole realm of nature mine,
> That were an offering far too small;

Love so amazing, so divine,
Demands my soul, my life, my all.

It was an experience never to be erased from memory, but Temple's teaching time and again did produce a comparable experience in his listeners and in a huge circle of followers who across the next generation of Christian life in this country would look to Temple in a way that they never looked to anyone else, and in a way that since his death there has been no one else quite to look to. His presence meant more than that of many another teacher. His legacy, sadly, can in consequence mean less.

It is truer to say of Temple than of most people that he never changed. His qualities were already extraordinarily apparent as a boy at Rugby both to his contemporaries and to us. Yet the very precociousness of his genius retarded, I believe, his maturity. The same might be said of other public school and Oxford geniuses of that delectably precious age, Ronald Knox especially. One has for years a feeling that Temple could not quite grow up and did not really want to. Even the First World War, while it made him more than usually over-active, did not mature him very noticeably. It is difficult to demonstrate such things but my impression is that his passion for meetings, addresses, missions, campaigns, only begins to give way to a cooler sense of pastoral responsibility as the central dynamo within his system well after he became a bishop in 1921 and still more noticeably after he moved to York in 1929. The Archbishopric of York may have been the one entirely suitable position he occupied in life. The trouble of the pre-1921 years had been the number of quite different jobs he had accepted and abandoned. York was right for him. Here was a cathedra for teaching, national, even international, rather than for formal ecclesiastical administration and political involvement. He was too briefly at Canterbury, and in the quite special circumstances of war, for us to be able to appraise him very satisfactorily as Archbishop of Canterbury. It was, of course, right that he should be translated from one to the other on Lang's retirement. He had no rival. And it is not true, as Henson claimed, that if he had lived he would have found he had outlasted his eminence. On the contrary. The post-war world would have suited him admirably and his role in it as the great presider and spokesman of the enlightened consensus in matters religious, not only for Britain but for the United States, Europe and the World Council of Churches would, undoubtedly, have been outstanding — a role no one person after his death could ever fill. Chairmanship was certainly one of his fortes. Nevertheless it remains true that he was weak in the political and administrative skills, manoeuvring within the corridors of power, which an Archbishop of Canterbury most needed, and that he was strongest in the more essentially public and oratorical skills of a ministry of teaching, personal, at once philosophic and popular, episcopal without doubt but more than ecclesiastical, a ministry which can really be exercised better at York than at Canterbury.

The York years are those on which above all Temple should be judged and they are the years of his three most valuable books — *Nature, Man and God*, his Gifford Lectures 1932-4, *Readings in St John's Gospel* and *Christianity and Social Order*. It is especially through these that Temple will endure, if he does endure, and it is from them and other contemporary evidence that we can best enter into his mind at its most profound. To help us here I will compare four passages from that last decade of his life which reflect upon the way he saw himself and the theological predicament about him.

The earliest is from the Preface to *Nature, Man and God*, dated June 1934. He first describes two types of thinker. The first lays out all he knows about a subject and 'piece by piece will work out his conclusion'. The second type, the intuitive, is the one to which Temple saw himself as belonging:

> All my decisive thinking goes on behind the scenes; I seldom know when it takes place — much of it certainly on walks or during sleep — and I never know the processes which it has followed. Often when teaching I have found myself expressing rooted convictions which, until that moment, I had no notion that I held . . . This characteristic must needs affect the philosophical method of him who suffers (or gains) from it . . . The two types described — are they the Aristotelian and Platonic, the Pauline and Johannine, respectively?

In his personal Introduction to the Report on *Doctrine in the Church of England* which he composed in October 1937, there is a slightly different dualism. The first part of the century, in which his own mind was formed, had concentrated upon 'a theology of the Incarnation rather than a theology of Redemption'. A theology of the Incarnation, he continued,

> tends to be a Christocentric metaphysic. And in all ages there is need for the fresh elaboration of such a scheme of thought or map of life as seen in the light of the revelation in Christ. A theology of Redemption (though, of course, Redemption has its great

place in the former) tends rather to sound the prophetic note; it is more ready to admit that much in this evil world is irrational and strictly unintelligible . . . If the security of the nineteenth century, already shattered in Europe, finally crumbles away in our country, we shall be pressed more and more towards a theology of Redemption . . . It is there that, in my own judgement at least, our need lies now and will lie in the future.

My third text is from the Preface to the First Series of *Readings in St John's Gospel*, dated December 1938:

For as long as I can remember I have had more love for St John's Gospel than for any other book. Bishop Gore once said to me that he paid visits to St John as to a fascinating foreign country but he came home to St Paul. With me the precise opposite is true. St Paul is the exciting, and also rather bewildering, adventure; with St John I am at home.

Finally, a passage from an article he contributed to *Blackfriars* in March 1944.[15] Here he contrasted two approaches to the theology of Aquinas, the first holding it decisively mistaken, the second

that his map needs correction in some important respects but that our most hopeful line of advance is to start with his work, making such corrections as we think it needs. To which of these two groups we belong is likely to depend on our admitting or repudiating the possibility of natural theology and the value of analogical argument from created nature, including human nature, to the nature of the Creator. It is not sufficiently understood in England that on the European continent this more than anything else is the point at issue between Catholicism and Protestantism. The Continental Reformers had so interpreted the Fall of Man as to leave in fallen human nature no capacity for recognising divine truth . . . In my own mind there is no doubt on which side of that division we should stand.

These four passages share something of a common structure. Each presents a contrast between two approaches or theologies; with one of which (type A) Temple each time identifies himself. In the first type A is characterized as intuitive, Platonic and Johannine; type B, argumentative, Aristotelian and Pauline; in the second type A is a theology of Incarnation, 'a Christocentric metaphysic', type

B a theology of Redemption, stressing the irrational and the prophetic. In the third text, type A is Temple at home in St John, Paul a bewildering adventure; type B Bishop Gore at home in Paul, a foreigner to John. In the fourth text, type A is Catholic Thomism stressing natural theology and type B Continental Protestantism stressing a fallen world and no human capacity for recognizing divine truth. Different as these four dualisms may seem in some way, I feel fairly sure that they are really, for the mature Temple, all of a piece. His theology throughout has been the Incarnational one fed on Plato and John, a Christocentric metaphysic which plays back and forth between nature and supernature, stressing the intelligibility and goodness of things, no need to be prophetic, but finding, especially in later life, that what had started out as idealism was ending up as Thomism, and what had seemed a species of liberal Protestantism, beefed up a bit with a dose of Anglican orthodoxy, was really a kind of classical Catholicism. In contrast he sees Paul and Gore and Barth, a theology of Redemption, the admission of a sinful crazy world, the call to prophecy rather than to philosophy, essentially the theology of Protestantism. It may seem rather too odd to claim Gore as the Protestant prototype, Temple the Catholic. I suspect there is a good deal in such an evaluation objectively enough, but the point is that it is how Temple was coming to read himself and his theological position. Of course by the late 1930s he is having his doubts. Barthianism seems to be spreading all around him. Too much in the world, he sees, simply has not got the intelligible character he had learnt to find in it with late nineteenth-century optimism. He clings to Natural Theology and Natural Law, is glad to find that as Hegel slips away he can turn instead to Thomas but somewhat alarmed at the seemingly rather irrational, almost Barthian, character of some of the young Anglican Neo-Thomists he meets.

In his Introduction to the Report on Doctrine he goes so far as to suggest that theology really needs to be moving away from his kind, type A, back to the other kind but he was recognizing too that if this was a need to be met by younger theologians, he himself could do little. 'I doubt if I can now *lead* them' he admitted, 'perhaps I might do a little in steering them . . . But is it really the function of an Archbishop to be a theological leader?'.[16] About the same time as he wrote that, he wrote to Dorothy Emmet in July 1942 suggesting a way in which rational and irrational might cohere:

What we must completely get away from is the notion that the world as it now exists is a rational whole; we must think of its unity not by the analogy of a picture, of which all the parts exist at once, but by the analogy of a drama, where, if it is good enough, the full meaning of the first scene only becomes apparent with the final curtain; and we are in the middle of this. Consequently the world as we see it is strictly unintelligible. We can only have faith that it will become intelligible when the divine purpose, which is the explanation of it, is accomplished.[17]

This he claimed was already there in *Nature, Man and God* but the total impression had remained static rather than dynamic. In this letter to Dorothy Emmet he seems closest to transcending the dichotomy between two approaches which he had himself set up, while still trying dialectically to defend the substance of his own ground. We see him in these last years coming a little sadly to recognize the non-contemporaneity of his own approach, though it may be that very much more of his approach did remain valid than the next generation was inclined to think. Certainly it is sad that Temple of all people should be driven to question whether an archbishop should be a theological leader. Of course almost no archbishop ever has been, but that is just where Temple seemed different. If the sense of crisis, sin and unreason unrooted him from his Idealist origins, it did not take him from St John and he could find in the Fourth Gospel, within his theology of Incarnation, a theology also of Redemption, darkness and prophecy. Take this splendid comment from his *Readings* on John 1.5 (7-9).

The divine light shines through the darkness of the world, cleaving it, but neither dispelling it nor quenched by it . . . It is always so. Take any moment of history and you find light piercing unillumined darkness — now with reference to one phase of the purpose of God, now another. The company of those who stand in the beam of the light by which the path of true progress for that time is discerned is always small. Remember Wilberforce and the early Abolitionists; remember the twelve Apostles and the Company gathered about them . . . As we look forwards, we peer into darkness, and none can say with certainty what course the true progress of the future should follow. But as we look back the truth is marked by beacon lights, which are the lives of saints and pioneers; and these in their turn are not originators of light but rather reflectors which give light to us because themselves they are turned towards the source of light . . . This darkness in which the light shines unabsorbed is cosmic. St John is most modern here . . . He does not conceive of Nature as characterised by a

Wordsworthian perfection, which is only spoilt by fallen mankind. To his deep spiritual insight it is apparent that the redemption of man is part, even if the crowning part, of a greater thing — the redemption, or conquest, of the universe.

In these words we hear Temple facing the darkness of the late 1930s, so different from the nineteenth-century security in which he had been brought up, with a deep alteration in mood but without the quite confusing and confused note to be found in a little article, 'Theology Today' published in *Theology* in November 1939,[18] in which, almost blandly, he committed himself to formulations painfully contrary to anything he had ever argued:

> We have to face this tormented world, not as offering a means to its coherence in thought and its harmony in practice, but as challenging it in the name and power of Christ crucified and risen; we shall not try to 'make sense' of everything, we shall openly proclaim that most things as they are have no sense in them at all. We shall not say that a Christian philosophy embraces all experience in a coherent and comprehensive scheme.

I confess I find it almost too painful to go on reading such repudiations of a life's work. Yet even in this article he was not quite carried away. Already he was wondering whether a Thomist scheme might not, after all, provide a new 'starting point' and, anyway, he remained sure that 'one day theology will take up again its larger and serener task and offer to a new Christendom its Christian map of life, its Christocentric metaphysic'. Even in that day, Temple was soon in point of fact busy once more attempting some part of that 'map of life' with his *Christianity and Social Order*, perhaps indeed the most enduring of his works. Here again he is dipping into the natural, stressing natural law, stressing the sort of rational order to be expected and sought in a divine and Christ-centred universe. Really the *Theology* article can best be dismissed as marginal to the interpretation of Temple's mind, a brief moment of lost confidence under the *Angst* of war.

> A man so broad, to some he seem'd to be
> Not one, but all Mankind in Effigy.

We have seen something of Temple's lifelong realization of what was intended as a caricature. He retained his passion for synthesis to the end, appealing in the last year of his life for 'a new integration of life: Religion, Art, Science, Politics, Education, Industry, Commerce, Finance'.[19] He retained too his optimism, his ability even while still 'in the middle' to see beacon-lights in the present and not only from the past. Thus his Enthronement sermon at Canterbury on St George's Day 1942 centred quite optimistically on 'the great new fact of our era', the Ecumenical Movement, whereby far from 'returning to the catacombs', the City of God 'again stands before us with gates wide open so that citizens of all nations may enter'. In some way, his repeated dualistic division of theological roles excluded him from Paul, prophecy and Protestantism. By and large that seems correct: Temple so often claimed as a prophet was not naturally one at all, unlike Gore or Bell. Yet we cannot simply place him as he often placed himself, upon the other Johannine, intuitive and harmoniously philosophic side. These binary categories really won't quite stand up on their own account, let alone when someone as broad as Temple is placed against them. Maybe archbishops are not theological leaders yet he undoubtedly tried to be one and no one in this country since Anselm more nearly succeeded. Maybe he was not a prophet, but many people found him stunningly prophetic.

Michael Ramsey, the only other good Canterbury claimant to such a role, was invited as a young theologian to Bishopthorpe by Temple in July 1936 with a galaxy of names — Emil Brunner and Reinhold Niebuhr, J. H. Oldham and Vissert 'Hooft — to help plan the ecumenical conferences of 1937. Ramsey came greatly to admire Temple but he admired Gore too and if at one time he thought Gore old-fashioned and Temple more contemporary, later he thought Temple dated and Gore still authoritative 'with the mysteriousness of a timeless authority'.[20] Theological fashion has its ins and outs. What is certain is that the three greatest theological names in twentieth-century Anglicanism have been Gore, Temple and Ramsey. Temple remains the man 'in the middle', his time cut off in war, still the most enigmatic of the three, the most difficult to make up one's mind about. Finally, when Ramsey was asked where he wished to be buried he replied 'I should like to be not far from William Temple'. Some of us, I believe, would be glad to say the same.

NOTES

1 'Absolute and Abitofhell', first published in the *Oxford Magazine*, reprinted in Ronald Knox, *Essays in Satire* (London, 1928), pp. 81-8.

2   W. Temple, *Studies in the Spirit and Truth of Christianity*, (London, 1914), Dedication.
3   F. A. Iremonger, *William Temple* (London, 1948), p. 22.
4   Iremonger, p. 31.
5   Iremonger, pp. 102-3.
6   Iremonger, p. 106.
7   E. V. Knox, Iremonger, p. 35.
8   W. Temple, *Religious Experience* (London, 1958), p. 189.
9   A. E. Baker in *William Temple: An Estimate and an Appreciation* (London, 1946), pp. 109, 95, 98.
10 Iremonger, p. 67.
11 O. Chadwick, *Michael Ramsey* (Oxford, 1990), p. 118.
12 Iremonger, p. 147.
13 Iremonger, p. 148.
14 Sidney Dark, *The People's Archbishop* (London, 1942), pp. 108-9.
15 Reprinted in *Religious Experience* (London, 1958), pp. 229-36.
16 Iremonger, p. 608.
17 Iremonger, pp. 537-8.
18 Republished in W. Temple, *Thoughts in War-Time* (London, 1940), pp. 93-107.
19 W. Temple, *The Church Looks Forward* (London, 1944), Preface.
20 P. Avis, *Gore: Construction and Conflict* (London, 1988), p. 4.

STEPHEN SYKES

The Genius of Anglicanism

I COULD SCARCELY imagine the phrase 'the genius of Anglicanism' upon the lips of the man we honour in this series of essays, and not merely because, so far as we know, the term 'Anglicanism' is a neologism of the 1830s. Indeed Dr Rowell has offered me the opportunity of citing Newman's dictum that 'a man of genius cannot go about with his genius in his hand'.[1] We would perhaps be better employed examining the truth of Anglicanism's claims, or analysing its role and outlining its prospects.

Indeed we may suspect that the title presages the kind of encomium we associate with an obituary. In praising Caesar are we not a little engaged in burying him too? There is a moment in the life of institutions when their problematic character provokes a certain kind of anxiety, an attention which itself signals imminent demise. Yet I find that 'The Genius of the Church of England' was the title of two lectures given at the Archbishop of York's Clergy School in July 1945 by Bishop Rawlinson of Derby and Canon Charles Smyth of Cambridge, and published in 1947. Here are no last rites, but the continuation of a vigorous apologetic tradition begun in the sixteenth century by John Jewel; in this case adorned with twenty pages of footnotes by Charles Smyth on every conceivable subject, including the salvation of archdeacons and the role of professional football in preserving England's immunity to a proletarian revolution.

Perhaps the title is ironic. We are closer to the ironical with a passage from William James cited in G. F. S. Gray's admirable sketch of *The Anglican Communion*. Anglicanism, James wrote, is

> So massive and all-pervasive, so authoritative and on the whole so decent, in spite of the iniquity and farcicality of the whole thing. . .Never were incompatibles so happily yoked together. Talk about the genius of Romanism. It is nothing to the genius of Anglicanism, for Catholicism still contains some haggard elements that ally it with the Palestinian desert, whereas Anglicanism remains obese and round and comfortable, and decent with this world's decencies, without one acute note in its whole life or history.[2]

Commentary of this kind on the 'yoking of incompatibles' has had an exceptionally long run. One loses count of the number of predictions of imminent collapse through internal incoherence, in the tradition of John Henry Newman's comment that Anglicanism was a paper, not a real, Church. Perhaps the following statement might also count as an example of the same basic genre:

> It would be more accurate to argue that the Anglican church, in the course of the long history of its reformations, incorporated into its basic documents an internal contradiction between Protestant and Catholic principles. There seems nothing to protect us from the conclusion that Anglicanism as it now exists is founded on an incoherent doctrine of the church; and that its attempts to resolve or conceal this gross internal antinomy has (sic) repeatedly led it into a series of chronic conflicts from which it barely escapes with any integrity.[3]

I fear that I cite myself. I thought this statement decently hidden in a group of essays published in Frankfurt, but it has returned in the altogether more exalted context of a Dominican study of Cardinal Ratzinger's theology,[4] and it will need a little glossing if its nuances are not going to be missed. The context is explicitly that of an *hypothesis* to the effect that Catholicism and Protestantism are mutually incompatible and antithetical ways of construing what it means to be the Catholic Church. That hypothesis I neither affirm nor deny. But in terms of that hypothesis Anglicanism, I argued, is bound to be seen as based on an internally incoherent doctrine of the Church. In this case the imperative driving Anglicans to interpret their communion in a constructive doctrine of the Church should be all but overwhelming.

In fact nothing of the kind has yet occurred. There are two reasons for this. One is that Anglicans formulated in the course of their external and internal controversies, the opinion that Anglicans have no distinctive doctrines; it follows, of course, that there can be no distinctive Anglican doctrine of the Church. Although this view is, I believe, manifestly and demonstrably incorrect,[5] its influence has effectively suppressed the theological enterprise which urgently needs to be developed.

The second reason for the failure to respond to the charge of incoherence is the absorption of so much time and effort, both leading up to and following the 1988 Lambeth Conference, in a largely fruitless effort to clarify the subject of authority in Anglicanism. It ought to have been obvious that it was impossible to arrive at theological or practical conclusions on authority *in* the Church without the help of a theology *of* the Church. But it has proved otherwise. And we have been painfully learning in the last decades, not least through ecumenical relationships, that we cannot borrow a doctrine of the Church from any other communion of Christendom, and pass it off as Anglican with a few minor adjustments. The very refusal of Anglicanism to oblige its critics by withering or splintering to death may in due course drag us, however reluctantly, to the task of ecclesiological self-interpretation.

II

TO THIS TOPIC I shall return at the close of this chapter but in the first place it seems to me only proper to articulate the case against Anglicanism. Viewed, as it should be, not against the privileged backdrop of an English cathedral and university city, but from the standpoint of a bemused Italian or Greek or German, the plausibility structures collapse, and we are bound to ask how credible its claims are.

To focus, first, on the Church of England, the charges are so familiar as to require only a very brief exposition.

The numerical decline in baptized, confirmed and regular church-going members is very marked. It has reached the point where the the Roman Catholic Church, which has far fewer baptized members, has now a larger number of Sunday-by-Sunday church attenders. This raises the question whether the Church of England has forfeited the right *de facto* to be regarded as the Church of the English people; whether its symbolic position in the person of the Sovereign, or the representation which it enjoys in Parliament, or the legislative role which Parliament occupies in its affairs any longer correspond to reality. Furthermore, it is asked whether the Church of England could ever survive as one denomination among many, shorn of the status and privileges which it so easily accepts, assumes, and then administers to non-Anglicans in culturally and socially condescending inclusion into the ranks of 'other Churches'.

The disputes which recurrently rack the counsels of the Church of England are not about minor details in the Christian faith, but concern its very heart and vitals. In 1947 Bishop Hensley Henson drew attention to two books by Anglican bishops, one by K. E. Kirk on *The Apostolic Ministry* (which he described as virtually Roman in 'type, temper and tendency') and the other by E.W. Barnes on the *Rise of Christianity* (which he designated 'not even, in any tolerable sense, Christian'); and he added, 'I do not think it possible that any Church can long cohere when such radical divergence on essentials is tolerated'.[6] Despite the fact that that was more than forty years ago, it is not unreasonable to ask whether the situation today is not worse than before, whether the slow erosion of Christian belief and practice in England is not closely connected to the incoherence of a Church which disputes publicly about its essential or fundamental doctrines, and whether the removal of the cement provided by establishment would not precipitate the end of the Anglican experiment altogether.

The uncertainty and irresolution displayed by the decision-making organs of the Church of England on urgent modern problems, such as the possession and threat to employ nuclear weapons, the eligibility of women for priestly and episcopal office, the status of the divorced in the marriage practice of the Church, and the attitude towards, and treatment of Christian homosexuals, are such as practically to disqualify it from the pretension to be a moral guide to the nation. The diverse and contradictory views of persons of weight and importance, and the vacillating and ambiguous pronouncements of its representatives, simply suggest that no one seriously expects the Church to teach on these matters, with authority. Instead it appears to be in constant retreat into long-winded complexity incapable of successful, popular communication. In this way it alienates the mass of the English populace, who have, in any case, long ceased to pay any attention. Has not the Church of England become a church without a structure of authority capable of speaking with authority, and worse, a church without vision, a church which has ceased to believe that its corporate decisions could be guided by the Holy Spirit?

So much, so familiar; but there is more to say about the international Anglican communion.

Precisely because of the past imperial association, international Anglicanism is now, it is said, in the throes of an identity crisis. No recent traveller to New Zealand, Australia, or Canada, for example, can fail to miss the element of sheer impatience with mother's apron strings which plays a distorting role in the quest for a genuinely local identity. Who, in the former Empire, wishes to be known as Anglican, once the meaning of the Latin phrase *ecclesia Anglicana* is explained? The Scottish and American Episcopal Churches, with their longer history of independence, know themselves under the non-imperial title 'Episcopalian', full of its own ambiguity. The sociologist, Dr Bill Pickering, has pertinently observed that 'many of the tensions in the contemporary Anglican communion seem analogous to those in the British Commonwealth'.[7] As the latter has lost its way, so has the former. There is no discernible agreement that the undeniably English (and Scottish) origins of the world-wide communion have bestowed on it lasting spiritual benefits. In particular those Prayer Books (the English and the Scottish) which previously provided much of the family ethos to the whole Church are now undergoing extensive revision on a purely local basis, each autonomous Province holding itself to be competent to revise its liturgy without reference to any other. The result is inevitably an apparently ever-increasing pluralism, without discernible restraint or boundaries.

Closely connected to the same complaint is the limited global membership of the Anglican communion. As Dr Pickering points out, it is difficult to give precise and at the same time meaningful statistics about any large religious group. But it appears that, despite the fact that there are Anglican churches in over 160 countries, one country, England, has more than half the total Anglican membership, and eight out of every ten baptized Anglicans in 1985 were white. This is a fact which can be concealed in international Anglican assemblies because they are rightly sensitive about the dominance of white members. But the demographic reality of Anglicanism, as compared with Catholicism or Orthodoxy, is comparatively parochial. Can such a Communion really have a global future, in a world Christianity which is increasingly orientated towards the southern hemisphere?

The much canvassed problem of authoritative decision-making procedures at international level must also be mentioned. In comparison to the Catholic Church's centralized government Anglicanism has no legislatively competent authorities above the level of a Province or group of Provinces. Thus decisions about even such important matters as the authorization of prayer books, or the passing of canons relating to the ministry, are legally made in local churches. The consultative status of the Lambeth Conference makes unified response to ecumenical documents exceptionally difficult, not least when one of those documents acknowledges the importance for the Church of a universal primacy. If Anglicanism is serious in envisaging the time when the whole Church will acknowledge such primacy, how can it at the same time suppose that its own informal and slow processes have any future? There are, moreover, in addition to the now hundred-year old tradition of ten-yearly conferences, two new and relatively untried organs, the Committee of Primates and the Anglican Consultative Council, whose uncertain status and competence cast further doubt on the clarity of the Anglican grasp of its own processes. These focus on the ambiguity attaching to the theology of the episcopate which has never received authoritative, or even classical Anglican treatment. Are the bishops of the Anglican communion apostles of the churches, confident enough to magnify their office and humble enough not to exalt their own persons, or are they 'men in purple shirts', to cite an English episcopal cynic?

III

THESE ARE SERIOUS charges, and I suppose that in 1977, when I wrote *The Integrity of Anglicanism*, I had little idea that I was stoking a debate which has seen, in the last decade, an astonishingly large number of contributions. What I wish now to do is to respond to the case against Anglicanism which I have sketched, by trying to evaluate where things now stand with the arguments I presented in that book.

The Integrity of Anglicanism was written in the year immediately following the publication of *Christian Believing* (1976), a Report by the Doctrine Commission of the Church of England, whose membership included most of my theological teachers. The inner story of that Commission's work has yet to be told, but I am informed that it brought one of its distinguished members nearly to the point of resignation. A whole generation of Anglican scholars, including the Regius Professors of Divinity at both Oxford and Cambridge, plainly found the greatest difficulty in coming to a common mind about the significance of the creeds for the beliefs of the modern Christians. They glossed over this problem by asserting that whatever conclusions they had personally reached in matters of belief, nonetheless they operated a common pattern or method of thinking. In *The Integrity of Anglicanism* I quoted, and took issue with, the following passage:

> The vital requirement for Christians today is not to force themselves to specifically agreed conclusions but to operate within the pattern — that is, to use in whatever way or proportion integrity allows the resources which the Christian community makes available.

But what was this pattern supposed to be? And what use was it to speak of 'the resources which the Christian community makes available', when one of the central elements of the discussion was the elimination of the creeds from worship?

The question, as many commentators made clear, was whether there were any limits in the Church to what might variously be called 'free enquiry' or 'unbelief'. My response to that was to argue that the Church of England as a whole had definite convictions and plainly insisted on a high degree of conformity to them. The definite convictions are those which inform its liturgical texts, and its insistence on conformity embodied in the canonical declaration made by every ordained person that he or she 'will use only the forms of service which are authorized or allowed by Canon'.[8] The Church itself, I argued, *has* a standpoint and the writings of its theologians will be characterized by that standpoint to the degree in which they subject it to painstaking scrutiny and interpretation, including, of course, the honest and truthful facing of many objections to it. Thus it is an error to deny that Anglican theology exists or should exist. There ought especially to be an Anglican theology of the Church. There is at least the beginnings of an Anglican standpoint on the dispersal of authority and the sheer inevitability of conflict in Christianity. The problem for Anglicans, I asserted throughout, was not that it had no standpoint, but that it had taken no trouble to study, analyse, criticize and reformulate it. There was a culpable intellectual failure here, the unintended consequence of F. D. Maurice's theory of Anglican comprehensiveness; a situation which only the restoration and recultivation of systematic theology (which I was then, by chance, professing) would mend.

There is much in the book which I do not regret. But there is also a certain amount of parade and folly for which I will doubtless have to suffer. An American woman meeting me for the first time said, 'I thought you would be older and crosser than you are'. There is a silly passage where I take considerable pains to discuss many possible but implausible meanings of some sentences from another work, and then elaborately excuse myself of pedantry. I was justly rewarded when the author of the said text pointed out that I had misquoted it.

One crucial issue which ought to have led to a good discussion, but did not, was the question of how I defined liberalism. 'Liberalism' continues, I think unforgivably, to be a battle cry in the polarized debates of modern Christians, Anglicans among them. My argument in *The Integrity of Anglicanism* to the effect that liberalism is not a substantive position, that one cannot be just a liberal, that one must be a liberal catholic, evangelical or believer of another positive stance, elicited a certain, but rather inconclusive discussion.[9] The implication of that view is, of course, that anyone who wants to know whether or not I am a liberal, will be told that the question is incapable of any clear answer. The sooner it is realized that polarization into liberals and conservatives is one of the main consequences of living in a modern and secular society, the sooner we shall free ourselves to examine calmly and in the light of history the many complex issues with which the churches are all faced.

IV

WE MUST NOW LAUNCH upon the attempt to answer the questions and objections I have made to modern Anglicanism

English Anglican condescension is simply intolerable. Much of it, of course, is quite unconscious, and if you are an Anglican and have no idea to what I am referring, then you will have to seek help from your non-Anglican friends. It is the effortless superiority of the *beati possidentes*, those who occupy the high ground of English culture — or who used to. We own the cathedrals and ancient parish churches of this land, produced those literary masterpieces, the Book of Common Prayer and the Authorized Version, claim for ourselves the rights of a pedigree of unbroken succession back to the Apostles, and crown the Sovereign of the land. We also, of course, helped to destroy Ireland and then forgot about it; persecuted and imprisoned Catholics and Non-Conformists whilst congratulating ourselves on our comprehensive middle way; and in our own day when our Government invited vast numbers of Afro-Anglicans from the Caribbean, we failed to make them welcome and to foster their contribution to the Church's life.

The justification for any confession, of course, is not the guilt which accompanies it, but the amendment of life to which it leads, or should lead. The root of the difficulty lies in the story we tell about our past; or even the story we assume without being con-

[234]

scious of any narrative at all. There is a great deal that should give us pause for thought in our history. In the interests of truth and of honesty we should take into account the fact that the victors in any conflict always tend to write a history justifying their successes, in which the losers are presented as deserving to, or being bound to fail. As Adolf von Harnack once said, 'Church historians become church politicians whether they like it or not'.

Even the very concept of 'Anglicanism' itself has a history. It was invented in the nineteenth century, possibly as an English adaptation of the (French) '*Gallicanisme*', an anti-papal tendency within French Catholicism. We are not surprised to find John Henry Newman in his High Church Anglican days as one of the first users, if not its inventor. But 'Anglicanism' is a term with no fixed content and it can be, and has been, used in a more or less blatantly one-sided way in the course of its history.

In either case the antidote has to be the study of Anglicanism, warts and all. It is not infrequently the case that Anglicans overseas take this more seriously than do English Anglicans. But it is a mistake to think that if one is English one has no need to study this history. A Church which has not examined its past, with the best methods of analysis and interpretation open to it, is liable to misinterpret its present situation. We live from our memories as well as our hopes, and our accustomed way of telling our own story needs to be purged of vanity and illusion.

The history of Anglicanism will show us, I believe, how dependent we are on our fellow Christians, on the Catholic Church and tradition for so much in our spirituality, on Lutherans and Calvinists for vital elements of our theology, on Congregationalism for so much of our modern thinking about the laity, on Methodist impulses wherever evangelical revival has been effective — and these are but a selection of possible ways of seeing our interdependence. It is important, I believe, now that we are quite clear about the importance of Anglican-Roman Catholic relations, not to be tempted to ignore or marginalize the Protestant Free Churches. We belong to one another in a complex ecological system, and there is a role for a national Church which is generous-minded and not condescending, and which is open-hearted and not imperialistic.

Is it scandalous that there should be open dispute between Anglicans about the fundamentals of the faith? Theologians and lay people have differing investments in the answer to this question. The theologian is absolutely right to point out that at no stage since the Reformation, when the idea of the fundamentals came into popular use, has it been possible for Protestants to agree what the fundamentals of the faith actually consist in. On the other hand the plain lay person has every right to demand that the public proclamation of the Christian faith be such as to be accessible to the theologically inexpert. Inevitably, then, there are different ways of answering this apparently simple question.

In my view, it belongs inherently to Anglican practice that the Scriptures of the Old and New Testament should be publicly read to the whole Church in the native language of the hearers, as part of the Church's normal worship. It is not, however, part of Anglicanism that the whole Scriptures should be considered to be infallible. Classic Anglicans of the Reformation and later eras did so believe and teach, but in the era of biblical criticism it was discovered that none of the Anglican confessional norms insisted upon verbal inspiration. If there are fundamentals which it is scandalous to challenge, they are not fundamental merely because they are taught in Scripture. Many Anglicans concluded that though there were fundamentals, no one could give an exhaustive list of what they were. This is a position which I consider to be fully defensible today, both theologically and practically. Anglican practice is to read the Scriptures, so that the whole people of God may hear the Gospel for themselves. They hear the Scriptures read, wrapped about by anthems and psalms articulating the praise of God, and crowned by the Creed. In this way is delivered to the Church the setting, the theme, the plot and the resolution of the narrative of God's way with His creation, in highly assimilable form.

But it is also true that every aspect of that narrative, beginning with the very word 'God' itself, is open to question and has been questioned and discussed by theologians within the Church from the very beginning. I would go still further and assert that it is impossible seriously to study the Old Testament without becoming aware that it reflects and contains the fruits of a centuries-long dialogue embracing the entire story of God's way with creation and humankind. Even in its much briefer time span the New Testament itself portrays a variety of theologies and modes of Christian discipleship, and frankly reveals (and, of course, deplores) the bitter acrimony with which the disputes were conducted. It is, in my view, the bitterness and inattention of the disputants which is scandalous to modern Anglicanism, as elsewhere. The disputes themselves are normal, and occur in every Christian church known to me.

We need have no hesitation, of course, in asserting that some matters in Christian faith and practice are much more important than others. We can also be quite confident in saying that there is a boundary between beliefs which are solidly part of the faith and those which are incompatible with it. It is a mistake to think that disputes about precisely where the boundary lies in relation to any given belief, or aspect of belief, threatens confidence in the existence of any boundaries whatsoever. From time to time it may be the duty of a bishop or bishops collectively, to draw such a boundary because something fundamental is at stake. But it would seem to me normal and appropriate in the Christian Church for such judgements, and the arguments on which they are based, to be subject to further thought and appraisal.

We move immediately to the issue of Anglicanism's alleged uncertainty and irresolution. It has become the easiest of journalistic clichés to accuse the leaders of the Anglican communion of sitting on the fence, fudging issues and woolly thinking. It is worth distinguishing pusillanimous behaviour, which simply lacks the courage to face a difficulty or the honesty to admit that one exists, with a fully justified refusal to fall into a neatly-set journalistic trap. 'We know you're a plain, honest-to-goodness, no nonsense kind of a teacher', they said to Jesus once, 'What about this tax, then; should we pay it or not?' And the meaning of Jesus' famous reply, 'Pay to Caesar what is due to Caesar, and to God what is due to God', an archetypal sound-bite, has been disputed ever since he uttered it. The refusal to give neat, categorical instructions on each and every issue is by no means a necessary sign of religious decay.

But it would be foolish to deny that the processes of decision-making which Anglicans have adopted in this century are public, slow and seem to lack authority. The question of authority we shall tackle next, but it ought to be asked by what processes is a church in a culture such as our own supposed to consider complex and controversial topics. There are those Anglicans who have too easily forgotten with what intensity and agony the issue of the control of conception by artificial means was discussed in the first half of the century. There are some Roman Catholics who have forgotten the heated rows about biblical criticism. In these matters it is important to preserve historical perspective. There is no doubt, for example, that biblical criticism was pioneered in Protestant Germany, and that it was Protestants who endured the fiercest battles about the mere possibility of formulating theories which today are discussed on every side with equanimity. Individual critics committed, of course, folly after folly, and there were those who argued that the method of so dangerous and uncertain an enterprise was rooted in unfaith. But in a real sense both critics and their opponents endured the fight on behalf of the whole Church, and the result is that, with the exception of the sternest fundamentalists, it is not nowadays thought that the mission of the Christian Church is impeded by holding that Moses did not himself write the Pentateuch, nor John, the Beloved Disciple, the Fourth Gospel.

Churches in modern cultures overhear one another's rows, and learn from them. The issue for Anglicanism is the truth, not the image; whether there is good Christian cause to argue about nuclear weapons, divorce, homosexuality and the rule restricting the priesthood and episcopate to males. My suggestion is that we be much less apologetic about being slow and careful, and public too, than we are. It does not follow that if we are criticized or mocked for this, we are in the wrong; nor even that if, in the debate, foolishness is on display with consequent disdain, we are not fulfilling a role in God's plan for His whole Church.

This brings me to my final charge concerning authority. Is Anglicanism a church without a vision, one which has ceased even to pretend to believe that its decisions are guided by God's Holy Spirit? Having written on this subject in the last years an indecent amount, two things are now absolutely clear to me. The first is that Anglicans cannot claim exemption from the sociological rule which determines that authoritative texts require authoritative interpreters. Even so-called non-hierarchical churches can be shown, on scrutiny, to have persons whose interpretative activity constitutes a centre of authority.[10] The issue for Anglicans is not whether, but who; and it is quite clear from the Thirty-nine Articles and the Ordinal that the Church has this authority, and that it pertains particularly to the episcopate.

In modern Anglicanism there has taken place, through the involvement of clergy and laity in synodical government, a practical experiment in expressing authority in a process, rather than in the issuing of definitive decrees. It is this experiment which has led to the expression of serious reservations. Nonetheless the question whether synodical government necessarily leads to incoherence and confusion is perhaps too frequently decided on the basis of unexamined political or managerial analogies. 'Where, in the Anglican system', it is asked, 'does the buck stop?' It is not asked often enough whether Christian faith is the same thing as a party's political programme, or a company's industrial strategy.

This leads me to my second observation, which is that the problem of authority for Anglicans is not so much in the external organs of authority, whether that be synods or bishops' meetings, but in the hearts and minds of members of the Church. Authority in a voluntary society does not issue simply from claims, but from general recognition. Even churches which have regularly claimed to be authoritative sometimes discover, as Roman Catholics do on the issue of the artificial control of conception, that recognition of authority is withdrawn. Authority in Anglicanism could not be conjured by fiat from resolutions or declarations. It has for too long entailed a process which includes the laity in one way or another; and if its latest experiment with structures has defects, the fundamental theology of the matter is, I believe, both clear and defensible.

It is rooted in a defensible, indeed plainly biblical theology, that God's gifts are given to the whole people of God, and that the gift of leadership is only bestowed within that context. The disputable element enters when a decision is taken to embody that doctrine in a specific structure. What that precise structure should be, however, is less important than the need for the theology to have a realistic sociological expression.

And behind that requirement lies a theology which includes what, I dare to think is, or ought to be, an Anglican theology of the Church (and here I should pause to add that it is not Anglican for the sake of its own distinctiveness, but for the sake of allowing other Christians who are not Anglicans to come to some understanding of why Anglicans persist in believing that God has things to accomplish in and through this communion of Churches).

It belongs to the heart of this theology that we maintain that God's action in His world involves an affirmation *both* of created sociality *and* of that which is new, surprising and unique. This is true, in differing ways and proportions, of the incarnate Christ and of His Church. If we apply this insight to the Church, we arrive at a way of thinking and speaking which Richard Hooker put memorably when he said that the Church was both a society and a society supernatural.[11] This is an important insight. For if the essence of the supposed division and incompatibility between Catholicism and Protestantism consists respectively in the affirmation and the denial that God commits himself to the instrumentality of persons and objects in the salvation of the world, then Anglicanism may well find itself in an uncomfortable position. Anglicans will see no reason to hesitate in saying that the Church itself, its ministry and its sacraments, are a divine gift to our world; but also no reason to doubt that this gift is embodied in sociologically ambivalent ways in time, history and culture. This is not a hybrid construct of the Church, as though it could be thought of as fifty per cent heavenly and fifty per cent earthly; but a way of seeing the Church as at one and the same time embedded in created sociality and the agent of God's new creation.

When Anglicans reflect upon the history of the Church of England and of the Anglican Communion instinctively they find many things to regret and repent of, and some things which are more encouraging. This both-and at the heart of their corporate sense reflects, I would judge, the ecclesiology I have been sketching. Its natural mode is to allow debate, disagreement, and conflict as a normal part of its life. It will provide a structure for the God-given gift of insight and leadership and for understanding and consent; and that structure will be appropriate to differing patterns of authority in different cultures at various times.

In doing so, we are bound to accept what my predecessor in the See of Ely called 'a consequential untidiness'

> ... given that the action were done in the integrity of obedience to the Christ — and we would trust that God's grace would hold us through our own conflicts and the attendant anomalies'.[12]

This is in itself an authentic twentieth-century version of Richard Hooker's 'harmonious dissimilitude of those ways, whereby his Church upon earth is guided from age to age, throughout all generations of men'.[13] This, together with, please God, the gift of patience, is the true condition of the Church. Whether or in what measure it be the genius of Anglicanism to embody that condition is for others to judge; it is perhaps enough that we should bear our testimony to it.

NOTES

[1] Letter to Stanislas Flanagan, 15. ii. 1868, quoted in J. D. Holmes, *The Theological Papers of John Henry Newman on Biblical Inspiration and on Infallibility* (Clarendon Press, Oxford, 1979), p. 158.

[2] G. F. S. Gray, *The Anglican Communion* (1958). The quotation from William James is cited without reference on p. 165.

[3] S. W. Sykes, 'Anglicanism and Protestantism' in *England and Germany, Studies in Theological Diplomacy* ed. S. W. Sykes, (P. Lang, Frankfurt, 1982), p. 127.

[4] Aidan Nichols, *The Theology of Joseph Ratzinger* (T. T. Clark, 1988), p. 166

[5] See S. W. Sykes, 'Anglicanism and the Anglican Doctrine of the Church' in *Anglican Theological Review*, Supplementary Series No. 10, March 1988, and J. Robert Wright ed., *Quadrilateral at One Hundred*.

[6] F. E. Braley ed., *Letters of Herbert Hensley Henson* (London, 1951), p. 204.

[7] S. W. Sykes and J. Booty eds., *The Study of Anglicanism* (London, 1988), p. 368.

[8] Canon C 15.

9   See M. Darrol Bryant ed., *The Future of Anglican Theology* Toronto Studies in Theology, Vol. 17 (Edwin Mellor Press, New York, 1984); see especially the essays of A. J. Reimer and F. G. Kreiger.

10 The classic study is that of P. M. Harrison, who investigated the American Baptist Convention, *Authority and Power in the Free Church Tradition* (Princetown, 1959).

11 *Of the Laws of Ecclesiastical Polity*, I, xv, 2.

12 P. K. Walker, *Rediscovering the Middle Way* (Mowbray, 1988), p. 109.

13 *Of the Laws of Ecclesiastical Polity*, III, xi, 8.

GEOFFREY ROWELL

A Sermon given in in the Church of St Mary the Virgin, Fairford, Gloucestershire on 25 April 1992 to mark the bi-centenary of the birth of John Keble (1792-1866)

> Keep as your pattern the sound teaching you have heard from me, in the faith and love that are in Christ Jesus. You have been trusted to look after something precious; guard it with the help of the Holy Spirit who lives in us.
>
> II Timothy i. 14

ON MAUNDY THURSDAY, 29 March 1866, John Keble died at Bournemouth. A week later, Easter week, a great concourse gathered at Hursley for his funeral. The evening before Canon Liddon and Tom Keble and others went to meet Keble's body as it was brought back to the parish whose revered and exemplary priest he had been. Liddon wrote in his diary: 'It was a beautiful starlit night: and the solemn movement along the road in front of the hearse filled one with wonderful thoughts . . . Before going to bed Dr Pusey, Tom Keble and I went into the study, where the body is laid out with a cross of white primroses stretching the entire length of the coffin and a cross and candles at the end. We remained there in prayer for an hour.' The next day was the funeral. Dean Church wrote that 'it was more like a festival than anything else. . . But the sun and the fresh keen air, and the flowers just coming out, and the beauty of the place and the church, and the completeness of that which had come to its last stage here, put all the ordinary thoughts of sorrow, not aside, but in a distinctly subordinate place.'

'Yet it was', he continued, 'a strange gathering. There was a meeting of old currents and new. Besides the people I used to think

[243]

of with Keble, there was a crowd of younger men. . . excellent good fellows, but who . . . looked upon us as rather *dark* people, who don't grow beards and do other proper things.'

That was the end of John Keble's life. It began seventy-four years earlier here in Fairford, where he was born two hundred years ago today as the second child and eldest son of another John Keble, vicar of the neighbouring parish of Coln St Aldwyn. Educated at home; imbibing the beauty of the Fairford countryside and the pattern of Christian symbol and story in the treasured glass of this church; of sharp mind, keen imagination, and winning spirit, John entered Oxford as a scholar of Corpus Christi when he was only fourteen. He carried off academic prizes — a double first in classics and mathematics, and a fellowship of Oriel, one of the university prizes of the day. But for Keble intellectual excellence was always subordinate to moral; to be clever was the gift of some, holiness was God's calling to all. As priest and pastor the pattern of Christian life as a school of holiness was Keble's overriding concern, whether assisting his father at Coln and Eastleach, or as Vicar of Hursley, or as the college tutor, who gave a new, pastoral understanding to the tutor's role.

What Keble taught he tried to live, and it was Keble the man who touched more, if we except his poetry, than Keble the writer. And yet the man remains, as he would have wished, elusive. John Henry Newman said of him, perhaps in some exasperation, 'How can one paint a man who will not sit for his portrait?' He was reticent and reserved on principle; he disliked the pushy and the showy; the religion of brash slogans and campaigns — and yet he could be firm, and stand on principle. His reserve was both a spiritual discipline and a recognition of the mystery at the heart of religion. His was a religion of the heart, but of a heart not worn upon the sleeve. 'In quietness and confidence shall be your strength' — the strength of the man of contemplative prayer, of disciplined spirituality, who lived in the presence of God, and so living knew himself unworthy to speak adequately of the God who was holy in majesty and awesome in love. When Liddon preached at the opening of our College Chapel at Keble, he said of John that 'no man perhaps ever lifted others to heaven without mentioning it more persuasively than he.' No blustering, no bragging, no knocking people over the head with dogmas, no thumping of Bibles, no multiplication of schemes and organizations — but an awareness that to worship is to adore, and that the prayer of adoration is the prayer of love, and that this inner core of our lives, our responsiveness to God, is a living out of a mystery, which always eludes our ability to express it in words. Keble gave men and women that awareness. When rebutting those concerned about what seemed to them undue veneration of the sacrament of the eucharist, he replied simply: 'Wherever Christ is, there he is to be adored.' And that meant also reverence in worship. He would warn against ecclesiastical gossip, the chit-chat of the sacristy, the dissecting of ritual and ceremonial, not because the outward signs of worship were unimportant for him, but because to treat them in this way was to miss the inner reality they were intended to convey.

This quality of reserve and reticence, combined with a strong faith, was (and is) seen by some as a limitation. In a sense that is right, if the measure of worth is a career ladder or a tally of publications. But for Keble the real ladder to climb was Jacob's, set between heaven and earth. In an Easter sermon he said: 'Each time you receive Christ's Body will be to you a step in a mysterious ladder, like that which Jacob saw, reaching from earth to heaven. The ladder is the Incarnation of God the Son; the steps are the blessed Sacraments; the Lord Himself, on the top of it, is Christ our Saviour calling us to Him, to be made for ever partakers through Him of a Divine nature and glory.'

In the history of the Christian church renewal and revival have often been opposed to order and structure — 'the letter kills, the Spirit gives life'. Yet the Spirit of God, though represented by the powerful symbols of desert wind, flickering flame and blazing fire, is also the orderer and shaper; the one who forms each one in the likeness of Christ, and the communion of the Church as the variety in unity of his body. Outward and inward, form and vitality, belong together. So Keble could remind his Hursley congregation — 'we must walk orderly before our God, we must set ourselves rules and try to keep them, and examine ourselves regularly how we have kept and are keeping them.' He was a wise pastor. 'Living by rule is not placing ourselves in a spiritual straitjacket . . . it is taking cautious account of what we know to be our human tendencies to give up too soon, or to become too enthusiastic and overreach ourselves.'[1] An important part of his understanding of poetry was that it disciplined and channelled raw emotion and wild feelings, directing them and giving them form and purpose. So the life of prayer which leads to holiness, is one of pattern, order and discipline, which enables us to see 'the trivial round, the common task', which make up most of our lives, as that which is given to us that we might have 'room to deny ourselves' and find it 'a road to lead us daily nearer God.' To see deeply into common things is to find both our humanity and the world around us signs and pointers to the love of God their creator and sustainer.

[245]

> New every morning is the love,
> Our wakening and uprising prove
> Through sleep and darkness safely brought,
> Restored to life and power and thought.

Our very sleeping and waking is, Keble says, in another Easter sermon, a pattern of Good Friday and Easter. 'Every evening we do in a certain way, in the way of type and parable, represent and enact the mystery of Good Friday, and no less plainly, every morning we enact the mystery' of Easter. The natural world was a book to be read as a parable of God the Creator.

> The glorious sky embracing all
> Is like the Maker's love.
> Wherewith encompassed, great and small,
> In peace and order move.

The silent refreshment of the morning dew is like the grace of God; the continuous roar of the waves evokes the angels' songs of adoration.

> Two worlds are ours
> 'Tis only sin, forbids us to descry,
> The mystic heaven and earth within,
> Plain as the sea and sky.

Of all the churches of the Reformation, the Church of England alone gave great prominence to the doctrine of creation. Its greatest theologian, Richard Hooker, whose works Keble edited, wrote that 'all things are partakers of God, they are his offspring, his influence is in them.' The world is important, matter is important; they are God's creation, and to be seen and known as such. The world is sacramental, pointing beyond itself to God. And the worship of the Church is inescapably sacramental, embodied. It was not for nothing that the rediscovery of the understanding of the Church as a divine society by Keble and the other leaders of the Oxford Movement went hand in hand with the rediscovery of sacramental embodied worship. Baptism the root and ground of our spiritual life; the eucharist as a sharing in the heavenly banquet.

If Keble shared with Wordsworth and Coleridge a vision of the glory of God in creation; he knew also that the world was fallen, and that sin and evil were not shadows but realities. 'Some persons think', he wrote, 'that because "God is love" there can be no severity in Him.' But the holiness of God and that very love is judging in a sinful and unloving world. And so the Christian life is penitence entwined with praise. Keble shrank from those who put him on a pedestal. He knew the truth of Jesus' words — 'How blest are those who know their *need* of God, the kingdom of heaven is theirs.' As Austin Farrer, a former Warden of Keble College, put it in a sermon on Keble:

> Keble is always repenting, and astonished or grieved to be thought a good man. But as he knows his penitence is accepted, he is light of heart and the most unaffectedly happy of all creatures. And this really is holiness, to have no defence against the full impact of the truth, and yet to sing for joy as one goes along . . . Keble has made his reckoning; he always knows the worst, and what is the worst? The worst, once faced, is redeeming love and a most dear Saviour, so why not sing?[2]

He made his confession; he was sought out for confession; he encouraged his people to open their sin and grief to him, that he might minister to them the healing grace of God. He knew confession to be an Easter sacrament, that penitence issues in praise, because in it the redeeming work that love has done is made actual in particular human lives.

Keble's sermon of 1833, which marked for Newman the beginning of the Oxford Movement, was a protest in part from a mind formed by his Tory father, a protest against necessary and useful reform of the established Church in Ireland, a Church with many bishoprics and much endowment in comparison with the population it served. Keble saw the proposed reform as secular and sacrilegious hands laid on the Church of God. Bishops were the successors of the apostles, ministers of Christ, not State officials. The Church of England had to be asked what kind of Church it was; the State had to be asked by what right it acted as it did. The occasion may have been misjudged, the context meant that Keble's words evoked response. So the Oxford Movement, which transformed the Church of England — and whose influence spread in every continent of the world wherever Anglicans were to be found — began. In another sermon a few years later in Winchester Cathedral, Keble spoke of tradition, of the responsibility of keeping and handing on the faith. He knew that it was possible to take a stance outside the Church, and look at it, as we would say, from the perspective of sociology or psychology, but the Christian priest and teacher was committed to a treasure which might be in earthen vessels, but

which was still a treasure. And so he warned against 'the habit of resolving the high mysteries of the faith into mere circumstances of
language, methods of speaking adapted to our weak understanding,
but with no real counterpart in the nature of things.' To be in the
truest sense a hander on of the faith was to see tradition, as the Eastern Churches do, as grounded in the living presence of the Spirit in
the Church and not as fossilizing, cabining and confining.

Keble's message for the Church in our own day may be summarized on the fingers of a hand. (1) Do not despise tradition, view
it perjoratively or make of it a party matter. For all Christians St
Paul's words are true, 'what have you that you have not received?'
(2) Remember that the church is not a bureaucracy, but a community of faith, a pilgrim people and a communion of saints; and the
saints are our contemporaries. (3) For the theologian, as for every
Christian, prayer must be at the centre. As Pusey said of Keble 'he
was all prayer at all times, though only those who narrowly observed him perceived it.' (4) Imagination, poetry, a sense of awe,
wonder and mystery, must be found in our worship as in our reverence for God's creation and in all our response to God. Head and
heart, body and soul, belong together. (5) Reserve and reticence
have their place and need to be valued as much as campaigns. They
lie at the root of God's gentleness towards us, and the pastor's and
every Christian's gentleness towards others. As St Paul might have
said, 'let slogans and caricature have no place among you.'

Keble the Victorian parish priest rebuking village lads who did
not tip their hats to him; Keble with his pupils at his reading parties,
where 'master was the greatest boy of them all'; Keble standing
writing at his desk in Hursley Vicarage, tracing image and allegory
in the writings of the Fathers; Keble following with close attention
the martyred John Coleridge Patteson's mission to the Pacific Islands; Keble restoring Hursley church and building two others;
Keble the poet with an eye for the minute particulars of the natural
world; Keble from whose eyes a strange power of light caught those
who met him — all these and more help us to capture the one
whose bi-centenary of birth we celebrate today. 'He has showed
you, O man, what is good; and what does the Lord require of you,
but to do justice, and to love kindness, and to walk humbly with
your God.' (Micah 6.8)

Come near and bless us when we wake,
Ere through the world our way we take:
Till in the ocean of Thy love,
We lose ourselves in heaven above.

NOTES

[1] Ralph Townsend, *Faith, Prayer and Devotion* (Oxford, 1983), p. 60.
[2] A. Farrer, *The Brink of Mystery* (London, 1976), p. 154.

RICHARD HARRIES

A Sermon given by the Bishop of Oxford in the Chapel of Keble College, Oxford on 26 April 1992 in Commemoration of the Founders and Benefactors of the College.

ON MY DESK AT HOME is a wooden writing-case, the kind in which you can keep notepaper and envelopes. A brass plaque says: 'Case used by Rev. John Keble (author of Christian Year)'. The writing-case is neat, practical, unostentatious. If there is a simple beauty about it, the charm is so workaday it can easily be overlooked. The case is designed for a purpose and all is subordinate to that purpose. Like Keble's poetry, like Keble himself, there are no frills and certainly no outward show.

Today we give thanks for the founders and benefactors of this College. Because this year is also the 200th anniversary of the birth of John Keble, it is fitting that we focus especially on him this evening.

Keble had a strong sense of beauty. He was deeply moved by the delights of nature and had a fine appreciation of the Greek poets. He was himself a poet. There has been a tendency in much theology to neglect the concept of beauty, to treat it at best as an optional extra to goodness and truth. The one exception to this lamentable neglect is Hans Urs Von Balthazar. In his great work *The Glory of the Lord* he has written about beauty: 'We can be sure that whoever sneers at her name as if she were the ornament of a bourgeoise past — whether he admits it or not — can no longer pray and soon will no longer be able to love'.

God is the uncreated light, who shines in the luminous beauty of his being. It is that glory, irradiating in divine truth and resplendent in divine goodness that haunts and draws us. Keble knew this and sought to express it.

His book of devotional poems, *The Christian Year*, went through 92 editions in his lifetime. It was highly acclaimed by the most distinguished critics of the time and widely appreciated by all sections of the Christian Church, including the most Evangelical. Taste has changed: 'No book was ever more to the liking of its own age or less to the taste of the present one', wrote Georgina Battiscombe. 'I will confess that I can only understand, with a bare assent of the intellect, the influence exercised by *The Christian Year*', wrote Owen Chadwick. I must leave to others the critical evaluation of Keble's poetry from a literary point of view. My point is simply that he sensed in an overwhelming way the beauty of God and sought to state it. As Professor of Poetry at Oxford from 1832 to 1841 he delivered 40 lectures, in Latin, the *Prælectiones*, which explored the nature of poetry and its relationship to religion. He believed that they were allies, that there was a hidden bond between them. Both sought to express thoughts and feelings beyond the power of prose to describe. Each had something to offer the other. As Keble put it: 'In short, poetry affords to religion its store of symbols and its metaphors; religion gives them back to poetry, but sparkling in their new light, (so to say) more sacraments than symbols'. We discern beauty in nature but our faith looking on that beauty sees it aglow with another light. Keble put it in a line of one of his poems: 'There is no light but Thee, with Thee all beauty glows'.

The second characteristic of Keble, present in his personality, his poetry and his theology, is his deep reserve. This reticence was deeply ingrained in his character. He was that kind of person we might say. More surprisingly, he makes it a central element in true poetry as well as true religion. The concept of reserve runs right through the *Prælectiones*. He argued that poetry is as much about concealing as revealing. Here, I believe, is still a profound truth. For what is fully stated and clearly understood cannot be God. Therefore it is what we do not say, what is only hinted at, which is as important as what is stated. This means that some of the most serious people, like Keble himself, will have a certain playfulness about them, a playfulness which exists because the hidden depths of which they are aware, are depths. I think of W. H. Auden, a person in so many ways unlike Keble yet like him in this, that both had a deliberate lightness, almost skittishness, in order to indicate that which merely serious words could not convey. Auden has a poem entitled 'The truest poetry is the most feigning'; it ends:

What but tall tales, the luck of verbal playing,
   Can trick his lying nature into saying
   That love, or truth in any serious sense,
      Like orthodoxy, is a reticence?

It was a thought that Auden derived from an Anglican Bishop friend of his. Perhaps it came down the line from its fount in Keble himself. 'Love, or truth in any serious sense, like orthodoxy is a reticence'.

A new book on the state of religion in Britain by Ian Bradley, *Marching to the Promised Land: Has the Church a Future?* points to the rise of militant forms of religion. It is entirely fair in recognizing this. However, it also points to an important set of values which are still preserved, in an unspectacular way, by some of the apparently less successful mainstream churches. 'They are values like understatement and reserve, genuineness and honest doubt, gentleness and humility. Almost alone among major organisations and institutions, the mainstream churches have as yet largely resisted the blandishments of management consultants and the burgeoning public relations industry. . . .' He argues that the first principle he would like to see guiding the Church in Britain into the third millennium is, and here I quote: 'The rather neglected doctrine of reserve — the preservation of a sense of reverence and awe in the face of the mystery of God.' It was with this sense as well as with an apprehension of the beauty of God, that this Chapel was founded.

Finally, I would select the simplicity of Keble. I do not of course mean stupidity, he was an extremely clever man, one of the brightest in the Oxford of his time. But he had the courage to be unadorned and straightforward before God, like that writing-case on my desk. A very different person, Kierkegaard, wrote that: 'Purity of heart is to will one thing'. Keble would have agreed, it is to will the will of God for one's own life and the world. Keble wrote:

> Religion and poetry are akin because each is marked by a pure reserve, a kind of modesty or reverence. To follow nature sensitively, you need to follow her unveiling part of herself. You are led upwards from beauty to beauty, quietly and serenely, step by step, with no sudden leap from depths to height. Beauty is shy, is not like a man rushing out in front of a crowd. Religion too, if it is wise, models itself upon the ways of Scripture, where the treasure of truth is hidden from the idle and unready, to be seen only when the eye of the mind is pure.

'When the eye of the mind is pure.' 'Blessed are the pure in heart for they shall see God.' Reserve is essential not only because what is fully stated hides God, when it needs to hint at him, but because to know God at all, to know the one who by definition makes a total difference to our lives, it is necessary to have an absolute integrity of heart and mind. It is never simply an intellectual quest. It is to seek in sincerity of purpose, aware of hidden motives and unconscious pressures. It is the simplicity of transparent sincerity that comes across to us from Keble's verses. They may not be great poetry but they have become great hymns.

> Still to the lowly soul
> He doth himself impart,
> And for his dwelling and his throne
> Chooseth the pure in heart.

> Lord, we thy presence seek;
> May ours this blessing be;
> Give us a pure and lowly heart,
> A temple meet for thee.

This Chapel was opened in 1876, and it reflects something of the strengths and triumph of the Catholic revival in the Church of England. That Catholic revival is no longer in the ascendant. We need to return to the virtues of Keble, which were the fresh springs of that movement, virtues which nourished and inspired so many of the founders and benefactors of this College. A sense of the beauty, the profound spiritual attractiveness of God; an awareness of what cannot be stated as well as what can in humility be said; above all, that simple, strong, steadfast sincerity of mind and will which leads us to put our entire trust in God and seek his purpose for the whole of our life.